Policy-making in the European Union

Traditional international relations-based approaches to the study of European integration, which have dominated the debate in recent years, have focused largely on the dominant role of national governments in the integration process and have centred on trying to explain Treaty-based landmarks in this process.

Policy-making in the European Union seeks to fill the gap in attempts to conceptualise the process of European integration. Laura Cram explores the impact of the day-to-day work of policy-makers, interest groups and bureaucrats in influencing the environment in which decisions on Treaty formulation and ratification are taken. Her book succeeds, where more traditional approaches have failed, in highlighting the wide range of policy areas in which the Commission of the European Union, often aided by the rulings of the European of Court of Justice, has succeeded in expanding the scope of EU competence despite national government opposition.

This is an illuminating study which emphasises the important role played by actors in the EU other than national governments in EU policy-making and in understanding major constitutional decisions. It will be of interest to those studying international relations, European integration, and comparative and European public policy.

Laura Cram is Jean Monnet Fellow in European Public Policy at the University of Strathclyde.

European Public Policy Series
Edited by Jeremy Richardson
Department of Government, University of Essex

Also available in the series:

European Union
Power and policy-making
Jeremy Richardson

EU social policy in the 1990s
Gerda Falkner

Democratic Spain
Reshaping external relations in a changing world
Richard Gillespie, Fernando Rodrigo and Jonathan Story

Regulating Europe
Giandomenico Majone

Policy-making, European integration and the role of interest groups
Sonia Mazey and Jeremy Richardson

Adjusting to Europe
The impact of the European Union on national institutions and policies
Yves Meny, Pierre Muller and Jean Louis Quermonne

Policy-making in the European Union

Conceptual lenses and the integration process

Laura Cram

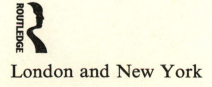

London and New York

First published 1997
by Routledge
11 New Fetter Lane, London EC4P 4EE

Simultaneously published in the USA and Canada
by Routledge
29 West 35th Street, New York, NY 10001

© 1997 Laura Cram

Typeset in Times New Roman
by Pure Tech India Ltd, Pondicherry, India

Printed and bound in Great Britain by Hartnolls Ltd, Bodmin,
Cornwall

British Library Cataloguing in Publication Data

A catalogue record for this book is available from the British Library

Library of Congress Cataloging-in-Publication Data

A catalog record for this book has been requested

ISBN 0–415–14625–9 (hbk)
ISBN 0–415–14626–7 (pbk)

For my Grandad, who would have liked to have seen this day so much

Contents

List of figures and tables	x
Series editor's preface	xi
Acknowledgements	xii
List of abbreviations	xiii
List of interviews	xvii
Summary	xix

Introduction | **1**
1 Rationale for the study | 1
2 The selection of policy areas: social policy and ICT policy | 3
3 Methods and sources | 4
4 Definition of key terms | 4
5 The research agenda | 5

1 Integration theory and the study of the European policy process | **7**
1 Introduction | 7
2 The evolution of European integration theory: the theoretical roots | 7
3 Developing integration theory in the 1970s | 20
4 Understanding recent constitutional developments | 22
5 Understanding the European Union as a polity | 25
6 Institutions, purposeful opportunism and the EU policy process | 27

2 The development of European Union social policy | **28**
1 Introduction | 28
2 EU social policy: historical development | 31
3 Learning and adaptation in the EU social policy process: the lessons of history | 57
4 Conclusion: the paradoxical nature of EU social policy development | 58

**3 The development of European Union information and
communication technology policy**   **61**
1 Introduction   61
2 Different conceptual lenses   63
3 The 1960s and 1970s: problems with the policy mix   69
4 Developing an institutional identity: from task force to DG   77
*5 ESPRIT and RACE: towards a European technology
    community*   79
6 Revitalising EU ICT policy in the 1980s   85
7 Maastricht and the information society   93
8 Conclusion   95

**4 Policy types and policy instruments in the European
Union policy process**   **98**
1 Introduction   98
2 EU legislation: categories and problems of definition   99
3 EU social policy: the legislative pattern   100
4 EU ICT policy: the legislative pattern   111
5 Conclusion: regulatory policy in the EU   120

**5 Collective action at the EU level: implications for the
integration process**   **123**
1 Introduction   123
*2 EU social policy: the commission as catalyst to
    collective action*   125
3 Collective action and the policy environment   132
*4 Collective action in EU social policy: towards a sense of
    Europeanness*   137
5 Business alliances in the EU ICT sector   139
*6 The rationality of collective action in the ICT sector:
    horses for courses*   148
7 Conclusion   152

**6 The institutional dimension of EU policy-making:
breaking down the monolith**   **154**
1 Introduction   154
*2 'Purposeful opportunism' and policy entrepreneurship in the
    European Commission*   155
3 Breaking down the monolith   157
4 ICT policy: dangling the carrot   158
5 EU social policy: undermining the opposition   160
6 The Commission as a 'multi-organisation'   162
7 Conclusion   166

**Conclusion: institutions, purposeful opportunism and the
integration process**   **168**
1 Introduction   168
2 Integration theory and the insights of the policy process   169
3 Institutions, agency slack and purposeful opportunism   170
4 Conclusion   176

Notes   177
Bibliography   188
Index   201

Figures and tables

FIGURES

1 Operational chart showing the implementation of the
   Agreement on Social Policy   48
2 Social policy: relative incidence of the four policy types   101
3 Social policy: regulatory policy by policy area   101
4 Social policy: regulatory policy by policy area and
   instrument of enactment   102
5 Social policy: regulatory policy by policy area over time   102
6 ICT policy: relative incidence of the four policy types   111
7 ICT policy: regulatory policy by policy area   112
8 ICT policy: regulatory policy by policy area and
   instrument of enactment   112
9 ICT policy: regulatory policy by policy area over time   113

TABLES

1 Overview of the main legal bases for social policy
   measures   44
2 Standards emerging from European standards
   organisations by year   113
3 The principal–agent relationship   174

Series editor's preface

One of the enduring puzzles of the process of European integration is that so much European level public policy emerges, despite the need to accommodate the diverse interests of fifteen member states, the degree of competition between European Union institutions and the EU's democratic deficit. Above all, the EU policy process is a series of multi-level games fought between an increasingly large number of policy actors – both public and private – who exploit the many opportunities presented by different policy arenas. The Union appears to pass though episodes of policy innovation and alleged sclerosis, but the trend is reasonably clear. There is some kind of internal dynamic which has the capacity to generate new policy proposals over time – sometimes in the form of conventional legislation and sometimes in the form of so-called 'soft law'. It is as though the Union has as internal 'engine' driving the process of integration forward.

Laura Cram's detailed study of two rather different policy areas – social policy and information technology policy – highlights some of the mechanisms at work in this seemingly inexorable march of European level public policy. The Commission is seen as a key institutional actor – the 'engine' in fact. Behaving like all bureaucracies, it is opportunistic in exploiting 'windows of opportunity' and mobilising diverse sets of policy actors in favour of policy change. Simply because the Commission is presented with different opportunities in each sector, the path of policy innovations exhibits major cross-sectoral variations. Another cause of these variations is, as she points out, the nature of the Commission itself. Again, exhibiting a well known attribute of modern bureaucracies, it is a multi-organisation, with each Directorate General having its own organisation culture, values and policy objectives.

Another important aspect of this study is the behaviour of the increasingly wide range of private actors in the EU policy process.

As is clear from the case studies, European level policy making has become a reality to the plethora of organisations and firms concerned with the two policy areas examined, whatever grand debates might be taking place in bodies such as the Inter-governmental Conference or between political parties at the national level. For an increasing number of organisations, their day-to-day public policy environment is largely determined at the European level. Hence, as is so clearly demonstrated in this volume, they are deeply engaged in trying to shape and influence European level policy debates and policy-making processes and in forming new representative structures through which they can participate at the Euro level.

Finally, this study has much to say about the process of integration itself and the role that day-to-day policy-making plays in it. Here, high politics and low politics meet in a process by which a European level policy system is being created. The analysis sheds much light on the interaction between these two types of politics, the ways in which they are linked via the collective action of diverse sets of private actors, the interests of institutions and the future opportunity structures available for facilitating European policy innovation.

Jeremy Richardson

Acknowledgements

I would like to thank the many people who have commented on the various drafts and papers which finally made up this book: Allan Cochrane, Kevin Doogan, Wyn Grant, Catherine Hoskyns, Gary Marks, Elizabeth Meehan, John Peterson, Mark Pollack, Graham Room, George Ross, Alberta Sbragia, Gail Stedward and Daniel Wincott. Special thanks are due to Rudolf Klein without whom my 'conceptual lenses' might have remained blinkers and to Jeremy Richardson from whom I learned so much. Last, but not least, to all my family: especially to James, for making sure this ever became a book, to Mum and Justin, who ploughed through some dreadful early drafts, and to Granny for being so proud of me!

Thanks also to the various funding councils which have generously supported the research that has contributed to this book: ESRC, Nuffield Foundation, British Academy, Carnegie Trust.

Abbreviations

BEUC	European Bureau of Consumers' Unions
BRITE	Basic Research in Industrial Technologies for Europe
Bull. EU	Bulletin of the European Union
CAP	Common Agricultural Policy
CBEMA	Computer and Business Manufacturers' Association
CBI	Confederation of British Industry
CEC	European Executive Confederation
CEEP	European Centre of Public Enterprises
CEN	European Committee for Standardization
CENELEC	European Committee for Electrotechnical Standardization
CEPT	European Conference of Postal and Telecommunications Administrations
CERD	European Research and Development Committee
CESI	Confederation of Independent Trade Unions
CEU	Commission of the European Union
COFACE	Confederation of Family Organisations in the European Community
COM	Commission Document
COMETT	Action Programme of the Community in Education and Training for Technology
COREPER	Committee of Permanent Representatives
COSINE	Cooperation for Open Systems Interconnection Networking in Europe
COST	Cooperation on Science and Technology
CREST	Committee for Research into European Science and Technology
CREW	Centre for Research into European Women
DG	Directorate-General

EACEM	European Association of Consumer Electronics Manufacturers
EAPN	European Anti-Poverty Network
ECAS	European Citizen Action Service
ECJ	European Court of Justice
ECMA	European Computer Manufacturers' Association
ECOSOC	Economic and Social Committee
ECSC	European Coal and Steel Community
ECTEL	Association of the European Telecommunications and Professional Electronics Industry
EEC	European Economic Community
EECA	European Electrical Components Manufacturers' Association
EFTA	European Free Trade Association
EIRR	European Industrial Relations Review
EMUG	European MAP Users' Group
ENOW	European Network of Women
EP	European Parliament
EPHA	European Public Health Alliance
ERASMUS	European Union Action Scheme for the Mobility of University Students
ERDA	European Research and Development Agency
ERT	European Roundtable of Industrialists
ESF	European Social Fund
ESPRIT	European Strategic Programme for Research and Development in Information Technology
ETSI	European Telecommunications Standards Institute
ETUC	European Trade Union Confederation
EU	European Union
EUCREA	European Association for Creativity by Disabled People (project within HELIOS programme)
Euratom	European Atomic Energy Community
EUREKA	European Research Coordinating Agency
EUROBIT	European Association of Manufacturers of Business Machines and Information Technology
EUROFORM	EU Initiative Concerning New Qualifications, New Skills and New Employment Opportunities
Eurolink Age	European network concerned with older people and the issues of ageing
EWC	European Works Councils
EWL	European Women's Lobby
EWOS	European Workshop for Open Systems

FAST 1	Forecasting and Assessment in the Field of Science and Technology
FEANTSA	European Federation of National Organisations Working with the Homeless
FORCE	EU Initiative on Continuing Vocational Training
FT	*Financial Times*
GSM	Global System for Mobile Communication
HELIOS	Handicapped People in the EC Living Independently in an Open Society
HORIZON	EU Initiative Concerning Handicapped Persons and Certain Other Disadvantaged Groups
IBC	Integrated Broadband Communications
ICT	Information and Communications Technology
IEC	International Electrotechnical Commission
IGC	Intergovernmental Conference
IRIS	Community Network of Demonstration Projects on Vocational Training for Women
IRS	Industrial Relations Service
ISDN	Integrated Services Digital Network
ISO	International Organization for Standardization
ISPO	Information Society Project Office
ITU	International Telecommunications Union
IUFO	International Union of Family Organisations
JRC	Joint Research Centre
LINGUA	Promotion of the Teaching and Learning of Foreign Languages in the EC
NGO	Non-Governmental Organisation
NOW	EU Initiative for the Promotion of Equal Opportunities for Women in the Field of Employment and Vocational Training
OJ C	Official Journal – Notices and Information
OJ L	Official Journal – Legislation
ORGALIME	Liaison Organisation for the European Mechanical, Electrical and Electronic Engineering and Metalworking Industries
OSI	Open Systems Interconnection
OSITOP	Open Systems Interconnection Technical and Office Protocols
PREST	Working Group of EEC Committee on Medium Term Economic Policy
PTTs	National Administrations of Post, Telecommunications and Telegraph

QMV	Qualified Majority Voting
R&D	Research and Development
RACE	Research and Development in Advanced Communications Technologies in Europe
RARE	Reseaux Associés pour la Recherche Européene
SAP	Social Action Programme
SEA	Single European Act
SEM	Single European Market
SMEs	Small and Medium Size Enterprises
Social Rep.	Social Report
SOCRATES	EU Initiative in Programmes and Vocational Training and Education
SOGT	Senior Officials Group for Telecommunications
SPAG	Standards Promotion and Application Group
TACIS	EU Initiative in the Area of Telematics
TEMPUS	Trans-European Mobility Scheme for University Students
TENS	Trans-European Networks
TEU	Treaty on European Union (Maastricht Treaty)
TUC	Trades Union Congress
UNICE	Union of Industrial and Employers' Confederations of Europe
VLSI	Very Large Scale Integration

Interviews

A total of sixty elite interviews were carried out for this research between March 1993 and September 1995. The organisations represented by the interviewees are listed below.

DGIII
DGIV
DGV
DGX
DGXII
DGXIII
European Council Secretariat
COREPER
European Commission Legal Services
Economic and Social Committee
European Parliament
CEN
CENELEC
EWOS
ORGALIME
ECTEL
EUROBIT
ECIF
EECA
BSI
DISC
ISPO
UNICE
IBM (UK)
IBM (EUROPE)
PHILIPS

OLIVETTI
HITACHI
NEC
ICL
COFACE
HELIOS
EUROLINK AGE
EUCREA
CREW
EUROPEAN WOMEN'S LOBBY
EUROPEAN ANTI-POVERTY NETWORK
EURO CITIZENS ACTION SERVICE
EUROPEAN PUBLIC HEALTH ALLIANCE

Summary

The underlying theme of this book is that to properly understand the process of European integration it is vital to understand the dynamics of the European policy-making process and the crucial role of the European institutions within this process. In this book the internal dynamics of the policy-making process within the European Commission in two directorates, DGV (Employment, Industrial Relations and Social Affairs) and DGXIII (Telecommunications, Information Industries and Innovation), are explored. It is argued that a vital characteristic of the Commission's ability to influence any policy sector is its ability to respond rapidly to any 'windows of opportunity' ripe for EU intervention or, indeed, to facilitate the appearance of these windows. Yet, the means required to achieve this end, and the degree of success they meet, vary from sector to sector. It is argued that the Commission has an important role to play in EU policy-making, and ultimately in the integration process, thus it is vital to develop a detailed understanding of the functioning of its constituent parts, of the interrelationships between them, and of the influence of their activities upon the actions of the Commission as a whole.

Introduction

1 RATIONALE FOR THE STUDY

This book seeks to redress an important gap in attempts to conceptualise the process of European integration. The impact of the European Union (EU) policy-making process, and the influence of the European Union institutions, on the wider process of European integration has largely been neglected by integration theorists.[1] In contrast, the underlying theme of this work is that to properly understand the process of European integration it is vital to understand the dynamics of the EU policy-making process and the crucial role of the European institutions and other interests within this process.

Traditional international relations-based approaches to the study of European integration, which have dominated the debate in this field in recent years, have focused largely upon the dominant role of national governments in the integration process and have concentrated on trying to explain Treaty-based landmarks in this process. This analytical focus has resulted in a neglect of the impact of the day-to-day work of policy-makers, interest groups and bureaucrats in influencing the *environment* in which decisions on Treaty formulation and ratification are taken by the heads of state or government of the member states. This approach also ignores, and, more importantly, fails to explain, the wide range of policy areas in which the Commission of the European Union (CEU),[2] often aided by the rulings of the European Court of Justice (ECJ), has succeeded in expanding the scope of EU competence despite national government opposition, with no basis in the founding treaties, or with only the most tenuous claim to legal justifications.

Viewed from a traditional perspective, in which national governments are considered to be the dominant actors in Union policy-making, a major preoccupation for scholars was, for a considerable period, whether or not the Maastricht Treaty would finally be ratified by the member states and thus whether its provisions would ultimately enter into force. However, 'different conceptual lenses lead analysts to different judgements about what is relevant and important' (Allison, 1971: 253). Viewed from a different conceptual angle, which takes into account the institutional dimension of policy-making, a more salient question might have been whether non-ratification would, in fact, have made a significant difference to the actual policies promoted by the Commission, or whether ratification would simply make justification of these policies simpler and their passage through the decision-making process somewhat quicker and smoother. Viewed from this conceptual angle, the Single European Act (SEA) and the Maastricht Treaty may simply represent the codification of (and occasionally the reinforcement of) trends and norms *already established via the policy-making process*. Many elements of the Maastricht Treaty might perhaps have been predicted had more attention been paid to the ongoing activities of the various Directorates-General (DGs) of the Commission.[3] Through day-to-day policy activity, the Commission and the Court had already gone beyond the existing Treaty basis in many policy areas (Cram, 1994a; Wincott, 1995a).

There has been a marked shift in recent years from the traditional emphasis by analysts on national governments as the key actors in EU policy-making towards a broader examination of the relative roles of the various actors involved in the EU policy process. The impact of lobbying by organised interests has come under scrutiny (Greenwood *et al.*, 1992; McLaughlin, 1994; Mazey and Richardson, 1993a) and there has been increasing attention paid to the role of policy networks at the European level (Bomberg, 1994; Peterson, 1992, 1995). The role played by European institutions themselves has received growing attention as an 'institutions-matter' perspective on EU policy-making has begun to gain ground (Bulmer 1994a, 1994b; Peters, 1992). However, these approaches tend to focus upon day-to-day events in the EU policy process or upon the functioning of the EU as a polity or system of governance. Attempts to explain the broader process of European integration, on the other hand, continue to be dominated by approaches drawn from the study of international relations. The argument developed in this book is as follows: even when attempting to explain major *constitutional* decisions, which may fundamentally alter the process of European integration, an examination of the *day-to-day* activities of the EU institutions and their relationship with other actors and interests, rather than concentration on the role of national governments, proves to be illuminating.

2 THE SELECTION OF POLICY AREAS: SOCIAL POLICY AND ICT POLICY

In this book the internal dynamics of the policy-making process within the European Commission in two directorates, DGV (Employment, Industrial Relations and Social Affairs) and DGXIII (Telecommunications, Information Industries and Innovation), are explored.[4] The differences and similarities in the ways in which these DGs have succeeded in influencing their respective policy sectors, the various constraints upon them, and their relationships with important sectoral actors are examined. The importance of the language of justification is highlighted, and the extent to which this has altered over time in both policy areas as new rationalisations for action have emerged is examined.

These two cases have been selected as they both present a challenge to traditional conceptualisations of the policy process in the EU. In both of these policy sectors, national governments have strongly opposed the extension of EU competence. Thus, traditional state-centred approaches to EU policy-making offer little insight into the reasons for the evident EU-level policy and legislative activity which has developed in these policy areas. In the area of social policy, national governments have traditionally opposed any attempt to upset the carefully established 'truces' which have evolved at the national level. In Information and Communications Technology (ICT), the policy of European governments has historically been one of protecting and promoting their national champion firms. While social policy had only an ambiguous basis in the founding Treaties, ICT policy had no formal legal basis at all until the Single European Act. Meanwhile, the two policy areas have attracted very different constellations of influential actors (for or against EU action). Critically, however, in both areas European Union legislation is having an increasing impact. How can this be explained and what are the implications of these cases for our understanding of the integration process?

In this book detailed studies of the two policy areas are presented. The contemporary situation is placed within a historical context. The changing cast of actors is explored and the pattern of legislative development is charted over time. Importantly, both political and legal aspects of policy development are examined. As a result of detailed empirical research into these two carefully selected policy areas a number of gaps in the existing literature have been identified.

3   METHODS AND SOURCES

The book begins with a critical review of the relevant literature on European integration theory and of attempts to understand the functioning of the EU as a polity or system of governance.[5] Drawing upon detailed empirical research compiled from a thorough analysis of primary documentation,[6] bureaumetric analysis of legislative patterns[7] and extensive elite interviewing,[8] a number of gaps in the existing literature are revealed. First, the selection of policy types and the instruments chosen for their implementation may have a significant impact on the responses made by national governments to proposals for action at the EU level.[9] Second, it is argued, the spill-over effects of collective action at the EU level may have important implications for the process of European integration.[10] Third, the European Commission must be treated not as a monolith but as a 'multi-organisation'.[11] Finally, how the links between the EU policy process and the process of European integration might be incorporated into attempts by theorists to comprehend the European integration process is addressed.[12]

4   DEFINITION OF KEY TERMS

There are five key terms referred to throughout this book.

Rhetoric   'Speech or discourse that pretends to significance but lacks true meaning' (*Collins English Dictionary*). The sources of member state rhetoric are derived from those documents to which the member states commit themselves collectively but without necessarily providing the substantive means for the implementation of their stated intentions: for example, from Treaty preambles, Summit Declarations, Conclusions of the European Council.

Soft law   'Rules of conduct which, in principle, have no legally binding force but which nevertheless may have practical effects' (Snyder, 1993a, 1993b) or 'the rules of conduct which find themselves on the legally non-binding level (in the sense of enforceable and sanctionable)' but which 'influence the conduct of member states, institutions, undertakings and individuals, however without containing Community rights and obligations' (Wellens and Borchardt, 1989: 285). The sources of soft law referred to are mainly those termed 'other acts' in the 'Directory of Community Legislation in Force' but may also refer to, for example, non-binding declarations of the Council such as the

Community Charter of Fundamental Social Rights for Workers (1989) (cf. Nielsen and Szyszczak, 1993).

Symbolic politics This refers to the 'symbolic reassurance' argued by Edelman (1985 [1967]) to encourage 'political quiescence'. According to Edelman (1985 [1967]: 206): 'In politics the names of goals are potent symbols. They are not "ends", for the world they promise never arrives, and their result is public acquiescence in current sacrifices'. In the context of the EU it is argued that member states require the acquiescence of their domestic interests, while the European Commission requires the acquiescence of the member states. In both cases, symbolic politics have played an important role in achieving this acquiescence.

Regulation A broad concept of regulation, or rule-making, is most usefully employed for the purposes of this book. Thus the regulation or regulatory policies and legislation referred to in this book may be described as 'the intentional restriction of a subject's choice of activity, by an entity not directly party to or involved in that activity' (Mitnick, 1980: 20).

Purposeful opportunism The strategy of an organisation which has a notion of its overall objectives and aims but which is quite flexible about the means by which these are achieved (Klein and O'Higgins, 1985).

5 THE RESEARCH AGENDA

This book takes as a starting point the assumption that member states are the key decision-makers in EU policy process with the power to approve or oppose the proposals of the CEU. The member state–Commission relationship may, moreover, be characterised as one of principal–agent. Member state principals delegate certain powers to the CEU agent.[13] However, member states have not always been able to anticipate fully the consequences of their actions. In recalling, for example, her part in the setting up of the Dooge Committee (established to examine the possibilities for improvement in political cooperation between the member states but which ultimately proposed that an intergovernmental conference be set up with a view to creating a 'European Union') Margaret Thatcher lamented the action as: 'one of those gestures which seem to be of minor significance at the time but adopt a far greater one in the light of events' (Thatcher, 1993: 549).

Thus, the member states may experience unintended consequences of their actions and these unintended consequences may have a major impact upon the process of European integration. Not least the attempts by the CEU to maximise its autonomy from the member states have been an important unintended consequence of member state actions.

The CEU's scope for action is at all times limited by the decision powers of the member states and by their ability to curtail the role delegated to the Commission as the agent of member state principals. It is in the interest of the CEU to avoid this outcome and, as becomes clear in this book, the Commission, acting as a purposeful opportunist, has learned to maximise its room for manoeuvre in the policy process while attempting to avoid direct conflict with the member states. Requiring the support of its member states for most actions, and lacking the range of policy instruments which national governments have traditionally employed as incentives or as sanctions against interests, it is argued in this book that the Commission has learned to make adept use of its crucial functional role in the policy-making process (see Cram 1993, 1994a) and has attempted to maximise its autonomy from its member states (Cram, 1995). It has learned to respond to opportunities for action as they present themselves, and has attempted to facilitate the emergence of these opportunities. Indeed, much of the activity of the European Commission might well be interpreted as an attempt to gradually expand the scope of its competence without alienating national governments or powerful sectoral interests. The Commission of the EU, acting within the many constraints upon it, has played an important role in shaping the environment in which policies are developed, in justifying a role for the EU, mobilising support for its action, and in selecting the types of policy intervention pursued by the EU.

The importance of these issues becomes clear as the two empirical case studies are elaborated in the book. In conclusion it is suggested that day-to-day events in the policy-making process must be understood as a fundamental aspect of the process of European integration: altering the environment in which major decisions are taken and even the very perceptions which actors, such as national governments, hold of their own interests. Major theoretical attempts to conceptualise the European integration process must, it is argued, take account of the important role played by opportunistic institutions and the impact of their activities on the integration process more generally.

1 Integration theory and the study of the European policy process

1 INTRODUCTION

In this chapter the development of European integration theory – its roots, development and the current state of the debate – is examined. The chapter presents a critical overview of the key theoretical approaches to the study of European integration. It concludes with the argument that the insights emerging from contemporary studies of the governance of the European Union might usefully be employed to enhance current attempts to conceptualise the integration process.

2 THE EVOLUTION OF EUROPEAN INTEGRATION THEORY: THE THEORETICAL ROOTS

During the Second World War and in its immediate aftermath, many scholars sought to elaborate a new type of political system which would facilitate cooperation between nations and the preservation of international (or at least Europe-wide) peace. Some theorists focused on the desirable end product of this cooperation (for example federalism and functionalism), while others focused on the background conditions which would be required for the establishment of a new transnational political community (for example, the transactionalist/communications school). Each, in their own way, contributed to the elaboration of later neo-functionalist attempts to explain the emerging process of European integration begun, in practice, with the establishment of the European Coal and Steel Community (ECSC) in 1951.

2.1 Federalism

For many scholars and politicians the solution to the conflict between European nations lay in the development of a European federation of nations. Throughout the Second World War, there were many references to the peace-making potential of a European federal political structure. The federalist movement had strong roots in the European resistance movement, and even further back, for example, in the writings of Coudenhove-Kalergi (1923, 1934, 1938). The development of the post-war federalist movement was championed by committed federalists such as Jean Monnet, Walter Hallstein and Altiero Spinelli (1966) who were to be disillusioned by the slow progress in Europe and the virtual abandonment of any attempt to create a true European federation. The end-product of the European integration process was to fall far short of the ideals of these federalists. While remaining a popular vision today, the 'federalist approach is more a strategy for fulfilling a common purpose and common needs than a theory explaining how these integrative forces arise' (Hodges, 1972: 13).

2.2   Transactionalism/communications school

In contrast, the work of Deutsch (1957, 1964, 1966, 1967), and other scholars working within the transactionalist/communications tradition, focused on the conditions necessary for political integration to occur. Mutual transactions or communications were for Deutsch a necessary, but insufficient, prerequisite for the development of a political community. Thus, travel, trade, telecommunications and postal links might, in themselves, lead to mutual relevance but, without creating mutual responsiveness, would fail to generate a sense of community. For Deutsch (1966: 96–97), mutually responsive transactions resulted from a complex learning process from which shared symbols, identities, habits of cooperation, memories, values and norms would emerge. Deutsch's vision of political integration did not insist on the presence of any specified institutional structure but rather depended on 'a historical process of social learning in which individuals, usually over several generations, learn to become a people' (Deutsch, 1966: 174).

The transactionalist/communication school approach was widely criticised, not least, for its methodological focus on transaction flow indices which did not provide an adequate picture of the multifaceted integration process (Inglehart, 1967; Puchala, 1970). However, Deutsch had highlighted the importance of the *socio-psychological* aspects of community formation (Hodges, 1972: 19) which were to be highly influential on subsequent work in the field of European integration: in particular, on Haas's neo-functionalism.[1]

2.3 Functionalism

Perhaps the most influential work of this period, both upon the European integration process and upon subsequent attempts to conceptualise this process, was David Mitrany's functionalism. Yet functionalism was not a theory of European integration. Indeed, Mitrany was directly opposed to the project of European regional integration. In his advocacy of a 'A Working Peace System', Mitrany (1966a: 68) proposed a universal, rather than a regional, solution to what he saw as the 'problem of our generation' : 'how to weld together the common interest of all without interfering unduly with the particular ways of each'.

A central tenet of Mitrany's work was his opposition to nationalism, and the territorial organisation of power which, like his contemporaries, he saw as a threat to world peace. Mitrany (1966a: 82) was vehemently opposed to the divisive organisation of states in the international system which he described as arbitrary 'political amputations'. Yet, while many of his fellow scholars were searching for European cooperative solutions to the problem of world conflict, Mitrany (1966a: 96) maintained that 'peace will not be secured if we organize the world by what divides it'. In the pursuit of peaceful, non-coercive, community-building, nationalism at the nation-state level must not, Mitrany argued, simply be replaced by nationalism at the European level.

In his 1943 edition Mitrany deals specifically with what he calls the 'perplexities of federalism'. Mitrany had a number of problems with this, the most frequently proposed, solution to the problem of conflict in Europe. First, he argued that the 'problems which now divide the national states would almost all crop up again in any territorial re-alignment; their dimensions would be different, but not their evil nature' (Mitrany 1966a: 46). Second, while he agreed with the federalists that 'cooperation for the common good is the task' (Mitrany 1966a: 97–98), he argued that it would be 'senseless' to tie this cooperation to a territorial authority. The number of necessary cooperative activities for Mitrany (1966a: 98) would remain limited while, he argued, 'their range is the world'. Further, as all proposed federal solutions were limited, either territorially or ideologically, there was no guarantee that the necessary political consensus could be achieved to create the new constitutional framework which a federation would require. A federation, by its very nature, would prove divisive: 'federation like other political formations, carries a Janus head which frowns division on one side in the very act of smiling union on the other' (Mitrany 1966a: 93).

A key factor in understanding Mitrany's functionalist vision is the distinction which he draws between political/constitutional cooperation and technical/functional cooperation in his advocacy of a new international society. For Mitrany (1966a: 58), the task was clear: 'our aim must be to call forth to the highest possible degree the active forces and opportunities for cooperation, while touching as little as possible the latent or active points of difference and opposition'. The political/ constitutional route had clearly failed to rise to this challenge. Mitrany was all too aware of the failings of recent peace pacts, international treaties and of international organisations (which retained states as members) like the League of Nations. In contrast, Mitrany advocated the development of technical international organisations, structured on the basis of functional principles,[2] which would perform collective welfare tasks. Internal political conflict and interminable debates about the boundaries of national sovereignty were to be sidestepped. The function to be carried out would determine the type of organisation best suited for its realisation. This 'technical self-determination' would, in turn, mean that there would be 'no need for any fixed constitutional division of authority and power, prescribed in advance'(Mitrany 1966a: 73). Indeed, 'anything beyond the original formal definition of scope and purpose might embarrass the working of the practical arrangements' (Mitrany 1966a: 73).

For Mitrany, it was rules, experts and the principle of 'technical self-determination' (1966a: 72), rather than territorial structures or national politicians, which would facilitate the decline of ideological conflict, the demise of nationalism, and would allow peaceful cooperation to develop on a world-wide scale. In Mitrany's words: 'It is no longer a question of defining relations between states but of merging them – the workday sense of the vague talk about the need to surrender some part of sovereignty' (Mitrany 1966a: 42). If the needs of society were revealed, Mitrany (1966a: 99) argued, 'quite starkly for what they are, practical household tasks' it would 'be more difficult to make them into the household idols of "national interest" and "national honor"'.

While not entirely opposed to some kind of formal international union in the future, Mitrany (1966a: 97) cautioned that, as yet, the 'political way was too ambitious'. Indeed Mitrany feared that the political/constitutional approach might even hamper progress towards a working international system. Only through cooperation in technical/functional organisations might it be possible to 'set going lasting instruments and habits of a common international life' (Mitrany 1966: 58). Without these habits, political/constitutional action could not be contemplated: while with these learned habits of integration such political/constitutional action may ultimately prove superfluous (Mitrany 1966a: 97). Although somewhat vague on the processes by which functional action would lead to international society, Mitrany (1966a: 58) argued that the 'growth of new habits and interests', as a result of functional cooperation, would begin to dilute persisting or emergent ideological divisions. Ultimately, 'every activity organised in that way would be a layer of peaceful life; and a sufficient addition of them would create increasingly deep and wide strata of peace – not the forbidding peace of an alliance, but one that would suffuse the world with a fertile mingling of common endeavor and achievement' (Mitrany 1966a: 98). With the 'working peace system' up and running, nationalism could, at last, be replaced by allegiance to the world community.

In the context of European integration, Mitrany's functionalism remains important not least because of its influence on two of the key architects of the European Coal and Steel Community: Jean Monnet and Robert Schuman. Monnet and Schuman, in creating the ECSC, borrowed key aspects of what might be termed the functionalist method, without adopting Mitrany's central goal: the dissolution of territorially based authorities. Thus Monnet and Schuman employed Mitrany's focus on technical, sector specific integration, and his emphasis on avoiding political debates about the surrender of national sovereignty, in order to facilitate the incremental establishment of a territorially based organisation and the creation of a new regional authority structure. For Schuman, the pooling of resources in the European Coal and Steel Community was 'a first step in the federation of Europe'.[3] Clearly, this was a very different end from that proposed by Mitrany.

In many ways this deracination[4] of Mitrany's approach to international cooperation (later perpetuated in many respects by the (mis) categorisation of neo-functionalist theory as a direct descendant of functionalism)[5] has led to Mitrany's vision surfacing in the literature on European integration more often as a caricature of itself than as a true reflection of Mitrany's functionalist ideal of an international society.[6] Mitrany directly opposed the re-creation of territorially based state structures at the European level except in so far as they represented unrelated responses to technical self-determination.

2.4 Neo-functionalism

Functionalism met with many criticisms: not least because of the rather naive belief that a neat division between technical/functional issues and political/constitutional issues could be sustained. Increasingly political scientists argued that the division between technical, non-controversial, economic issues, on the one hand, and political issues, on the other, was untenable: 'economic integration, however defined, may be based on political motives and frequently begets political consequences' (Haas 1958: 12). Likewise, while Mitrany had prescribed the necessary development of a new world community, quite how the transition from functional action to international society would take place was never clearly specified and relied on a rather organic process of expansion which was not consistently observable in practice. By the late 1950s Ernst Haas (1958: 4), in *The Uniting of Europe*, described western Europe as a 'living laboratory' for the study of collective action between European states. A wide range of organisations, which required the collaboration of European governments, operated in western Europe.[7] Yet, as Haas (1958: 4) noted: 'detailed data on how – if at all – cohesion is obtained through these processes is lacking'. It was this very process which Haas set out to investigate with the development of neo-functionalism.

In many ways the title neo-functionalism is something of a misnomer or 'a case of mistaken identity' (Groom, 1978). Developed, in part, to address the gaps in existing functionalist theory and practice and, in part, as a pluralist critique of the realist school,[8] which had hitherto dominated the study of international relations, the neo-functionalist approach is of very mixed intellectual parentage. Neo-functionalism, as well as addressing some of the shortcomings of Mitrany's functionalism, also represents a clear divergence from some of the central tenets of Mitrany's functionalism in a number of important respects. Although incorporating many elements of the 'functionalist method', as practised by Monnet and Schuman on the basis of their deracinated version of functionalist theory, neo-functionalism also draws upon some of the central tenets of both the communications school and of the federalist school of integration theory.

Focus on the process of developing a new political community in Europe

Neo-functionalism, in its early articulation, focused specifically upon the integration project in Europe. It sought to explain what was happening in Europe, and to provide a conceptual framework within which developments in Europe could be understood.[9] For Haas, it was not the necessary background conditions nor the end product of cooperation between the nation-states which were the focus of his study.[10] Rather, the focus of study for neo-functionalists was the process of political integration itself. For Haas

> Political integration is the process whereby political actors in several distinct national settings are persuaded to shift their loyalties, expectations and political activities toward a new centre, whose institutions possess or demand jurisdiction over the pre-existing national states.
>
> (Haas 1958: 16)

In terms of the relationship between Mitrany's functionalism and the neo-functionalism developed by Haas, it is important to note that for neo-functionalists the basic unit of analysis remained the territorially based state system so vehemently opposed by Mitrany (Groom, 1978: 21). There was no concept in neo-functionalism of transcending the traditional territorial division of states: these were simply to be supplemented/replaced by new territorially based organisations at the European level.

The role of supranational institutions

In terms of the intellectual parentage of neo-functionalism, Haas viewed a central government as 'essential institutionally' and a national (in this case European) consciousness as 'essential socially' (Haas, 1958: 8). The links with the federalist and communications schools respectively are clear.[11] Although recognising the importance of the insights developed by Deutsch, and in particular of the importance of an emergent European-centred belief system, for Haas (1958: 7), 'the existence of political institutions capable of translating ideologies into law [is] the cornerstone of the definition'. The contrast with Mitrany's functionalism is stark. Mitrany specifically warned against the creation of territorially based supranational authority structures: 'for an authority which had the title to do so would in effect be hardly less than a world government; and such a strong central organism would inevitably tend to take unto itself rather more authority than that originally allotted to it' (Mitrany, 1966: 75). In contrast, in Haas's neo-functionalist approach, the very propensity of organisations to maximise their powers is an important element of the process through which a political community is formed. Indeed, the supranational institutions are allotted a key role as potential 'agents of integration' (Haas 1958: 29). The supranational institutions were expected both to facilitate the transfer of elite loyalties to the European level and to play the role of 'honest broker' facilitating decision-making between recalcitrant national governments (Haas, 1958: 524).

Interests, learning and authority-legitimacy transfers

The neo-functionalist approach shares with Mitrany's functionalism a focus on social actors and technical experts. However, Haas did not share Mitrany's vision of politically neutral actors carrying out technical/functional tasks unaffected by political conflict. Less idealistic, Haas's pluralist-based neo-functionalism recognised the continuing importance of national political elites, and emphasised the key role played by interest-based politics, in driving the process of political integration. National political elites might, for example, become more supportive of the process of European integration as they learned of the benefits which might ensue from its continuation.[12] In turn, a re-evaluation of the interests of the political elite (whether in favour of, or in opposition to, the European project) would result, ultimately, in the transformation of traditional nationally centred belief sytems:

> As the process of integration proceeds, it is assumed that values will undergo change, that interests will be redefined in terms of regional rather than a purely national orientation and that the erstwhile set of separate national group values will gradually be superseded by a new and geographically larger set of beliefs.
>
> (Haas, 1958: 13)

In its focus upon the learning of integrative habits, as a result of prior cooperation, neo-functionalism displays a clear link with both the functionalist and communication schools. For Haas, however, this was not a one-way process. Although the attitudes of national political elites would influence the development of the integration process, supranational political elites also had a role to play in encouraging the process of integration. Thus, 'decision-makers in the new institutions may resist the effort to have their beliefs and policies dictated by the interested elites and advance their own prescription' (Haas, 1958: 19). It was through a complex interaction of belief systems that Haas envisioned that the reorientation of the activities of national political elites, in response to European-centred interests and aspirations, would take place.[13] Ultimately, Haas argued that as 'beliefs and aspirations' were transformed, through the interaction of supranational and national belief systems, 'a proportional diminution of loyalty to and expectations from the former separate national governments' could be expected (Haas, 1958: 14). A shift in the focus of national loyalties and, importantly, of expectations towards the new supranational authority structure would similarly be expected.

The central importance of the transfer of loyalty in early neo-functionalist explanations of the process of political integration is undisputed. However, in his later work, Haas (1970: 633) recognised the difficulty of measuring this transferral and welcomed the contribution of Lindberg and Scheingold (1970) who stressed the importance of the extent to which authority for decision-making had been transferred to the European level. The degree to which 'authority-legitimacy' transfers had taken place would, they argued, provide a measurable indicator of progress towards a new political community. The authority-legitimacy transfer was not, however, the sole defining criterion of political integration identified by Haas. Crucially, the process of political integration encompassed not only a change in the focus of the 'loyalties' of the political elite but also in the focus of their 'expectations and political activities' (Haas, 1958: 16).

The reorientation of the interests of the political elite, Haas argued, may result as much from their opposition to, as from their support for, the integration process. It is the reorientation of national expectations and political activities in response to supranational developments in Europe, or to the pull of the new centre, which are crucial for the process of political integration, not simply the extent to which the political actors are in support of the process of integration. Haas (1958: 288) considered that although elites with 'long-run negative expectations' of supranational activity might appear irreconcilable to the 'unification pattern', in fact, 'even the consistently negative-minded may be persuaded to adjust' (Haas, 1958: 296). Meanwhile, groups with short-run negative expectations who mobilise in response to specific supranational policies which they oppose 'may, in self defence, become a permanent institution with a common – albeit negative – body of expectations' (Haas, 1958: 288).

Any shift in loyalties, in response to the activities of the new centre, need not be absolute or permanent. Multiple loyalties may continue to exist. Hence, for Haas (1958: 15–16), it is was more likely to be the convergence of a very disparate set of interests which would drive the process of integration and result in the establishment of a new political community, than any mass conversion to the doctrine of 'Europeanism'. Ultimately, a self-interested shift in loyalty, or in the focus of political activities, by the political elite will increase the dynamic towards the development of the new political community whether it results from positive or from negative long-term expectations of the integration process (Haas, 1958: 297). It is this process which is usually referred to as 'political spill-over'.

Spill-over v technical self-determination

It is the process of political 'spill-over' which is, perhaps, most closely associated with the neo-functionalist approach to the study of European integration and which represented the most significant advance upon Mitrany's functionalist method. Political spill-over, in short, consists of a convergence of the expectations and interests of national elites in response to the activities of the supranational institutions. This, in turn, may result in a transfer of loyalties (authority-legitimacy transfers) or, at minimum, in a transformation in the political activities of national elites (for example, a rise in European lobbying) in favour of, or opposed to, new supranational policies. Crucially, political spill-over could be positively or negatively inspired and was expected to increase as supranational policies were revealed to be of increasing relevance to national elites.

The concept of political spill-over was a major advance upon Mitrany's functionalist focus on the notion of 'technical self-determination', and on his reliance on a rather organic process in which successful cooperation in one area would encourage cooperation in another area. Haas, however, continued to recognise the importance of functional or sectoral spill-over which, he argued, was based on a quite different logic from that which drove political spill-over: 'sector integration . . . begets its own impetus toward extension to the entire economy even in the absence of specific group demands and their attendant ideologies' (Haas, 1958: 297). In neo-functionalist terms, the process of functional or sectoral spill-over referred to the situation in which the attempt to achieve a goal agreed upon at the outset of cooperation, such as the harmonisation of coal and steel policy, becomes possible only if other (unanticipated) cooperative activities are also carried out, for example harmonisation of transport policy or economic policy. In this way cooperation in one sector would 'spill-over' into cooperation in another, previously unrelated, sector.

Haas increasingly sought to refine his understanding of the dynamics of the process of functional or sectoral spill-over and to move away from the automaticity inherent in the concept of 'technical self-determination'. Haas (1960: 376) argued that there was no 'dependable, cumulative process of precedent formation leading to ever more community-oriented organizational behavior, unless the task assigned to the institutions is *inherently expansive*, thus capable of *overcoming the built-in autonomy of functional contexts* and of surviving changes in the policy aims of member states' (quoted in Lindberg 1963: 10–11, emphasis added). With his focus on inherently expansive tasks, Haas clearly distinguished his neo-functionalism from Mitrany's functionalism. Far from focusing on the very separate demands of different functional tasks, Haas focused on the potential linkages between sectors. It was this focus on linkage politics which, in part, contributed to the image of the political integration as an inexorable process: a snowball, constantly gathering momentum as the process of integration rolled on.

Importantly, the snowball effect identified by neo-functionalism was not limited only to political, or to functional/sectoral spill-over, but also incorporated what Haas (1958: 317) referred to as 'geographical spill-over'. Haas recognised that cooperation between one group of member states was likely to have some effect upon excluded states, not least by altering existing patterns of trade. In turn, the responses of non-member states might, he argued, influence the process of integration. In this context, Haas (1958: 314–317) referred particularly to the integrative effects which UK participation in the European Free Trade Association (EFTA) had had upon the UK government's attitude towards European cooperative ventures. By 1957, the UK government had recognised that at least 'qualified association' with the European Economic Community (EEC) was necessary. Haas (1958: 317) noted that 'a geographical spill-over is clearly taking place'. This is an aspect of neo-functionalist spill-over which is often overlooked but which has clear resonances today as the EU seeks to accommodate an increasing range of demands for membership.

The heyday of neo-functionalism

Initial evaluations of the neo-functionalist approach appeared favourable. As the ECSC 'spilled-over' into the EEC and the European Atomic Energy Community (Euratom), in many ways it seemed that neo-functionalism had rather neatly encapsulated the process of European integration.

> Economic integration – with its evident political implications and causes – then became almost a universal battlecry, making complete the 'spill-over' from ECSC to Euratom and its promise of independence from oil imports, from sector common markets to the General Common Market.
>
> (Haas, 1958: 298)

Not only had the Rome Treaties been signed in 1957, providing a good example of *sectoral spill-over*, but, by the early 1960s, a number of members of the competitor European Free Trade Association had begun to apply for membership of the EEC. Hence a type of *geographical spill-over* had also begun.[14] *Political spill-over* was in clear evidence, as interest groups mobilised, for example, around the issue of the Common Agricultural Policy (CAP). Not least, the European Commission, with Walter Hallstein as President, had adopted an active constitutional role for itself and was a committed 'agent of integration'. As the goals of the first transition phase were achieved, it was decided that the second phase could be shortened. At the time it appeared that 'the spill-over may make a political community of Europe in fact even before the end of the transition period' (Haas, 1958: 311).

Very shortly, however, it became clear that the picture was not so simple as neo-functionalism had painted it. Within a few short years, De Gaulle had vetoed the UK membership application (hence curtailing the process of geographical spill-over); the French 'empty chair policy' of 1965 had put paid, at least in the short term, to any notion of Commission activism and its encouragement of political spill-over; and, finally, the oil crisis and recession of the early 1970s had brought even the automaticity of sectoral spill-over into question. Clearly, forces other than those identified by Haas were at play and now had to be explained.

2.5   The realist/intergovernmentalist approach

The study of international relations more generally had been dominated, in the post-war period, by the realist model of world politics. The most influential text in post-war international relations, *Politics Among Nations* (Morgenthau, 1967), identified a world system in which the dominant actors were rational unitary states, prepared to use force to achieve their goals, and for whom the maintenance of military security lay at the apex of their hierarchy of goals (see Keohane and Nye, 1977). From a realist perspective the interaction between states in a conflictual international environment was central and the balance of power was constantly shifting. From this perspective, cooperative ventures between nation-states were likely only to constitute a temporary equilibrium, from which the partners were at liberty to withdraw should they no longer feel that their interests were best served by membership.

While there have been many criticisms of the realist approach, it is perhaps unsurprising that one of the most powerful early critiques of the neo-functionalist approach to the study of European integration should have had roots in this tradition of thought. While acknowledging the shortcomings of the realist school, not least the fact that states could in no way be characterised as unitary actors, Stanley Hoffmann (1966) in his intergovernmentalist critique of the neo-functionalist approach developed upon some of the insights of the realist school.

Hoffmann emphasised the importance of the international environment and the role which nation governments played within the global system. The role of national governments was to promote the interests of their peoples to the best of their abilities within an adversarial world system. The implications of this for the study of regional politics (such as the process of European integration) were important. First, the importance of regional politics was, Hoffmann (1966: 865) argued, far less important to national governments than 'purely local or purely global' concerns. Within the global international system 'regional subsystems have only a reduced autonomy' (Hoffmann, 1966: 865). Second, Hoffmann highlighted the contingent nature of any transnational cooperation. While 'extensive cooperation is not at all ruled out', there 'would be no assurance against a sudden and disastrous reversal' (Hoffmann, 1966: 896). For Hoffmann, national governments were more 'obstinate' than 'obsolete' in the process of European integration. This was clearly a serious challenge to the snowball effect of cooperation proposed by the neo-functionalist approach.

Hoffmann (1966: 886) also drew attention to the 'limits of the functional method' or, as he referred to it, the 'Monnet method' (Hoffmann, 1966: 885). Crtically, Hoffmann criticised the logic of integration implicit in the 'Monnet method', and which Haas had incorporated into his neo-functionalist approach. Hoffmann argued that, in fact, it was the 'logic of diversity' which prevailed and which would set limits to the 'spill-over' anticipated by the neo-functionalists (Hoffmann, 1966: 882). In areas of vital national interest, Hoffmann argued, national governments were not willing to be compensated for their losses by gains in other areas. Crucially, some issues were more important than others. Instead, national governments would choose to minimise uncertainty and would maintain tight control over decision processes when vital interests were at stake.

> Russian roulette is fine only as long as the gun is filled with blanks. . . . Functional integration's gamble could be won only if the method had sufficient potency to promise an excess of gains

over losses, and of hopes over frustrations. Theoretically, this may
be true of economic integration. It is not true of political integration (in the sense of 'high politics').

(Hoffmann, 1966: 882)

Hoffmann's distinction between issues of 'low politics' (economic and
welfare policies) and matters of 'high politics' (foreign policy, security
and defence) was central to his critique of the neo-functionalist
approach. The ambiguity implicit in the neo-functionalist 'logic of
integration' might appear acceptable to national governments when
taking decisions about tariffs, and almost sufficed for discussions on
the issue of agriculture. When it came to the discussion of matters
of 'high politics', however, clear and consistent goals would be
required (Hoffmann, 1966: 883). National governments would not
be persuaded to accept anything less.

3   DEVELOPING INTEGRATION THEORY IN THE 1970s

There have been many attempts to reassess and revitalise neo-functionalism. Many of these resulted in important refinements to Haas's
original work (see for example, Haas, 1964; Lindberg, 1963; Lindberg
and Scheingold, 1970; Nye, 1968; Schmitter, 1970). Increasingly, it
was recognised that integration was not an inexorable process, in
which national governments found themselves caught up, but a process which might just as easily 'spill-back' or 'spill-around'. However,
in the context of the late 1960s and early 1970s it was difficult to make
a case for the neo-functionalist approach. Indeed, while in 1970, Haas
was reflecting upon the 'Joys and Anguish of Pre-theorizing', by 1975
he was declaring the 'Obsolescence of Regional Integration Theory'.
As the EEC faced a period of stagnation, shaken by international
events and the actions of domestic leaders, the snowball of neo-functionalism seemed to have melted.

The study of European integration was clearly less fashionable in
this 'doldrums period' (Caporaso and Keeler, 1995: 13). For a number
of years scholars of European integration, having observed the apparent stagnation of the integration process and the consignment of neo-
functionalist and communication school approaches to the theoretical
wastelands, were, understandably, somewhat hesitant to generate
'grand theories' of European integration. However, as Caporaso and
Keeler (1995: 16) argue, the scholarship generated during this period
deserves more attention and respect than it has received. As well as
providing many important insights into the integration process, the

studies of this period provided the foundations for later studies of both the integration process and of the functioning of the European Union as a polity or system of governance. Case studies of European policy-making proliferated, significantly enhancing understandings of how the European institutions and member states interacted. Meanwhile, a number of theoretically distinct developments were to play a significant role in facilitating a more synthetic approach to the study of European integration in the late 1980s and the 1990s.

3.1   Domestic politics approaches

First, scholars recognised the importance of domestic politics and of the political concepts developed in the context of domestic politics in enhancing our understanding of European policy-making. In 1975, Puchala questioned the snowball effect of neo-functionalism and argued that national governments remained important determinants of the integration process. In 1979 Wallace, Wallace and Webb edited a detailed series of case-studies into the process of policy-making in the European Community. They concluded that national governments were the central actors in the integration process and that an understanding of the internal domestic politics of the member states was crucial to any rounded understanding of the integration process. This approach was further developed in 1983 when Bulmer sought to move away from the 'supranationalism versus intergovernmentalism' debate and to explain the 'linkages between the domestic and EC tiers' (Bulmer, 1983: 349). Bulmer criticised the persistent focus on the European Community solely as an international organisation and argued that the analytical tools usually applied to the study of national politics could usefully be applied to the study of the behaviour of member states in the European Community.

3.2   Interdependence/regime theory

Meanwhile, the study of international organisations more generally was undergoing some radical changes. Students of international relations, rejecting the realist model of international relations, began to attribute to international organisations a degree of dynamism, not solely attributable to the interests of nation states (Keohane and Nye, 1974, 1977). Interdependence theorists recognised the fragmented nature of the nation-state, the importance of transnational actors (including for example multinational companies) and the effect on national governments of participating in international regimes.

Cooperation between member states in an interdependent world is unavoidable, and membership in international regimes may help to minimise the uncertainties inherent for nation-states in international collaboration. Crucially, however, in this interpendent world 'recurrent interactions can change official perceptions of their interests' (Keohane and Nye, 1977: 34). Although, the interdependence school did not focus specifically on the European Community, but more broadly on the creation of international regimes, this approach generated a number of important insights which have been incorporated into subsequent attempts to understand the process of European integration.

3.3   Law and integration

Finally, the study of European institutions was being presented with some new challenges. Increasingly, scholars argued that the study of European institutions needed to encompass an examination of the role of the European Court of Justice and of the impact of European law in the process of European integration. During this period Weiler (1982) and Stein (1981) began to draw attention to the relevance of the law to any study of the European integration process. While the other institutions might have been going through a doldrums period, this was hardly the case for the ECJ:

> Tucked away in the fairyland Duchy of Luxembourg and blessed, until recently, with benign neglect by the powers that be and the mass media, the Court of Justice of the European Communities has fashioned a constitutional framework for a federal-type structure in Europe.
>
> (Stein, 1981: 1 cited in Wincott, 1995a)

4   UNDERSTANDING RECENT CONSTITUTIONAL DEVELOPMENTS

Since the relaunch of the Community (now European Union) with the Single European Act and the Maastricht Treaty, the study of European integration has enjoyed a renewed momentum. As Caporaso and Keeler (1995: 22) note, 'to a striking extent, however, the new debates parallel the old': the central division remains that between state-centric and non-state-centric approaches to the study of European integration. Recent attempts to conceptualise the process of European integration, from both perspectives, have sought to incorporate the strengths of earlier approaches, while addressing their weaknesses and building upon some of the theoretical insights developed in the 1970s.

Some of the most ambitious studies have emerged as an attempt to explain the negotiation of the Single European Act, a key constitutional event in the history of European integration. In '1992: Recasting the European Bargain', for example, Sandholtz and Zysman (1989) incorporate some of the key insights of the neo-functionalist approach. They argue that, in the run up to the Single European Act, the European Commission played a crucial leadership role, acting as a 'policy entrepreneur'.[15] Aided by a transnational industry coalition which was in favour of the single market, they argue, the Commission was able to persuade an important coalition of national governments of the benefits of market unification (Sandholtz and Zysman, 1989: 96). The critical role played by European business elites – in setting the agenda for the 1992 project, in mobilising support and in overseeing its implementation – has also been demonstrated by Cowles (1995).

Crucially, Sandholtz and Zysman (1989) also address one of the most powerful critiques of the neo-functionalist approach: that it neglected the impact of the international environment. For Sandholtz and Zysman (1989: 100), changing international and domestic conditions – the rise of Japan, the relative decline of the USA and the evident failure of existing national economic policies in Europe – were the very events which made 1992 possible: 'international and domestic situations provided a setting in which the Commission could exercise policy entrepreneurship, mobilizing a transnational coalition in favour of the unified internal market'. Thus, as well as drawing upon the insights of the neo-functionalist school, Sandholtz and Zysman incorporate aspects of the 'domestic politics' approach and recognise the vital catalytic role played by changes in the international environment.

However, in 'Negotiating the Single European Act', Moravcsik (1991) argued that it was not an elite alliance between European officials and the European big business elite which had made the SEA possible. In contrast to the revised neo-functionalist interpretation of the SEA advocated by Sandholtz and Zysman, Moravcsik (1991: 42), drawing on the insights of realist and intergovernmentalist approaches, argued that interstate bargains between Britain, France and Germany were the key determinants of the negotiation of the SEA. Moreover, the bargains struck represented the 'lowest common denominator solution' achievable only because of the convergence of national interests. Each government had closely guarded its national sovereignty and had placed strict limits on any future transfer of sovereignty (Moravcsik, 1991: 46–48). While acknowledging the influence of the realist school of thought (states as the principal actors in the international system), and of the regime school of international relations (shaping interstate politics by providing a common framework which reduces transaction costs and minimises uncertainty), Moravcsik (1991: 48) differentiates his 'intergovernmental institutionalism' by stressing the importance of 'domestic politics' in influencing the changing preferences of states.

Moravcsik (1993) further develops his argument in 'Preferences and Power in the European Community'. In this work on liberal intergovernmentalism, he argues that 'state behaviour reflects the rational actions of governments constrained at home by domestic societal pressures and abroad by their strategic environment' (Moravcsik 1993: 474). The preferences of national governments, which determine their positions in international negotiations, are determined, he argues, by domestic societal forces: 'the identity of important societal groups, the nature of their interests and their relative influence on domestic policy' (Moravcsik, 1993: 483). Within the framework of liberal intergovernmentalism, however, Moravcsik (1993: 484 and 488) allows for a degree of what he terms 'agency slack'. Thus, within the principal–agent relationship, in which domestic societal principals delegate power to governmental agents, there is on occasion some limited discretion allowed to those agents. Where the interests of societal groups are ambiguous or divided, the constraints upon government are loosened, allowing politicians 'a wider range of *de facto* choice in negotiating strategies and positions'.

National governments have not, he argues, simply passively enjoyed the benefits of the occasional discretion allowed to them by divided or unclear domestic pressures. They have actively sought to maximise their room for manoeuvre. Thus, Moravcsik (1993) has argued that national governments have used EU institutions as part of a two-level game (cf. Putnam, 1988) to increase the policy autonomy of national governments in relation to domestic interests: 'particularly where domestic interests are weak or divided, EC institutions have been deliberately designed to assist national governments in overcoming domestic opposition' (Moravcsik, 1993: 515). Thus, in his more recent work Moravcsik (1994: 47) has argued that far from supranational elites tying member states into a process to which they are resistant, the European Union may in fact strengthen the state by allowing, for example, chief executives 'to manipulate their own domestic constituents into accepting common policies'.

Sandholtz (1993) has criticised the presentation of the debate about European integration as a dichotomy between intergovernmentalist and institutionalist approaches. Although decisions are taken in intergovernmental institutions (therefore analysis of intergovernmental bargaining processes is important), the preferences on the basis of which national governments influence EC policies 'are themselves influenced by EC institutions and law' (Sandholtz, 1993: 3). In emphasising the endogenous nature of preference formation, Sandholtz not only recalls the insights of Haas, who argued that participation at the European level would alter the perceptions which national elites held of their own interests, but also emphasises the development of shared identity, norms and behaviour patterns developed within the context of an international regime (in this case, the European Monetary System). Examining the decision of the member states to commit themselves to monetary policy in the Maastricht Treaty, Sandholtz argues that there is an important link between participation in the EU policy regime and the formation of government preferences:

> membership in the EC has become part of the interest calculation for governments and societal groups. In other words, the national interests of EC states do not have independent existence; they are not formed in a vacuum and then brought to Brussels. Those interests are defined and redefined in an international and institutional context that includes the EC.
>
> (Sandholtz 1993: 3)

5 UNDERSTANDING THE EUROPEAN UNION AS A POLITY

Attempts to understand major constitutional decisions, as landmarks in the integration process, are now accompanied by a growing literature examining the functioning of the EU as a system of governance. Drawing on approaches from the areas of comparative politics and policy analysis (Bulmer, 1994a, 1994b; Majone, 1993; Marks, 1992; Mazey and Richardson, 1993c; Peters, 1992, 1994; Peterson, 1995; Sbragia, 1992):

> increasingly scholars assume that some institutional structure is in place and examine what goes on inside these structures. Politics and policy-making within institutions have assumed an analytic place alongside the politics of institutional change.
>
> (Caporaso and Keeler, 1995: 43)

It is increasingly recognised that it is important to focus, not simply on the process through which major institutional change takes place in the EU, but also on the day-to-day functioning of the EU as a polity.

In the early 1990s studies revealed the crucial role which interest groups have played in the EU policy process (Greenwood *et al.*, 1992; Mazey and Richardson, 1993a). Other studies demonstrated how EU institutions have influenced the agenda-setting, policy formulation and implementation processes, for example the role of bureaucratic politics in the EU (Peters, 1992); the role of the Commission as agenda-setter (Peters, 1994; Pollack, 1995a, 1995b); and the Commission's role in the promotion of the EU regulatory regime (Bulmer, 1994a; Cram, 1993; Dehousse, 1993; Majone, 1989a, 1991a, 1991b, 1992a, 1992b, 1992c, 1993). Likewise, the role of the European Parliament as 'conditional agenda-setter' has been examined (Tsebelis, 1994). Increasingly too, scholars have begun to assess the important political role played by the European Court of Justice (Burley and Mattli, 1993; Garrett, 1992; Garrett and Weingast, 1993; Shapiro, 1992; Weiler, 1991; Wincott, 1995a) and, importantly, to examine the critical interactions between the Court and other institutions within the policy process (Alter and Meunier-Aitsahalia, 1994; Wincott, 1995b). Scholars have, meanwhile, been forced to recognise the complexity of the role played by EU institutions. Analysts have, for example, cautioned against over-generalisation concerning the role of 'the Commission', which is a highly differentiated structure (Cram, 1994a), or of the impact of the European Parliament, as its influence varies between policy sectors (Judge *et al.*, 1994).

These policy-based studies have important implications for evaluations of the most appropriate 'conceptual lenses' (Allison, 1971) through which to view the integration process. Peterson (1995: 71), for example, conceptualises the European Union as a multi-tiered system of governance. He distinguishes between the different types of decisions taken, the different actors which dominate and the different types of rationality which inform their actions, at the various levels of analysis identified within the EU. Peterson concludes that no single theory can explain EU governance at all levels of analysis. Broad 'macro' approaches to the issue of integration (such as neo-functionalism or state-centred 'intergovernmentalist' approaches) are particularly useful for explaining the major 'history-making' decisions of the EU. When it comes to explaining 'policy-setting' or 'policy-shaping' decisions, however, 'macro-theories tend to lose their explanatory power' (Peterson, 1995: 84). Indeed, as our understanding of the EU policy process, and of the process of European integration more generally, becomes more sophisticated, it may increasingly be the case that 'our explanatory goals are best served by specifying the analytic strengths – and limitations – of approaches that work better in combination than alone' (Sandholtz, 1993: 39).

While scholars have argued that it is necessary to distinguish between the politics of the EU policy process, and the process of European integration (Hix, 1994), or between history-making and day-to-day decisions (Peterson, 1995), it is important not to overstate the division between the two. It is clearly useful to distinguish between different levels of analysis for analytic purposes. It is important, however, to remember that this divide is not clear cut. The relationship between the politics and processes which accompany day-to-day decision-making, as opposed to 'constitutional' or 'history-making' decisions, is, in many respects, reciprocal. From this perspective, the studies of the 'normal politics' of the EU, identified by Caporaso and Keeler (1995: 42), might most usefully be viewed, not simply as occurring alongside the development of integration theory but, rather, as performing a crucial role by enhancing existing understandings of the process of European integration and of the various influences upon the environment in which major history-making decisions are taken.

6 INSTITUTIONS, PURPOSEFUL OPPORTUNISM AND THE EU POLICY PROCESS

The critical role which EU institutions have come to play in the EU policy process is increasingly recognised. Studies have revealed how EU institutions have influenced the agenda-setting, policy formulation and implementation processes. There is considerable evidence that institutions, as purposive actors, have an important influence on EU policy-making. The central argument of this book is that the insights of these studies are crucial in facilitating the development of a more rounded understanding of the integration process. The question is no longer do institutions and the day-to-day politics of the policy process matter but how do they matter and in what respects do they influence the policy process and ultimately the process of European integration?

2   The development of European Union social policy

1   INTRODUCTION

> The results of institutional change cannot be evaluated with reference to discrete, isolated decisions, but must be assessed in terms of sequences of interdependent decisions taken by a variety of actors over time. This assumption of continuing relationships among policy actors introduces a temporal dimension that is absent in the one-time choice situations usually considered in policy analysis.
>
> (Majone, 1989b: 98)

A snapshot picture of the current situation in European Union social policy appears straightforward. The legislative profile of EU social policy, as recorded in the most recent 'Directory of Community Legislation in Force and other Acts of the Community Institutions' (June 1995: Section 05.20: 521–547), indicates the limited extent of binding legislation in the area of EU social policy: twenty-four Regulations; forty-two Directives; forty-nine Decisions. These few Regulations, Directives and Decisions are, moreover, strictly limited in scope. Most of the binding provisions in the social field are devoted to the establishment of an institutional framework at the EU level: establishing decision-rules (such as those governing the operation of the European Social Fund), setting up advisory and standing committees; or creating permanent organisations such as the European Foundation for the Improvement of Living and Working Conditions. Of the very limited number of provisions which directly affect the well-being of European citizens, these include a relatively small number of regulatory policies: in the areas of Health and Safety; Equal Treatment of Men and Women; Protection of Workers and Social Security for Migrant Workers; as well as a number of small-scale EU social programmes involving direct EU expenditure such as the HELIOS Programme for people with disabilities (see Chapter 4 and Cram, 1993: 138–140). A broader range of social issues such as public housing, elderly people, education and public health are, meanwhile, the subjects of an array of non-binding, or soft law (Wellens and Borchardt, 1989), provisions implemented via 182 'other acts'. These 'other acts' include, for example, non-binding Commission and Council Resolutions, Declarations, Recommendations and Opinions. In this context, it is easy to understand how the European social space could be dismissed as 'Heavy on Symbolism... and Light on Substance' (Tsoukalis, 1993: xiii).

As always, the picture is not so clear cut as it first appears. The paucity of binding legislative achievements in the social field, and the restriction of these provisions to a narrow range of issues, belies the many far-reaching declarations made by the Heads of State and Government expressing their commitment to the social dimension of European integration. Since the creation of the European Economic Community in 1957, a stream of Treaty preambles, Summit Declarations and, more recently, of Conclusions of the European Council has stated the significance which the Heads of State and Government of the European Union attribute to the social dimension. Yet, there has long existed a tension between the declarations of the member states and the reluctance of the same member states to turn their rhetoric into reality via the introduction of binding EU legislation in the social field. In the area of European Union social policy there is 'many a slip 'twixt the cup of general ideas and the lip of concrete applications' (Venturini, 1989: 23). Thus, while the goals expressed in the preamble to the Treaty of Rome (1957) exhibit broad aims concerning the nature of the new socio-economic order in the making,[1] the actual social provisions of the Treaty, Articles 117–128 (Part 3, Title III), are vague and often ambiguous. Only those referring to: freedom of movement for workers; social security for migrant workers; freedom of establishment and equal treatment for male and female workers require binding legislation. Meanwhile Articles 117 and 118, in particular, are highly ambiguous and have caused intense inter-institutional wrangling, between the Commission and the Council of Ministers, over their interpretation (Holloway, 1981: 41–48).[2] Although the Commission has always taken a dynamic approach in interpreting these (Collins, 1975: 188), this has not always proved successful.

Broad statements of commitment to social progress, although perhaps less ambitious than those in the Treaty of Rome, figure, once again, in the preamble to the Single European Act.[3] In contrast, the social provisions of the revised Treaty remained vague. Actual advances in the social provisions are rather confusing. Article 118A, for example, allowed for majority voting on matters of health and safety for workers, while Article 100A stated that matters concerning the 'rights and interests of workers' must be subject to unanimous voting. The few changes implemented, as predicted, have led to 'interminable political controversy over their appropriate use' (Rhodes, 1991: 253).

There has never been consensus among the member states as to the role of the EU in the social field. However, commitment to the social objectives of the integration process has always been, at least, symbolically important. Even the very public opt-out by the UK government from certain social aspects of the Maastricht Treaty was focused more on the UK government's objection to the means proposed to achieve social ends than upon a total rejection of the ends themselves.[4] The UK government, in fact, endorsed the goal stated in the preamble of the Maastricht Treaty 'to promote economic and social progress for their peoples'. Likewise, the UK government endorsed Article 2, Title II, of the Maastricht Treaty, which declares the intention of the EU to move 'towards a high level of employment and of social protection, and the raising of the standard of living and quality of life'.

The most surprising feature of European Union social policy is, perhaps, that there should be any at all. There is a general consensus in the literature that national governments are the dominant actors in the EU policy process, and much evidence that these dominant actors have until recently been resistant to any extension of the EU's social policy role. At the same time, however, an increasing EU presence in social affairs is making itself felt. The output of the EU in the field of social policy has increased significantly since the mid-1980s and this trend seems likely to continue alongside the process of completing the internal market. Meanwhile, EU competence in the area of social policy was considerably enhanced by changes brought about by the Maastricht Treaty. In this chapter, the paradoxical nature of social policy development in the EU is explored. It is suggested that the European Commission, or the Directorate-General for Employment, Industrial Relations and Social Affairs (DGV) within the Commission, has behaved in the manner predicted for all bureaucracies by Anthony Downs (1967) and has played an active role in expanding the scope of EU social policy.

2 EU SOCIAL POLICY: HISTORICAL DEVELOPMENT

2.1 The 1960s: benign neglect or testing the water?

Early Commission intervention in the social field, from the inception of the European Economic Community in 1957 until the late 1960s, has been referred to as a phase of 'benign neglect' (Mosely, 1990: 149) or 'low key convergence' (Taylor, 1983: 199) in the social field. Certainly during this period the role of social policy in overall EU policy was minor (Shanks, 1977: 3). However, while there were few binding legislative advances, the area of social policy was by no means neglected. Perhaps a more accurate characterisation of this period is that the newly established Commission of the European Union was attempting to define its relationship *vis-à-vis* the Council of Ministers in the social field. In understanding the approach which the Commission adopted at this time, it is critical to appreciate the nature of the Commission as a bureaucracy with a mission: a body charged by the founding Treaties with the mission of promoting the integration process. Critically, the CEU is no ordinary bureaucracy. As Usher (1994: 149) argues, 'as a civil service, the Commission would naturally give way to its political masters. As an independent political animal, the Commission is keen to extend its power and play a politically strategic role in setting the goals of the Community itself'.

The Commission from the outset attempted to define its relationship with the member states to allow itself maximum flexibility in the social field. In 1958, the Commission stated that 'the governments had allotted the Community its own role in social affairs' (1st General Report, 1958: 79). The Rome Treaty, drawn up just a year earlier, was interpreted as a declaration of the member states' ambitions in the social field and the Commission consistently sought to hold the member states to ransom over their Treaty commitments. Far from waiting for the member states to clarify their intentions, the CEU thought it 'important to keep the Council and member governments informed of what the Treaty implied for the Commission' (6th General Report, 1963: 21). The ambiguities in the Treaty's references to social policy, in particular those embodied in Articles 117 and 118 (see note 2), were interpreted as providing increased scope for Commission action. Thus, the CEU stated that the 'comparative lack of precision in the Treaty forces the Commission to interpret certain of the articles...it is not the Commission's intention that the interpretation shall be restrictive; it cannot conceive that the Community has not got a social purpose' (2nd General Report, 1959: 107). In particular, the CEU chose to support a broad interpretation of the aims expressed by the member states in Article 117 (2nd General Report, 1959: 107), while attempting to sidestep the potential restriction of its actions by the limited provisions of Article 118: 'the sphere of action of the institutions in social matters has no strict limits, the problems listed in Article 118 being in no way exclusive' (1st General Report, 1958: 78). Further, the CEU argued that

> The European Commission realises that it bears particular responsibilities in this field and intends to neglect no sphere in which it may prove possible to 'promote close collaboration between member states' (Article 118) and it will use all appropriate procedural methods.
>
> (1st General Report, 1958: 79)

This last statement was particularly significant considering that there was no consensus among the member states as to what constituted 'appropriate procedural methods'. There was no agreement as to which 'procedures' were implied by Article 117, as to whether the functioning of the internal market would suffice to bring about a degree of harmonisation of social systems, or whether more interventionist methods would be required. Indeed, there was no consensus concerning the necessity of harmonisation, rather than the coordination of national systems, in this field at all (Holloway, 1981: 17–27).

In pursuing its goals in the social field the Commission noted that it was '*counting* on the support not only of governments and of the international organisations but also on that of professional organisations representing the world of labour' (1st General Report, 1958: 80, emphasis added). From early on the CEU sought to draw in non-governmental actors to support its work on the harmonisation of social systems. Trade unions, employers' associations and member governments participated in *ad-hoc* committees to examine 'ways and means of attaining these ends' (5th General Report, 1962: 180). Working parties, composed of representatives from both sides of industry, examined the problems of collective bargaining, protection at work for women and young workers and the length of the working week (5th General Report, 1962: 180). Throughout, this period, the Commission showed scant regard for the opinions of the member states. On the part of the member states, meanwhile, 'such moves by the Commission suggested that governments might be bypassed and action encouraged which was unwelcome to them' (Collins, 1975: 191). In December 1962, for example, the Commission organised the European Conference on Social Security aimed to draw a range of public and private bodies into the discussion on the harmonisation of social systems (Bull. EU 2/1963: 51–52). Significantly, the member states refused to participate other than as observers (Holloway, 1981: 53). Nevertheless, in October 1963 the Commission issued a preliminary draft programme for the harmonisation of social security schemes on the basis of the conclusions of the Conference (Bull. EU 12/1963: 36). The Commission also issued Recommendations based on Article 118 concerning the employment of young workers and the rationalisation of invalidity costs, although these were opposed by both employers and the member states because of the costs involved (Collins, 1975: 191–192). Ultimately, the member states signalled their discontent by refusing to cooperate with the CEU. No meetings of the Council of Ministers for social affairs were held between October 1964 and December 1966 (Collins, 1975: 195; Holloway, 1981: 54).

On 19 December 1966 the deadlock situation was finally resolved on the basis of the Veldkamp Memorandum.[5] The subsequent agreement, struck in the Council of Ministers, strictly curtailed the role of CEU in social affairs and represented a clear triumph for the Council over the Commission (Collins, 1975: 196; Holloway, 1981: 55). Ultimately, 'members did not wish to see Community proposals which might encourage or justify claims they did not wish to satisfy' (Collins 1975: 197). As a result, the Commission's approach to social policy in the late 1960s and early 1970s was inevitably more restrained. Notably, the Commission's 'Preliminary Guidelines for a Community Social Policy Programme' (Bull. EU Supplement 2/1971: 55),[6] issued in 1971, include a section on 'Community Action: *Justification and Limits*' (emphasis added). The recognition that there was a need to justify the Commission's activities in social affairs, and that there were limits to its responsibilities, was far removed from the expansive interpretations contained in its earlier documents.

By the early 1970s there was clear Commission recognition of the need for political support from the member states for Commission actions in the social field. Commission Vice-President Levi-Sandri, in his address to the European Parliament in 1970, argued that 'the flimsiness of the Treaty provisions will be no obstacle if the political will to advance along the road indicated has been affirmed at the start' (Bull. EU 5/1970: 27–28). More generally, in the late 1960s and the early 1970s, the Commission began to change its approach towards the Council. Rather than engaging in direct conflict, which might result in a further curtailment of its powers, the Commission sought to provoke the Council into supporting CEU action in the social field: 'Further propaganda and prodding will be necessary to generate the political will required to overcome the difficulties arising from the frequently vague and loose provisions of the Treaties on social subjects' (Bull. EU Supplement 2/1971: 55).

The evident shift in the Commission's approach after the Veldkamp Agreement has also been portrayed as the triumph of the economic view over the social vision. Thus, 'the outcome of the clash marks not only an institutional defeat for the Commission, it also marks the defeat of the "harmonisation for social progress approach" .... the Commission's work after 1966 has been increasingly economic in nature' (Holloway, 1981: 57). Justifications for Community action employed by the Commission post-Veldkamp are heavily couched in economic terms and repeatedly stress the close relationship between social policy and economic and monetary union. In its 1971 'Guidelines', for example, the Commission stated that it had 'based its choice of priorities on the fact that social policy must play an effective part in the steady advance towards economic and monetary union, which, in turn, takes on its full significance by its contribution to the fulfilment of the great social objectives' (Bull. EU Supplement 2/1971: 55). Commissioner Albert Coppe, meanwhile, stressed the need 'to move on to the fresh stage of social policy which is a necessary corollary of the decision to establish economic and monetary union' (Bull. EU 5/1971: 5). The references to the direct achievement of social objectives are less frequent and it is argued that 'at a time when the Community is resolutely taking the road to economic and monetary union, social policy is seen in a new light' (Bull. EU 5/1971: 13). Writing at the end of the 1970s, and examining this apparent U-turn, Holloway (1981: 63) asked whether the Commission had undergone a 'complete reversal of its earlier policy?' and concluded that the 'tentative answer to this important question must at this stage be: yes'.

Viewed over time, and in the light of subsequent events, however, it becomes increasingly clear that a change in the Commission's language, or even of its purported ambitions, should not be confused with a change in its overall purpose: that of expanding its competence. Crucially, a 'purposeful opportunist' knows where it wants to go but is fairly flexible about how it gets there.[7] Observed through this 'conceptual lens', the evident changes in the CEU's position may be viewed as changes less of substance than of strategy: in short, as a Commission foray into the realm of symbolic politics.

2.2 The Commission U-turn: ideology or opportunism?

Both the Commission and the member states were faced with a problem at the end of the 1960s. Clearly, the Commission's interpretation of the ambiguities of the Treaty provisions in the social field did not comply with that of the member states in the Council. However, to equate the positions adopted by the Council and the Commission as the economic versus the social approach respectively is to seriously underestimate the crucial role which symbolic politics have played in the EU policy process. If the member states had a clear and unambiguous commitment to the economic approach, then a clear and unambiguous interpretation of the Commission's role could have been delegated to it by the member states. Likewise, if the Commission had an ideological commitment to the social progress approach it might have been expected that it would not have altered its stance and adopted the economic rationale so readily. In practice, neither the Commission's nor the Council's position is this clear cut.[8] As always, 'multiple realities are inherent in politics and so are the rationalisations that justify particular interpretations of the political scene' (Edelman, 1985: 199).

National governments clearly have to generate the support, or acquiescence, of their domestic principals (i.e. domestic interests) if they wish to continue to pursue their goals at the European level.[9] This support is often achieved by the use of symbolic politics. Similarly, the Commission requires the support of its member state principals if it wishes to retain its role in the social field and the Commission may also resort to symbolic politics in its relations with the member states. Viewed from this perspective the Commission's approach to social policy may most usefully be characterised as more pragmatic than ideological. The Commission's early high-profile support for the social dimension may have been less a sign of its commitment to social progress than a means by which it sought to expand the scope of its competence in this field. When it became clear that the member states were unwilling to support a broad interpretation of the Commission's activities in the social field, but would continue to issue ambiguous statements of support for the social dimension, the Commission sought to justify the extension of its activities by emphasising the social aspects of economic integration.

As member states have been less equivocal about the role of the CEU in economic integration and the completion of the internal market, the symbolic references made by the CEU to economic rationalisations for its actions in the social field have allowed it to engage in a range of activities in the social field which would otherwise have been impossible. While Commission activities in the social field have often been justified in economic terms, this link has sometimes been stretched gossamer thin. Spicker (1991: 10) notes, for example, the Commission's argument for aluminium controls to protect migrant dialysis patients. As he argues, this proposal is less concerned with the freedom of movement of workers than it is with establishing a precedent for future Community action in the field of public health. Symbolically, however, being seen to have made a U-turn may in itself have been a judicious move. Importantly, 'much problem solving takes the form not of altering any state of affairs but of altering people's perceptions and evaluations' (Lindblom, 1990: 4).

2.3 The 1970s: preparing the ground for future action

A number of factors can be said to have influenced the manner in which the Commission has tackled the subject of social policy. The Community process is vulnerable to a variety of external factors, to changing economic circumstances, to the state of world markets and to the prevailing attitude to European integration. Not least of the influences upon the Commission role in social policy, however, has been the continual battle between the Commission and the Council over the interpretation of the social responsibilities of the Community. In interpreting its responsibilities, as derived from the founding Treaties, the Commission has always adopted a dynamic approach. In the case of social affairs the Commission has continually striven to maximise Community competence (Holloway, 1981: 52–53). As has been seen, the early 'head on' approach to social policy by the Commission resulted in institutional stalemate on social matters and the curtailment of the Commission's powers in this area.

To a large extent the result of this battle can be said to have been a triumph for the Council and, consequently, of national over Community interests. The Commission, reluctant to clash with the Council once again, adopted a notably more circumspect approach to social affairs, concentrating far more on technical matters and provisions stipulated in the Treaty. However, to refer back to Allison's important observation: 'different conceptual lenses lead analysts to different judgements about what is relevant and important' (Allison, 1971: 253).[10] Viewed through an institutionalist lens, a change in the activities of the Commission does not necessarily indicate that it had lost its integrationist ambitions or become simply the servant of its member state principals. Although in the early stages, following this débâcle, little progress appeared to be made in social policy, this may have been more to do with the inexperience of the Commission as an institutional actor than an indication of a change in perspective. During the 1970s and early 1980s, however, the Commission adopted a lower profile approach and learned to make more sophisticated use of its bureaucratic skills.

Not least, the Commission learned to capitalise upon the rhetoric of the member states. It quickly learned to couch its proposals in the language of economic and monetary union favoured at the Summits held at The Hague in 1969 and in Paris in 1972. In Paris, for example, the member states had declared their intention to 'strengthen the Community by forming an economic and monetary union, as a token of stability and growth, as the indispensable basis of their social progress and as a remedy for regional disparities' (Bull. EU 10/1972, Point 2). The Commission was asked to draw up an action programme by 1 January 1974, 'providing for practical measures and the means for them' (Bull. EU, 19/1972, Point 3).

In response to this request from the Council, the Commission continued to assert its independence in the social field: 'It is emphasised that the Commission considers that the guidelines laid down in the Council Resolution of 21 January 1974 do not constitute a limit to the Community's activity in the social field and that the Commission always retains its right of initiative to make proposals as and when necessary' (Social Rep. 1974: 13). In practice, however, it took a pragmatic approach to the elaboration of the Social Action Programme (SAP) which 'consisted of measures for which it was felt, rightly or wrongly, that there was a broad political consensus among the nine member governments' (Shanks, 1977: 13). Until 1975, the SAP seemed to run according to plan but even in 1974 and 1975, when progress was still being made, there was a growing tendency for the member states to water down policies which involved the expenditure of Community resources. By 1976 progress on the SAP had 'slowed to a trickle' (Shanks, 1977: 16). Each of the Commission's thirty-six proposals had to be argued separately through the Council and already, by the mid-1970s, the political will to pursue an active Community social policy seemed to have waned. In contrast with the situation a decade earlier, however, in 1976 it was declining economic circumstances which had the effect of making national governments more protectionist rather than the over-zealous activities of the Commission.

In this context, little major binding legislation was passed in the late 1970s and early 1980s. However, the Commission was able to continue its catalytic research activities (during this period the Poverty Programme (OJ L 199, 30.7.1975) and the Action Programme for Health and Safety (OJ C 13, 12.2.1974) were established and entered into their second phases (OJ L 2, 3.1.1985 and OJ C 67, 27.2.1984)) and to promote the institutional development of EU social policy. A number of EU organisations and committees in the social field were, for example, established during this period, for example, Standing Committee on Employment (1970), European Foundation for the Improvement of Living and Working Conditions (Regulation 1365/ 75), Social Problems of Agricultural Workers (74/442/EEC), Inland Navigation (80/991/EEC), Equal Opportunities for Men and Women (82/43/EEC), Railways (85/13/EEC) and Road Transport (85/516/ EEC).

By establishing research projects, and small-scale social programmes, issuing communications and drawing a range of actors into the EU policy process (whether formally or informally), the Commission engaged in what Majone (1992c: 6–7), building on Kingdon's (1984) work, has called a 'softening up process': paving the way for the Commission's preferred course of action should a 'policy window' open up. At the same time, the Commission carried out extensive analysis and comprehensive evaluations, both of its own actions and programmes in the social field, and, perhaps more importantly, of the policies of the member states at the national level. In this context, the persuasive role of policy analysis is worth recalling. For some, 'policy analysis is no longer an alternative to a play of power; it becomes largely an instrument of influence or power....Policy is analysed not in an unrealistic attempt to reach conclusive determinations of correct policy, but simply to persuade' (Lindblom, 1968: 117). Part of the softening up process is the preparation of data which require action and, moreover, which demonstrate that the most suitable action will be that which favours the interests of the CEU: that is, action which expands the competence of the CEU in the social field. Majone's (1989b: 117) observation, that 'demonstrating that there is a problem which can be attacked by one's favourite instrument is a very real preoccupation of participants in the policy process', is nowhere more true than when applied to the activities of the DGV during this period.

The Commission was, thus, well prepared to make good use of the opportunity for action when a renewed declaration of support for EU intervention in the social field came from the Council of Social Affairs Ministers in 1984:

> the Community will not be able to strengthen its economic cohesion in the face of international competition if it does not strengthen its social cohesion at the same time. Social policy must therefore be developed at Community level on the same basis as economic, monetary and industrial policies.
>
> (Bull. EU 5/1984, Point 2.1.68)

The Commission's new Medium-Term Social Action Programme was approved by the Fontainebleau European Council in June 1984 and provided the Commission with a basis upon which to build its plans for the social dimension (Bull. EU 6/1984, Point 5). Carefully couched in language which emphasised the importance of social policy for the completion of the internal market, the currently popular rationale for EU intervention, the action programme sought to revitalise the 'social dialogue', between employers and and trade unions. Jacques Delors, then President of the European Commission, argued that negotiation between management and labour (the 'social partners') should constitute one of the cornerstones of the revitalised 'social area', or 'L'Espace Sociale', in the EU.

On Delors's initiative, what became known as the 'Val Duchesse Dialogue' was launched in 1985. Intended to be an important step towards revitalising the social dimension in the Community, and to draw an important constituency of actors into the EU social policy process, the Val Duchesse talks proved disappointing in practice. Hesitation on the part of employers to participate in any dialogue which sought to reach a binding agreement scuppered the Commission's ambitious intentions. The 'Joint Opinions', finally issued, were vague and loosely worded and committed neither party to any specific action. Employers agreed to sign the final texts only on condition that the Commission would not make use of the joint opinions as the basis for any legislation (Brewster and Teague, 1989: 96–97). However, 'Delors knew that the exercise would initially be more about confidence building than about immediate results' (Ross, 1995: 377). Indeed, subsequent developments in both the SEA and in the Maastricht Treaty bear testimony to the way in which the role of the social partners has developed and become institutionalised in EU social policy process.[11] As so often, the initial faltering steps initiated by the Commission have proved to have a lasting impact on the development of EU social policy.

2.4 The SEA to Maastricht: a step too far?

The softly, softly approach adopted by the Commission throughout the late 1970s and early 1980s allowed the Commission to prepare the ground for future action. By the mid-1980s, a more experienced and sophisticated bureaucracy had a series of viable proposals at the ready, research had been done, actions programmes run and many of the most important actors had been softened up. The negotiations over the Single European Act and the future direction the EU was to take provided the window of opportunity which the Commission required to launch a renewed offensive on the social dimension.

One of the most sophisticated aspects of the Commission's approach to the negotiations over the Single European Act was the packaging of innovations in the potentially conflictual social dimension as matters of procedure rather than of substance. Arguably one important reason for the relative lack of conflict over the issue of social policy during the SEA negotiations was the rather low-profile approach adopted by the Commission and the focus it encouraged on procedural, rather than substantive issues. The Commission early on dropped its plans for major social reforms and focused on 'efficiency' issues (such as amendments to the voting procedure on matters of health and safety) rather than those which would draw attention to the 'distributive' implications of social policy innovations. Advances in the social dimension were extremely limited in the SEA and the few new provisions were ambiguous and vague.[12] However, this very vagueness may have facilitated the agreement by member states on procedural reform in this area. Arguably, the focus on regulatory and efficiency issues, promoted by the Commission, allowed national governments to sign up to these proposals without fully understanding or anticipating the potential uses to which the procedures would be put. In a very short time, however, member states were to become aware of the implications of their actions.

While the UK government, in particular, strongly opposed Commission intervention in social affairs, some concession in this area was the price which had to be paid for the economic benefits expected from the internal market. The concessions made to the inclusion of social policy in the SEA are, as noted above, extremely limited. Meanwhile, Mrs Thatcher, then UK Prime Minister, insisted that the procedural changes in the SEA did not effectively change the right of individual countries to veto proposals considered contrary to their national interest (Brewster and Teague, 1989: 39). However, the stated commitment to economic and social cohesion in the Community provided an important starting point for Commission action. As Andriessen (1986: 17), then Vice-President of the Commission, stated at the signing of the SEA:

> Our task now is to make real progress within this new framework. The value and scope of the Act now to be opened for signature will

be judged by the results. For its part, the Commission is determined to take advantage of what the Single Act has to offer and, to quote Mr Delors, to make the compromise dynamic.

(Andriessen, 1986: 15)

The Commission's revived attempts at a dynamic interpretation of its role in EU social policy rapidly succeeded in alienating, in particular, the UK government. Conscious that to be seen continually blocking Commission social policy initiatives was bad politics, and anxious to influence the direction of Community social policy, the UK government, with the support of Ireland and Italy, had presented its own 'Action Programme for Employment Growth' in 1986 (Brewster and Teague, 1989: 98–99). The basis of this proposal was for a non-interventionist EU policy, based largely on improved training, help for the self-employed and entrepreneurs and encouraging labour market flexibility. It went through the Council with little difficulty. Minor amendments were made to the text to incorporate the 'social dialogue' principle and the programme was ratified unanimously (Bull. EU 12/ 1986, Point 2.1.137). In theory this was a major achievement for the UK Conservative government, since proposals which are not supported by the Commission are rarely adopted by the Council. However, the six-monthly progress reports required of the Commission indicate the Commission's efforts to countervail the programme's objectives of decentralisation and deregulation. The Commission divided the Action Programme into separate initiatives and classified them under existing Community programmes and initiatives. The radical UK programme thus appeared as little more than an adjustment to existing policy aims:

It appears that the Commission is using its role as helmsman of policy development to frustrate the key objectives of the UK government by identifying proposals in the Action Programme which correspond broadly with previous EU initiatives.

(Brewster and Teague, 1989: 99)

Meanwhile, the SEA was rapidly followed up by a high-profile onslaught by the Commission on the social dimension. The SEA provided the basis for the Delors initiative which sought to give substance to the social dimension of the Internal Market (Venturini, 1989: 27). The UK government was so disturbed by the use made by the Commission of its new-found powers in the social area, that it chose not to sign up even to the non-binding Community Social Charter in 1989.[13] The UK government feared that the social proposals, emanating from the associated Commission action programme (COM (89) 568 Final), would be linked to Article 100a, thus allowing for qualified majority voting in the Council (Rhodes, 1991: 262). This position was supported by employers who feared the generalised use of qualified majority voting (QMV) (Tyszkiewicz, 1989: 23). These reservations were proved to be justified when the then Commissioner for Social Affairs, Vasso Papandreou, announced that the Commission would also use Article 118a (also allowing for QMV) as a basis for the implementation of the action programme wherever possible. In the event, the latest Commission White Paper (COM (94) 333 Final: 21) records that the Commission action programme (COM (89) 568 Final) 'foresaw 21 proposals for directives, most of which were based on Article 118a. The Commission has proposed all of these and 13 have been adopted'. Clearly, these 13 Directives form a significant proportion of the only 42 Directives currently in force in the social field.[14]

The low-profile approach adopted by the Commission, it appears, facilitated the agreement of national governments on the relatively minor procedural advances agreed in the SEA which in retrospect have been of some importance. In turn, the high-profile relaunch of the social dimension, and the Commission's manipulation of the SEA provisions, may have contributed, by 1991, to the UK decision to 'opt out' of the rather limited provisions of the Maastricht social agreement. Critically, if the overarching goal of the Commission is viewed as the expansion of its competence, rather than of progress in the social field, then the opt-out amounts effectively to the curtailment of the Commission's powers in this field. Although enhanced procedures have been provided for policy development among the remaining eleven signatories, the Commission considers the opt-out, and the curtailment of the geographical scope of its competences, as a negative development:

> the Commission's principal objective is to promote the development of a European Social Policy which will benefit all citizens of the Union and will therefore enjoy, as far as is possible, the support of all member states. The Commission hopes, therefore, that Community social policy will once again be founded on a single legal basis. A major opportunity to achieve this will be the conference of representatives of Member State governments in 1996.
>
> (COM (93) 600 Final: 9–10).

This clearly raises the question: has the Commission become a victim of its own success?

2.5 Changes in the legal basis for action: the Maastricht Treaty, the Social Protocol and the Social Agreement

The Maastricht Treaty brought about two sets of changes with significant consequences for the legal basis for EU action in the area of social policy. First, changes were made to the main body of the EU Treaty which may affect the social policy activities of all of the member states (including the United Kingdom). Second, a Social Protocol (Protocol 14) was signed by all of the member states (again including the UK) entitling the EU member states, with the exception of the United Kingdom, to press ahead with social policy in the areas identified by, and using the instruments specified in, the attached Agreement on Social Policy. The Social Agreement is, the Protocol states, to facilitate the activities of the member states which have declared that they wish 'to continue along the path laid down in the 1989 Social Charter'. The UK is not entitled to participate in the deliberations or adoption of proposals made on the basis of the Protocol and Agreement. In turn, legislation adopted on this basis is not applicable to the UK nor is the UK to incur any financial costs as a consequence of such legislation.[15]

As a result of the Maastricht Treaty EU social policy is now, in the words of the European Commission, 'subject to two free-standing but complementary legal frames of reference' (COM (93) 600 Final: 9). The Commission has identified the main legal bases for social policy measures as shown in Table 1.

The Maastricht Treaty

When the Maastricht Treaty entered into force in November 1993 what was previously *Title III on Social Policy* became *Title VIII* of Part Three of the Treaty ('Community Policies') entitled *Social Policy, Vocational Training and Youth*. As is clear from Table 1, changes to the main body of the EU Treaty in the area of social policy were relatively few and, for the most part, fairly minor. As well as some small changes to Article 118a, which covers social issues open to majority voting (importantly health and safety), the Maastricht Treaty included procedural changes for the European Social Fund (Article 125) and new provisions on vocational training (Article 127). While vocational training (previously Article 128 of the EC Treaty) has always been an important aspect of EU social policy, its development was hampered by the lack of a clear implementing procedure (Collins, 1975: 24). Vocational training now enjoys a strengthened position as a result of its changed Treaty status.

Table 1 Overview of the main legal bases for social policy measures[16]

Maastricht Protocol and Social Agreement	EU Treaty
Qualified majority (52/77) possible (Article 2(1))	**Qualified majority (62/87) possible**
Improvement in particular of the working environment to protect workers' health and safety	Article 49: free movement of workers
Working conditions	Article 54: freedom of establishment
The information and consultation of workers	Article 57: mutual recognition of diplomas
Equality between men and women with regard to labour market opportunities and treatment at work	Article 125 (new) ES (application decision)
	Article 127 (new) vocational training
The integration of persons excluded from the labour market	Article 118A: health and safety at work
	Article 100A, Article 43: agriculture; Article 75: transport
Unanimity (14) required (Article 2(3))	**Unanimity (15) required**
Social security and social protection of workers	Article 51: social security (measures necessary for freedom of movement)
Protection of workers where their employment contract is terminated	Aryicle 100: internal market
Representation and effective defence of the interests of workers and employers, including codetermination	Article 130D: tasks, priority objectives and organization of the structural funds
Financial contributions for the promotion of employment and job creation	Article 235
Explicitly excluded from Community jurisdiction (Article 2(6))	
Pay	
Right of association, the right to strike, the right to impose lock out	

Although not included in the Commission's table of legal bases, there were also some broader developments in EU competence in the social field which deserve a mention. For the first time the term 'education' appears in an EU Treaty (Lenaerts, 1994: 7). In Article 126, the Community is given explicit competence to act in the area of education, an area in which the issue of EU intervention has been highly controversial. In practice, however, the provisions of Article

126 are rather familiar. While the term 'education' may not have been officially sanctioned prior to the Maastricht Treaty, many activities in the field of educational did, in fact, take place. The Commission Task Force on 'Education, Training and Youth', for example, predated the Maastricht Treaty and the activities of this body were, in effect, codified in the Maastricht Treaty (see CEU, 1989).

The Community is charged in the new Article 126 with promoting cooperation between the member states and with supporting and supplementing their actions in the field of education. In particular, action is to be aimed at: language teaching (a longstanding goal of the highly controversial LINGUA programme); encouraging the mobility of students (previously ERASMUS and TEMPUS programmes); facilitating recognition of educational qualifications (Article 57: Mutual Recognition of Diplomas); encouraging cooperation between educational establishments (previously, for example, the COMETT programme); to develop the exchange of information and experience on education systems between member states (in 1987 Article 128 was ruled by the European Court of Justice to be the proper legal basis for 'Community information projects and promotional activity' in the area of education: Lenaerts, 1995: 19);[17] to promote youth exchanges (previously, for example, Youth for Europe); and to encourage the development of distance education (a longstanding project entailing cooperation between DGV and DGXIII).

Not only is there little new to be found in the provisions on EU education policy but also, under Article 126, the legislative powers of the EU remain limited in the area of education: 'acting by a qualified majority on a proposal from the Commission [the Council] shall adopt recommendations' (Article 126(4)). Thus EU action is limited to the implementation of non-binding recommendations. Meanwhile, the 'harmonisation' of policy measures is specifically excluded (Article 126(4)). However, the inclusion of a Treaty article on education, viewed as distinct from vocational training, is an important example of the institutionalisation of existing policy actions on the part of the Commission. Viewed from this perspective, the way in which the new Treaty basis has helped to legitimise the transformation of the Task Force (mentioned above), into a new Commission Directorate-General (DGXXII – Education, Training and Youth) is significant. The new Directorate-General was established on 23 January 1995. As so often in the history of EU social policy, while the Treaty provisions initially appear limited, their effect may ultimately be far-reaching.

A further extension of the formal powers of the EU is to be found in the new *Title X* on *Public Health*. As with the case of education, for the first time the Treaty gives the EU institutions an explicit competence in the area of public health. However, once again, the Treaty provisions are fairly weak: the Council is limited to enacting recommendations in this field, albeit by qualified majority, and harmonisation measures are again excluded (Article 129). Meanwhile, the new Treaty powers are largely a codification of existing practice. As the proceedings of the Council of Ministers reveal, a section of the Council's report annually lists the activities of the EU in the area of public health.[18] The participation of the EU in the fight against cancer, drug dependency and AIDS, for example, all predate the Maastricht Treaty and the formal extension of EU competence. Similarly, in commenting on the development of its AIDS strategy in the pre-Maastricht era, the Commission specifically observed that an 'AIDS strategy is an expression of a public health policy' (Commission, 1991: 28 cited in Altenstetter, 1994: 413). However, the Commission has now begun to extend its activities on the basis of its newly recognised powers in this field. On 23 October 1995, the Commission, acting on the basis of a proposal from Commissioner Padraig Flynn (social affairs) and Commissioner Yves-Thibault de Silguy (economic affairs), adopted a new five-year programme (1997–2001) on public health (Agence Europe no. 6590, 23/24.10.95: 13). The programme, with a budget of 13.8 MECU, will monitor the health of European Union citizens. Importantly, it is precisely this type of research project which has in the past been used by the Commission to justify a further extension of its competence in the social field.[19]

The Social Protocol and the Social Agreement

The changes brought about by the Social Protocol and the attached Social Agreement, like the earlier changes to the social provisions of the Single European Act,[20] were largely changes in procedure rather than of content. Indeed, the 'innovation of the provisions lies in the provision of new legal bases for the adoption of secondary legislation' (Whiteford, 1993: 207).

Importantly, the overall role of EU social policy, as declared by the member states, does not differ dramatically between the main body of the Maastricht Treaty (signed by all of the member states) and the Social Agreement (from which the UK is excluded). Thus, in Article 2 of Part One of the Maastricht Treaty (Title II), establishing the 'Principles' upon which the EU is to be based, all of the member states declare their commitment

> towards a high level of employment and of social protection, and the raising of the standard of living and quality of life, and economic and social cohesion and solidarity among Member States.

While in Article 1 of the Social Agreement the member states, with the exception of the UK, support

> the promotion of employment, improved living and working conditions, proper social protection, dialogue between management and labour, the development of human resources with a view to lasting high employment and the combating of social exclusion.

Similarly, the specific areas of action laid out in Article 2 of the Social Agreement (see Table 1) are less of a bolt from the blue than a codification and extension of existing practice. The CEU had long been active in all of these policy areas. However, the extension of qualified majority voting to those areas listed in Article 2(1) and the creation of an *explicit* competence for the EU in the areas specified in Article 2(3) potentially represent a considerable enhancement of the Commission's powers in the area of EU social policy.[21]

The main innovation of the Social Agreement is undoubtedly the key role assigned to the social partners in the negotiation, agreement and implementation of EU social policy (see Figure 1). In Article 3 of the Social Agreement the Commission is charged with the task of promoting the consultation of the social partners and with facilitating the progress of the social dialogue between management and labour. To this end, the CEU must consult the social partners on the overall direction of EU social policy and upon the desirability of any specific social policy action at the EU level. If the CEU then decides to draft a proposal, it must consult the social partners on the specific content of the proposal. At this stage in the consultation procedure, the social partners may inform the Commission that they wish to negotiate an agreement between themselves using the procedure provided for in Article 4 of the Social Agreement. Any such agreement may be implemented either 'in accordance with agreements and practices' (unspecified) specific to management and labour within the member states or, in those areas covered by Article 2 of the Social Agreement, by a Council Decision.[22] In either case the procedure 'shall not exceed nine months'.[23] During this period the CEU suspends its own legislative activities.

While, at first sight, Articles 3 and 4 appear to represent a radical departure from the existing approach to EU social policy, viewed in historical and organisational context the changes appear less dramatic. First, the new provisions reflect the institutionalisation of the growing role of social partners, a process set in motion in the 1970s

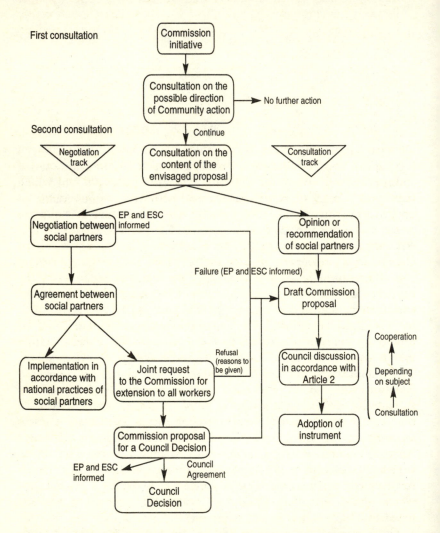

Figure 1   Operational chart showing the implementation of the Agreement on Social Policy

Source: *Social Europe* 3/94: 208 'Two Years of Community Social Policy: July 1993–June 1995'

with the establishment of the Standing Committee on Employment and of the various Sectoral Committees attached to DGV and continued, in the 1980s, with the Val Duchesse dialogue and the inclusion of Article 118b in the Single European Act:

> the Commission shall endeavour to develop the dialogue between management and labour at European level which could, if the two sides consider it desirable, lead to relations based on agreement.

Second, not only did the Commission play an important role in setting the social dialogue ball rolling but also it has constantly sought to maintain some control over the direction it travels and the impact it has.

Articles 3 and 4 of the Social Agreement reproduce, in almost identical terms, the agreement concluded on 31 October 1991 between UNICE (Union of Industrial and Employers' Confederations of Europe), ETUC (European Trade Union Confederation) and CEEP (European Centre of Public Enterprises) within the *ad-hoc* group set up by the Commission for the purpose of defining the role and place of the social dialogue in the new Community framework (COM (93) 600 Final, 14 December 1993: 1).[24] However, two, apparently minor, changes to the draft text ensured that the CEU retained a gatekeeper role with respect to the functioning of the social dialogue. First, the draft agreement from the social partners specified that, should the social partners decide to request the implementation of an agreement by a Council Decision, the Commission proposal should follow exactly the agreement as issued by the social partners. This stipulation was dropped from the final text of the Social Agreement, allowing the CEU considerable room for manoeuvre (EIRR (European Industrial Relations Review) 241, February 1994: 30). Second, under the Social Agreement, the Commission must agree before any extension of the nine-month negotiation period between the social partners is granted. In contrast, the social partners had suggested a bilateral agreement between management and labour with no Commission involvement (EIRR 241, February 1994: 30). The Commission has argued that its involvement will prevent 'any prolongation of fruitless negotiations which would ultimately block the Commission's ability to regulate' (cited in EIRR 241, February 1994: 31).

The Commission quickly sought to interpret its role of supporting and promoting the social dialogue in its 'Communication Concerning the Application of the Agreement on Social Policy' (COM (93) 600 Final). The gatekeeper role of the Commission is once again emphasised as the CEU identifies its role as one of deciding which groups may be recognised as social partners and on which particular issues specific groups should be consulted. Further institutionalisation of the social dialogue has, meanwhile, been assured with the establishment, on 20 October 1995, of the European Centre for Industrial Relations in Florence. Bringing together trade unions and employers, the centre is to 'promote apprenticeship of the European dimension in social relations' (Agence Europe, 20.10.95, 6588: 12). However, while the Commission has been quick to place its stamp on the social dialogue proceedings, it has not been an altogether enthusiastic supporter of the Protocol procedure.[25]

The implications of the Social Protocol and the Social Agreement for the future of EU social policy are not yet entirely clear. Certainly

> the agreement can be regarded as a considerable advance on the existing legal provisions of the Treaty because not only are there a number of new legal bases for the adoption of Community social legislation, but for the first time a substantial role is created for the Community in the social sphere. Specific power is now granted for the adoption of measures throughout the spectrum of social issues related to employment.
>
> (Whiteford, 1993: 211)

However, there has been considerable debate among legal scholars regarding the legal status of the Social Protocol and Agreement, in particular, concerning the relationship between measures adopted pursuant to the Agreement and the *acquis communitaire* (Watson, 1993; Weiss, 1992; Whiteford, 1993). As was noted at the signing of the SEA:

> The signature of the Act does not mark the close of a chapter, but the beginning of a new one. What will count is how life is breathed into the Treaties.
>
> (Alber, 1986: 12)

Similarly, the impact of the new Protocol procedure will, in practice, be mediated by the activities of the key actors: the institutions, the social partners and the member states.

> All in all, treaty-base problems have not been resolved; there is ample scope (perhaps even more than before the adoption of the agreement for member states to contest EU competence and for the Commission to engage in 'creative regulation'.
>
> (Rhodes, 1995: 114)

The obvious question is how will the protocol procedure be brought to life?

2.6 The emerging pattern of social policy post-Maastricht

Since the Maastricht Treaty entered into force, the procedures by which social policy can be introduced by all the member states, with the exception of the United Kingdom (UK), have been significantly relaxed, potentially allowing for significant policy machination on the part of the CEU.[26] In particular the extension of QMV in Articles 2(1) and 2(2) of the Social Agreement is potentially important for the enhancement of the role of the Commission (see Table 1). In practice, however, the CEU has initiated very little new legislation since the Maastricht Treaty. The 1994 legislative programme was sparse in the area of social policy and the Commission's White Paper on Social Policy (COM (94) 333 Final, 27.7.94) specifically emphasises the CEU's unwillingness to launch a new legislative programme at this time. As Padraig Flynn, Commissioner for Employment and Social Affairs, stated in a speech to the CBI, 'the White Paper on Social Policy indicates clearly that the Commission has concluded that there is no need for a major new programme of legislation in the coming period' (Agence Europe, 7/8.11.94, 6352: 12). Meanwhile, the most recent Medium-Term Social Action Programme (1995: 6) stresses both its break with the 'head on' approach adopted by the CEU in 1989 and its non-legislative focus.

Those proposals which have been brought forward have largely been instigated by the various Council presidencies. For example, the Belgian Presidency of July to December 1993 tried to push through the backlog of social measures and tested the ground for the use of the protocol procedure by resurrecting a number of proposals which had remained blocked in the Council for a number of years (EIRR 240, January 1994: 24). In the latter half of 1993 the Belgian Presidency issued a compromise text aimed specifically to unblock the debate on the issue of European Works Councils (EIRR 242, March 1994: 13). The Council of Ministers under the Presidency of the German Minister, Norbert Blüm, subsequently agreed that the parental leave directive should proceed on the basis of the protocol procedure while the CEU was asked to investigate the best strategy for the pursuit of the directive on the burden of proof (Agence Europe, 24.9.94, 6322: 6).[27]

Meanwhile, the European Parliament has stated unequivocally that the protocol procedure should be used whenever possible:

It advocated strict application of the Protocol in the absence of consensus and was in favour of the Council adopting Directives in the social sphere by a qualified majority rather than diluting their content to satisfy the United Kingdom.

(Bull. EU 1/2/1994: 57)

Moreover, the European Parliament 'regretted that the Commission had given too little consideration to social affairs in its legislative programme for 1994' (OJ C 20, 24.1.94; Bull. EU 12/1993: 71).

Although the Commission was quick to make use of the new protocol procedure in the case of European Works Councils (EWC),[28] it has generally been less enthusiastic about the use of this procedure. Padraig Flynn, Commissioner for Employment and Social Affairs, declared his disappointment at the Council's decision to go ahead without the UK on the parental leave directive and stated that the CEU would think about the most appropriate response to UK opposition over the burden of proof directive (Agence Europe, 24.9.94, 6322: 6). Only in July 1995 did the CEU launch the first stage of consultation with the social partners on the issue of the Burden of Proof (Agence Europe, 6.7.95, 6516: 15). After a blockage of over a year in the Council of Ministers, the Commission also began the first stage of consulation with the social partners over the issue of atypical work in September 1995. However, Commissioner Flynn again expressed his disappointment with the Council's inability to move forward as one when it appeared to be 'close to a solution' (Agence Europe, 28.9.95, 6572: 15). Meanwhile, the CEU appears to be hedging its bets on the issue of national information and consultation. The CEU has issued a Communication which both consults the EU institutions and the social partners on the desirability of action in this area and is to serve as the first stage of consulation of the social partners *if* the Commission decides to trigger the protocol procedure (EIRR 264, January 1996: 18).

Importantly, the CEU has not launched a series of new legislation in its reinforced areas of competence but has almost reluctantly been drawn into pressing through old issues or bringing back issues 'from the dead' (EIRR 240, January 1994: 24). This presents something of a puzzle for analysts. How can the Commission's evident resistance to trigger the protocol procedure be explained? Is the CEU no longer the activist it once was or was the initial analysis of its role flawed? As usual, neither of these is quite the case. The development of EU social policy since the Maastricht Treaty can, as always, be viewed through different conceptual lenses.

On the one hand, the relative inaction of the Commission may simply serve as a confirmation of the intergovernmentalist thesis. Opt-outs, effectively the veto of the 1990s, amount to a geographical curtailment of the Commission's competence. Most actions pursued under the protocol procedure have been initiated by the member states (i.e. by the various Council Presidencies) and the Commission has, quite simply, been forced to toe the line. From this perspective, a period of consolidation with few new initiatives from the Commission is only to be expected. However, this approach cannot explain why the Commission appears to be actively resisting the activities of the fourteen member states in their attempts to make use of the protocol procedure.

Viewed from an institutional perspective, on the other hand, it becomes clear that the protocol procedure presents both threats and opportunities for the development of the competence of the Commission in the area of EU social policy. As a result, the Commission has been very cautious about pursuing this route. Although the CEU has actively developed the role of the social partners as a welcome constituency of support for CEU action, there are dangers for the Commission inherent in a more corporatist arrangement. Not least, the social partners have proved in the past to be rather unreliable partners. There is, for example, a very real danger of UNICE participation in the social dialogue only in an attempt to avoid the imposition of EU legislation (EIRR 241, February 1994: 33)! Meanwhile it is not yet clear that the social partners have the required mechanisms and experience to negotiate viable alternatives to legislation.[29] Finally, there is a danger that the social dialogue route will be so fraught with negotiation and implementation problems that the incremental softening up already done by the CEU will be wasted.

A more convincing explanation in the light of the history of the Commission–Council relationship is, once again, that the Commission's activism in the area of EU social policy, and its evident desire to enhance the scope of its competence, should not be conflated mistakenly with a desire to raise social standards in Europe. Proceeding via the protocol procedure, higher common standards may be achieved by fourteen member states but the precedent for future action becomes unclear.[30] Arguably it is better from the CEU's point of view to proceed at a low level by fifteen than to achieve higher social standards as fourteen. Arguably too, the fewer measures passed under the protocol procedure, the easier it will be for the UK to opt back in,[31] and for EU social policy to be subject once more to a single, more coherent, set of legal bases. The Commission made this point explicitly, in its contribution to the Reflection Group preparing for the 1996 Intergovernmental Conference (IGC) when it stated that:

> Permanent exemptions such as that now applying to social policy, which in the last analysis have had the effect of excluding the Social Charter from the Treaty, create problems, as they raise the prospect of an *à la carte* Europe, to which the Commission is utterly opposed. Allowing each country to pick and choose the policies it takes part in would inevitably lead to a negation of Europe.

2.7   The protocol procedure in practice: threats and opportunities for the Commission

On 22 September 1994 the first Directive to be agreed on the basis of the protocol procedure was adopted unanimously by the Council of Ministers, excluding the United Kingdom.[32] The new Directive, providing for European Works Councils or information and consultation 'mechanisms', 'procedures' and 'structures' (OJ L 254 30.9.94), has proved to be something of a success story from the Commission's perspective:

> The success of the Directive on European Works Councils adopted by the Council on 22 September 1994, will reside in the fact that its provisions will never need to be implemented.
>   (Padraig Flynn cited in Agence Europe, 17/18.7.95, 6524: 11)

By July 1995, sixty of the largest companies in the European Union had already set up information and consultation mechanisms on a voluntary basis (more than a year before the deadline for transposing the Directive into national legislation on 22 September 1996). Moreover, all of the companies which have reached agreements with their employees have included their UK workers. Indeed, some UK-owned multinationals such as United Biscuits and Coats Viyella have concluded their own information and consultation agreements (Agence Europe, 17/18.7.95, 6524: 11). However the European Works Councils case has a long history and the progress of this Directive through the protocol procedure remained largely under the control of the CEU.

One of the main threats to the Commission's position when the social dialogue track is pursued is that UNICE may simply choose to negotiate in order to avoid legislation. In this particular case, however, the Commission was well aware that there were entrenched divisions between the representatives of management and labour at the European level. Moreover, there were clear divisions emerging within the employers' camp.

There was an early breakdown in employer unity over the draft EWC Directive and some evidence of a division between employers and their representatives. Discussions between ETUC and UNICE broke down at the second stage of the consultation process provided for in the Social Agreement (see Figure 1). However, thirty-two companies had already implemented EWCs on a voluntary basis. The economic costs of implementing information/consultation procedures turned out to be lower than initially estimated by the CEU,[33] in unofficial discussions with ETUC, a number of employers stated that they regretted the failure of the negotiations between ETUC and UNICE. As the Secretary-General of ETUC claimed:

> None of the 32 multinationals which so far have established European Works Councils on a voluntary basis consider it a handicap. On the contrary.
>
> (Agence Europe, 22.9.94, 6320: 14)

Meanwhile, although the CBI took an extreme position by directly opposing the Directive, and withdrawing from the UNICE delegation which was to debate participation in the Commission's consultation exercise (IRS Employment Trends 561, June 1994: 12–13), many UK-owned companies were, in fact, fairly ambivalent about the implications of the Directive.

The Commission had, moreover, been softening up the reception of the EWC Directive for some time. A myriad of transnational links between management and employee representatives in multinational companies already existed and these had boomed in recent years due, at least in part, to the Commission's funding of transnational representatives' meetings under the Commission's Budget Line B3 4004 (IRS Employment Trends 561, June 1994: 10). Indeed, although the UK was specifically excluded from legislation emerging from the protocol procedure, and thus would not be party to the proposed directive on Europe Works Councils, in 1993 the Trades Union Congress (TUC) received 206,000 ECU to run a project on 'Information and Consultation in Multinational Companies' (IRS Employment Trends 561, June 1994: 11). The sum allocated to the TUC by the Commission (approximately £190,000) was to be used to promote the establishment of works councils by transnational companies operating in Britain (IRS Employment Trends 552, January 1994: 3).

Meanwhile, the UK opt-out was under attack from another direction. Following infringement proceedings brought by the

Commission, the European Court of Justice (Cases 382/92 and 383/92) found that the UK government must ensure that adequate information and consultation procedures for UK workers were in place in order to comply with two long-standing EU directives on 'Collective Redundancies' (75/129/EU) and 'Transfer of Undertakings' (77/187/EU). The ECJ found that the prevailing voluntaristic approach in the UK failed to ensure that employers consult workers' representatives and failed to provide adequate sanctions in the event of an employers failure to inform and consult workers' representatives (Bull. EU 6/1994: 132).

The EWC Directive provided an excellent opportunity for the CEU to make use of the protocol procedure. First, the Directive had largely been adopted without the need for EU legislation thus the CEU managed to avoid the 'meddling Eurocrat' label. Second, the breakdown in the social dialogue allowed the CEU to retain its central position in the negotiation of the proposal. Third, the voluntary implementation of the Directive by UK-based multinationals undermines the UK opt-out from the protocol procedure and makes it easier for UK to opt in at the IGC in 1996. Finally, it may prove difficult for the UK not to take some similar action on information and consultation procedures in the light of the rulings of the Court of Justice.

However, if the EWC Directive is an example of the opportunities available to the CEU in the post-Maastricht era, the Parental Leave Agreement illustrates some of the threats to the CEU's role in social policy inherent in the protocol procedure. Signed on 14 December 1995 the Agreement reached by ETUC (for trade unions), UNICE (for private sector employees) and CEEP (for public sector employees) has now to be submitted by the Commission to the Council to be transformed into binding legislation (EIRR 264, January 1996: 3). However, those organisations which represent management and labour, more generally, have strongly criticised their exclusion from the negotiation of the agreement. The European Executive Confederation (CEC) claimed, for example, that the procedure excluded

> interprofessional organisations representing certain categories of workers, including the executives who are, however, recognised as a category of specific importance in social dialogue by the European Parliament.
>
> (Agence Europe, 10.8.95, 6540: 2).

Meanwhile, the Confederation of Independent Trade Unions (CESI) has argued that only the broadest approval of the results of the social dialogue will guarantee the acceptance of the legislation by European citizens (Agence Europe, 8.9.95, 6558: 13). Eurocommerce has since gone even further by arguing that the Parental Leave Agreement is 'undemocratic and not representative for commerce which has been excluded from participating in the negotiations'. Moreover, Eurocommerce has argued that the Council should apply the Agreement to commerce only if Eurocommerce has given its 'explicit consent' (Agence Europe, 11.11.93, 6603). Clearly, the range of threats and opportunities inherent in the protocol procedure are only just beginning to emerge. Not least, the implications of Article 4(2) of the Social Agreement have yet to be discovered:

> this arrangement implies no obligation on the member states to apply the agreements directly or to work out rules for their transposition, nor any obligation to amend national legislation in force to facilitate their implementation.

3 LEARNING AND ADAPTATION IN THE EU SOCIAL POLICY PROCESS: THE LESSONS OF HISTORY

If there is one thing to be learned from the history of CEU activities in the social field it is that the CEU has proved to be remarkably adaptable. In the 1990s the CEU may simply have been forced to adopt a new strategy. This time a heavy emphasis has been placed upon the process of consultation. In many respects, the current CEU strategy, following the UK opt-out, strikes a chord with the low-profile approach adopted in the late 1960s and early 1970s, following the Veldkamp Memorandum. In 1971, the Commission's 'Preliminary guidlines for a Community Social Policy Programme' (Bull. EU Supplement 2/1971: 5), stressed the non-legislative nature of the action programme and the need for Council support:

> These preliminary guidelines should not be read as formal proposals but as a substantial contribution to a wide-ranging discussion, without which it would be impossible to achieve the required consensus and the essential political will.

In a similar vein, the Medium-Term Social Action Programme stresses that

> This social action programme opens a new phase in the development of social policy. It differs from the 1989 social action programme – which had a largely legislative focus – in that it

presents a broader and more detailed overview of action in the social policy field. This new action programme sets out an important and substantial agenda for the coming years. It is not a static 'blue print'.

(COM (95) 134 Final: 6)

The Commission has once again recognised the need to adopt a lower profile, to play a catalytic role and to mobilise support for its actions (COM (94) 333 Final: 6). The latest Commission strategy in the social field is perhaps best exemplified by the issuing of the consultative Green Paper ('European Social Policy – Options for the Union': (COM (93) 551) which elicited more than 500 responses from a wide variety of actors (COM (94) 333 Final: 3). Indeed, in the action programme (COM (95) 134 Final: 8) reference to support from consultative partners is accorded almost equal status with references to, for example, Council conclusions. Thus, the 'wide ranging consultative process highlighted a broad agreement on a number of key themes which underpin this action programme'. While the UK opt-out presents a serious threat to the autonomous action of the Commission, it appears that the CEU has found a renewed source of pressure to bring to bear on the member states, opening up a new path to its ultimate destination: the expansion of the scope of its competence.

4   CONCLUSION: THE PARADOXICAL NATURE OF EU SOCIAL POLICY DEVELOPMENT

Two basic paradoxes lie at the heart of European Union social policy. First, given that Title III of the Rome Treaty (subsequently amended by the Single European Act) and now Title VIII of the Maastricht Treaty are devoted to the subject of EU social policy, why has a comprehensive EU social policy not developed? Second, since it clearly has not, why is there any EU social policy at all?

EU social policy has a basis in the Treaty of Rome (1957: Articles 117–128). Yet advances in EU social policy have been slow and inconsistent, for long periods even non-existent. In particular, national governments are generally willing to allow an EU presence in social policy only in so far as it can be proven to be directly relevant to the functioning of the internal market. Intervention by the Commission in the social field is justified as being instrumental to the smooth implementation of the single market and as intended to ameliorate the potential social and economic dislocations which this process may bring about. The evident lack of a comprehensive EU social policy has been explained in terms of the essentially intergovernmental nature of the EU, with member states as the dominant actors in the policy process. National governments have, for a variety of reasons, generally been unwilling to allow a significant EU presence in the social field (Taylor, 1983: 222–223). With their effective right of veto in the Council of Ministers, member states have then been able, until recently, to prevent the development of any significant EU social policy.[34] Crudely, 'intergovernmentalism', from this perspective, should prevent the emergence of a significant body of EU social policy.

Safe in the expectation that the UK government could veto most social measures at the EU level, many countries have until recently, however, felt able to indulge in 'cheap talk' (Lange, 1992: 242). Social ambitions, expressed by national governments in the European Council, may then be a means of increasing their electoral popularity at home in the certainty that the actual proposals will never be passed in the Council and that the government will never have to face the economic implications of the implementation costs. Notably, when the veto is relaxed (for example, when qualified majority voting applies, when the UK refused to sign the 1989 Social Charter, and again when the UK opted out of some of the social aspects of the Maastricht Treaty) proposals and declarations are usually significantly watered down. Ostensibly this is done to try and coax the UK into participating. However, the earlier, more stringent, versions of the proposals are rarely resurrected: even when it is realised that the UK is not to be moved! Symbolic politics are likely to remain a central feature of Council activities in the social field. However, as will become clear, even those actions which are intended to remain symbolic, at least by some member states, often provide the necessary cloak under which to smuggle in Commission actions in the social field.[35]

The careful ambiguities evident in the social provisions of the EU Treaties reflect both the diversity of approaches to social policy within the various member states as well as the dual role which national governments are forced to play: on the one hand, as members of the EU promoting its development, and on the other hand, as national leaders protecting the status quo in their countries (Rifflet, 1985: 23). Critically, national governments maintain their position in the EU only as long as they remain electorally popular at home. Political rhetoric in the Council is important as it allows the member states to declare broad ambitions for social progress in the Community, while power in the Council permits the same member states to veto unwelcome proposals and to protect their perceived 'national interest'.

This leads us, however, to the second paradox: EU social policy is expanding both in scope and effect, despite the reluctance of national governments to concede a role to the EU in this area, and despite the requirement, until recently, of unanimity in most social policy decisions. The state-centred, or intergovernmental, explanation cannot sufficiently explain this development. Collins (1975: 199) has argued, for example, that the role of the European Commission may have been particularly significant in the development of Community social policy where lines of policy have had to be created and did not flow directly or unambiguously from the Treaty. Neither can the state-centred approach explain the importance of the various types of policy emerging in the social field or of the timing of their appearance. Thus another key question to be addressed is why the Commission favours particular policy options and why these particular options are passed by the Council of Ministers. The nature of the legislative and policy output of the EU policy process has been left largely unexamined. Although there is a well-developed literature on the theories and practice of regulation and the importance of the various types of policies which emerge from the policy process, there have few attempts to apply these concepts to the case of the EU (but see Majone, 1989a, 1991a, 1991b, 1991c). There have been no attempts to disaggregate the various types of policies (for example, regulatory, redistributive, symbolic) which are emerging from DGV and the relative significance of these policy types for the various actors concerned.[36] The heavy symbolic dimension of EU social policy, the restricted scope of binding legislative provisions in the Treaties or resulting from secondary legislation, and the emphasis on 'other acts' or non-binding soft law, make it easy to dismiss the EU social dimension as simply rhetoric or 'symbolic' politics. However, when the pattern of EU social policy is examined over time it becomes clear that 'cheap talk' (Lange, 1992: 242) may not be as cheap as it at first appears.

3 The development of European Union information and communication technology policy

1 INTRODUCTION

The evolution of EU ICT policy presents something of a puzzle for analysts.[1] National ICT policy has traditionally been bound up with broader notions of national sovereignty as well as with more specific notions of industrial policy. Individual governments have thus developed a variety of means of promoting national champion firms in the ICT sector. The key role which ICT firms are perceived to play in the national economy has led national governments to guard control over these firms jealously. Cooperation by ICT firms at European Union level has, moreover, been fraught with the difficulties outlined by Olson (1971) regarding collective action. For industry, a series of conflicting pressures discouraged cooperative action at the EU level. Problems of competition, the often more profitable alliances to be forged with US and Japanese firms, and their unwillingness to jeopardise their special relationships with their own governments, generally mitigated against a willingness to cooperate with other EU firms.

During the early 1960s and 1970s there was overt hostility to attempts by the European Commission to develop an EU policy in the ICT field: from many national governments; from national champion firms and from National Administrations of Post, Telecommunications and Telegraph (PTTs). Not surprisingly, perhaps, there was little enthusiasm on the part of member states for an active ICT policy at the EU level:

> Arguments among governments, differences of national policies and priorities and difficulties in establishing effective management formulae were all major constraints.
>
> (Sharp and Shearman, 1989: 38)

In this context, most theories of international relations would also have predicted virtual inaction at the EU level. If, on the one hand, national governments are taken to be the dominant actors in international policy-making, issues of national sovereignty might have resulted in a total lack of cooperative action at the supranational level, or action on a global scale might have been expected in order to reap the benefits of truly free trade. If, on the other hand, multinational companies are viewed as the major actors in the ICT field, global cooperation would again appear most advantageous, there being no coincidence between technical innovation and geographic boundaries. In either case, EU, as opposed to European or international, cooperation appears something of an anomaly. Indeed, examining the collective responses of western European governments to international technology-related problems in the late 1960s and early 1970s, Nau (1975: 631) was led to the conclusion that:

> In changing times, the tendency seems to be to emphasize familiar organizations and goals (ie., the institutional framework). For the moment, this tendency has diminished interest in and the evolution of Community organs (structural framework).

Yet by the late 1980s and early 1990s, the situation in the ICT field appeared quite different. Once again the sector was in crisis and once again the member states, and some key industrial actors, were divided in their responses to that crisis. Yet, since the mid-1980s there has been increasing collaboration between European firms in the context of EU R&D programmes and, particularly in recent years, a growing body of EU regulations and technical standards has emerged in the ICT sector.

The role of the EU in the ICT field was confirmed in the Single European Act and is reinforced by the Maastricht Treaty. Moreover, firms and non-governmental actors have been drawn closely into the EU policy process in the ICT field. There is now a comprehensive institutional policy framework for the elaboration of EU ICT policies and an increasing range of EU regulations in this field. The European Union has increasingly become a focal point for policy actors intent on influencing the direction of ICT policy and there could now be said to exist a European Union Technology Community (Sharp, 1990; Sharp and Shearman, 1989). EU legislation is also constraining national policy instruments (such as public procurement practices) with which the nation-state has traditionally steered firms and industry (see Thatcher, 1994: 458). Importantly, these policy developments, by creating a regulatory vacuum, enhance the *regulatory* role of the EU institutions. This has been a vital means of expanding the scope of the Commission's direct influence without over-extending its budgetary capacity (Majone, 1990; Peters, 1992).[2] This incremental regulation has not been without controversy, particularly in the area of telecommunications where PTTs remain cautious in their support for EU action. Despite this, however, 'the Commission's progress toward a liberalised telecommunications market is astonishing' (Darnton and Wuersch, 1992: 124).

In the late 1980s and 1990s the response to policy failure and crisis at the national level was the development of an extensive and powerful EU ICT policy. This led Sandholtz to argue that

> international organisations register the greatest impact on interstate cooperation during periods of policy adaptation. When national leaders confront policy failures that compel them to rethink their objectives and/or the means chosen to pursue them, they adapt by searching for alternative approaches.... Policy crises provide opportunities for activist, entrepreneurial leaders to marshal states behind a cooperative solution.
>
> (Sandholtz 1992b: 252)

Member states remain divided in their responses to the global pressures on the ICT market,[3] as do major ICT firms.[4] In the 1980s and 1990s, however, rather than rejecting the emergence of new collective institutions, as was the case in the 1970s, there is evidence of the evolution of a thriving institutional framework for the development of EU ICT policy. Further, the response of a number of member states, and of some key industrial actors, has been to push for greater institutionalisation of EU ICT policy and the establishment of new, centralised, authorities at the European level.[5] Within this dynamic policy environment the Commission has come to occupy a crucial functional position. The question is clear: first, how can the development of a dynamic EU ICT policy sector be explained and, second, how was it possible in the late 1980s and 1990s to develop a central institutional role for the CEU in the area of ICT policy when it had proved so difficult in the 1970s?

2   DIFFERENT CONCEPTUAL LENSES

As always, the development of EU ICT policy, between the late 1960s and the 1990s, can be viewed through a variety of conceptual lenses.

2.1   National governments and the demise of the national champion strategy

First, viewed from a state-centric perspective, national governments may simply have altered their attitude towards cooperation at the EU level as the failure of the national champion strategy became increasingly clear. In the critical economic environment of the early 1970s, most national governments within the EU remained firmly committed to traditional protectionist policies in the ICT sectors, in the hope that national flagship companies would ride out the recession and oil crisis and would emerge as the engine of economic recovery. The logic of these policies was that the ICT sector was central to general economic growth and that it would be a strategic error to allow foreign interests to dominate the sector. National champion firms were happy to accept this analysis, of course, as the existing policy framework effectively gave them a national 'franchise'. At this stage, consumer interests, including business users, were not mobilised or organised to challenge this conventional wisdom.

Already by the late 1970s, however, it had become clear, that the existing national champion policies were making little impact upon the competitive position of European countries. The gap between European industry and Japan and the US continued to increase. With a resurrection of interest in the 'technology gap' (identified, for example, by Servan-Schreiber, 1968) a belief in the strategic importance of the ICT sector, long recognised at the national level,[6] began to emerge as a collective EU interest. National governments began to seek cooperative solutions to this familiar problem, in the face of continued decline.

The speed of technological advance was outstripping the ability of European industry to compete on an international scale. The comparatively small scale of national markets in Europe was not considered to provide the economies of scale on which US and Japanese industry could depend. European industry had already recognised the need to find research partners, to enable it to limit the increasing R&D costs generated by ever more ambitious technological projects, and to cushion it from the effects of the diminishing life cycle of ICT products. International cooperation agreements could, moreover, help to secure access to important foreign markets. By the 1980s, European industry had, on its own initiative, begun to seek out partners for cooperative R&D ventures in the ICT sector, simply as a means of survival. It was probably inevitable, therefore, that public policy had to accommodate this reality, sooner or later.

Clearly, a reassessment of traditional approaches to ICT policy and practice was underway in the late 1970s and early 1980s. Both national governments and industries had recognised that the traditional protectionist approach to industrial policy was no longer suited to this increasingly global policy sector. Decline had set in, all of the actors were being squeezed by global and technological trends, and many began to see the logic of cooperation. Unless ICT firms were to be allowed to die, or alternatively to become totally independent (of the state) actors, national and EU policy-makers had to act. Initially, the telecommunications sector was slightly different. Although facing significant policy adaptation, the PTTs were far slower to respond to the growing internationalisation of the sector and to the speed of technological advance, preferring to hang on to their own 'franchise'. It was not until the ideology of liberalisation began to gain currency throughout the countries of Europe, in the mid-1980s, that the monopoly position of PTTs came under serious threat. Even so, resistance on the part of the PTTs to international cooperation has been fairly strong.

While the changing position of national governments has clearly been important, it has been a slow and contradictory process. This presents a number of challenges to the state-centred approach. First, it does not explain why collaboration at the EU level took place in the 1980s and not in the late 1960s: 'Technology gaps became a cause célèbre in Europe in the 1960s, but collaboration did not follow' (Sandholtz, 1992a: 3). Second, as always, actors have more than one choice when faced with a crisis. Indeed, even when national governments had been drawn into cooperation at the EU level, for example in the ESPRIT (European Strategic Programme for R&D in Information Technology) and RACE (R&D in Advanced Communications Technologies in Europe) programmes in the early 1980s,[7] they continued to be suspicious of the Commission's role in the ICT field and to promote the simultaneous development of intergovernmental programmes.[8] Why then did national governments choose to co-operate at the EU level at all? Why not simply cooperate intergovernmentally, in Europe or internationally? Without the combined lobbying strength of the Commission and the key industrial actors, in the 1980s, it is not clear that action at the EU level would have taken place at all: far less that the EU ICT sector would have emerged as a central element of the current activities of national governments in the ICT field.

2.2   The technological imperative

A second potential explanation of the expansion of the ICT sector at the EU level is that it was simply a response to the technological imperative. Indeed, the Commission has frequently rationalised Community action in the ICT field as a response to the technological imperative and to the increasing globalisation of the ICT sector: 'Europe's response to today's technological challenge must be to set up a European Technology Community' (Bull. EC 6/1985: 23).

The importance of technological development in explaining regulatory reform in ICTs at the national as well as the supranational level is undeniable. New technology affects the economic parameters of supply and demand and the conditions under which demand is brought into play (Cawson *et al.*, 1990). It also modifies the behaviour of the various actors in a process in which the stake is the sharing out of the added value produced by the sector. These changes led the authorities involved to seek out a new organisational framework through which the ICT market could be optimised (Koebel, 1990: 111). New technological developments clearly require new types of regulatory response. It is not clear, however, that this, in itself, explains the emergence of an EU ICT policy. It cannot, for example, be assumed that the content of public policy was determined by the technological imperative and that the actual policy instruments eventually chosen were inevitable. Once again, it should be recalled that member states have a range of choices available to them when responding to the drive of new technology. The important question is why member states selected one option and not another (Sandholtz, 1992a: 12). Indeed, no organization was more aware of the options available to member states, when responding to the speed of technological change, than the Commission:

> The magnitude of the changes taking place, the problems they engender and the uncertainty of future prospects are all factors which, in the absence of a Community industrial policy, could result in uncoordinated national measures and reorganisation on an exclusively national scale, thus jeopardizing the benefits that follow from the establishment of the Common Market.
>
> (Bull. EC S7/73: 5)

It is not clear that responses to the technological imperative and globalisation would lead to a need for EU rather than global standards and regulations. If there is a logic of globalisation in the ICT sector, there is likely to be a 'logic of regulation' which, in the end, also leads to global regulation. EU-specific standards and regulations present another barrier to international free trade, to the detriment of consumers, and might slow down the rate of innovation. In practice, EU activities in the ICT sector, if not the rhetoric, reflect the global reality. Non-EU participation in supposedly EU initiatives is a recurrent aspect of the Commission's attempts to create an EU-based ICT policy. Both non-EU European firms and foreign-owned firms operating within the EU participate in many EU initiatives (Wyatt-Walker, 1995: 430–431). For example, the COST (Cooperation on Science and Technology) programme was centred on the EU but included seven non-member countries – Austria, Switzerland, Norway, Sweden, Finland, Turkey and former Yugoslavia.[9] Similarly, in the standard-setting process more generally – both in ICTs and other sectors – the EU participates in the activities of non-EU standards bodies.[10] There are, moreover, close links between the standards which emerge from the European Standards Boards and international standards.[11] Thus, to some degree EU participation *per se* may be partly symbolic when one examines the origin of standards and when one identifies the key actors. Nevertheless, the reinforcement of a central role for the CEU in this process has been crucial for the development of ICT policy at the EU level.

In practice, firms did prove willing to forge their own collaborative alliances and industrial cooperation had already begun to emerge in the early 1980s prior to the main thrust of EU policy. However, the direction that this cooperation took lacked a particular EU focus. Although a small number of EU firms had begun to cooperate with each other, cooperation with extra-EU firms was, in fact, far more common (Mytelka and Delapierre, 1987: 241). This gives some indication of the global direction which the development of the ICT sector might have taken of its own accord if firms were left as entirely independent actors, untramelled by regulation or by incentives. Once again, a variety of choices were available to both firms and national governments: the question remains, why did a dynamic EU ICT sector develop in the 1980s and 1990s?

2.3 Global competition and the ICT sector

Commission intervention in the ICT sector has often been rationalised in terms of the competitive position of European industry *vis-à-vis* Japan and the USA:

> in view of the technological challenge to Europe constituted by the United States and Japan, the Community must make a quantum

leap in the R&D field; such a leap must have an immediate impact and must be made in the Community context.

(Bull. EC 6/1985: 23)

Certainly, this has been a powerful argument in prompting governments to support intra-EU collaborative efforts. Importantly, however, Europe extends beyond the European Union. Also, as Kay (1990: 261) has pointed out, 'firms, rather than trading blocs, compete for consumers and markets'. In order to promote the competitive edge of European companies, cooperation with non-EU countries may be more advantageous for European firms. Just as there are many advantages to be gained by US firms collaborating in EU programmes – advance information, increased market access and subsidies (Goldenstein, 1991) – so too EU firms are more and more likely to seek extra-EU partners for joint ventures as the internal barriers to trade continue to decrease in the Single European Market (Kay, 1990: 265).

The reality is that it has become increasingly difficult to identify an exclusively EU policy for ICT. Thus, EFTA countries, even prior to the enlargement of the EU in 1994, were involved in a large number of cooperative agreements in the Community ICT sectors. Meanwhile, US, and occasionally Japanese, subsidiaries operating in Europe may participate in EU R&D programmes (Wyatt-Walker, 1995: 430–431). It has proved impossible, in practice, to contain cooperation in ICT within the geographical boundaries of the EU. Simply, the pace of technological development, the increased market pressures, and the relative independence of firms, the key players, all combine to cause a mismatch between political boundaries and the reality of the process of technological innovation. Cross-national linkages are so complex that the EU is faced with a similar problem to national governments. Yet importantly, the European Union has emerged as an important forum through which some of these complex interactions can be mediated. Complexity and uncertainty also breed a desire to achieve stability, or at least manageability. Hence the EU, particularly the Commission, has provided a useful participative structure for the key actors whether EU based, more broadly European or even international.

2.4   The institutionalist approach

While each of the approaches identified above highlights important factors which have faciltated the development of an active EU ICT policy, none of these approaches is able to explain the development, timing and nature of ICT policy development at the EU level. The responses of the member states to crises have been different at different times: in the early 1970s there was a clear reaction against the development of more EU institutions, while in the 1980s and 1990s, a flurry of EU regulations and standards have emerged and there is even a push, from some quarters, for increased powers for the CEU and for the establishment of a new regulatory authority at the EU level. Rather than representing an inevitable response to global competition and technological advance, a more convincing explanation of the development of EU ICT policy is that technological advance and the politics of progress presented the Commission with a set of opportunities. This has allowed the CEU to develop a role for itself (Fuchs, 1994; Hills, 1991; Sandholtz, 1992a) and, gradually, to emerge as a central actor in the ICT field. The Commission in the 1980s and 1990s has learned to exploit these opportunities in a manner for which it was ill equipped in the late 1960s and early 1970s. Having already softened up the policy area, mobilised the key actors and, crucially, having developed a clear institutional identity in the ICT field,[12] the Commission was able to capitalise on the legitimising concept of the Single Market and the 1992 project, in the mid-1980s. Viewed over time, it becomes clear that a crucial aspect of any interpretation of the development of an EU ICT policy is the gradual institutionalisation of the Commission's central role in the ICT sector.

3 THE 1960s AND 1970s: PROBLEMS WITH THE POLICY MIX

Commission attempts to create a centralised EU ICT policy have been fraught with difficulties. There is a long history of EU interest in the area of high technology. Jean Monnet's Action Committee for a United States of Europe (established in 1955), for example, called for the establishment of a new institution, in conjunction with the Commission, to promote technologial cooperation (Sharp and Shearman, 1989: 26). Advocates of EU action in the ICT field have, however, always been divided as to the objectives of such intervention. There has always been

> tension between the free-marketeers, whose emphasis throughout has been on competition and the diminishing of internal barriers to free competition within the Community, and the mercantilists, who have constantly warned against Europe's increasing dependence on

US (and latterly Japanese) technology, and whose vision centered on a more positive and interventionist approach.

(Sharp, 1990: 102)

As a result, the legal basis for Community intervention in the fields of ICT and Research and Development (R&D) has been highly controversial. The Treaty of Rome (1957) served only to reinforce this division. On the one hand, the Treaty provided powers which could be used to determine the regulatory framework and to shape the market environment. On the other hand, it included no explicit powers which might allow the EU institutions to promote either industrial or technology policy (Sharp, 1990: 102). The Commission thus lacked both the resources and, until recently, the policy instruments with which to influence the actions of industry through public policy.

Apart from nuclear power, covered by the Euratom Treaty, and coal and steel, covered by the Treaty of Paris, there was no specific legal basis for Community intervention in advanced technologies prior to the Single European Act 1986.[13] Any policies implemented in this field had, therefore, to be carried out on the basis of Article 235 of the Treaty of Rome. This catch-all article, providing for additional EU powers where they have not been specifically laid out in the founding Treaties, requires unanimity in the Council of Ministers. Given that the Commission could operate only where there was consensus in the Council of Ministers, and given the strength of national protectionism and the competing perspectives of the national governments in this area,[14] the 'stop-go' nature of EU activity in the ICT sector is perhaps not surprising (Sharp, 1990: 102). The Commission, nevertheless, attempted from the outset to pursue an active approach to the development of an EU ICT policy.

From the late 1950s the Commission produced proposals for collaborative European R&D programmes based on its own priorities. Early Commission attempts to create a role for itself in the EU ICT sector were based mainly on Commission direction of, and subsidy for, particular collaborative efforts, for example, in nuclear research and aerospace (Barry, 1990: 119). It was, of course, difficult for the Commission to tackle science and technology issues except as they related to the economic aspects of integration as laid out in the EEC Treaty and this was reflected in its activities. It was not until 1967 that the Council of Science Ministers held its first meeting. It began, almost immediately, to commission research in the ICT field (in the areas of metallurgy, oceanography, transport, telecommunications, environment and data processing: Sharp and Shearman, 1989: 27). In October 1967, meanwhile, a working group of the EEC Committee on Medium Term Economic Policy (know as PREST) was set up to examine the development of European cooperation in advanced technology (Nau, 1975: 631).[15] Again, developments in science and technology were closely related to the broader economic matters in which the Commission could claim to have explicit competence.

In 1969, however, Christopher Layton, (from DGIII, Industrial Affairs), one of the most active and influential Commission actors in the ICT field, published his book, *European Advanced Technology: A Programme for Integration*. Included in his fifteen recommendations for the development of EU industrial policy in the area of advanced technologies were the development of a European agency to promote mergers; common purchasing measures; industrial Community contracts for R&D; a European Advisory Council; and a Technology Assessment Centre (Sharp and Shearman, 1989: 26). From the late 1960s, moreover, the Commission was promoting the now familiar causes of 'the elimination of technical barriers to trade' and of 'mutual recognition of checks' and linking these to ICT policy.[16] In 1969 these measures were first passed as Council Resolutions. Although Resolutions are soft law measures, and thus entail no direct legal obligation, they are often of considerable political significance and, as is clear in this case, may act as 'precursors to binding legislation' (Wellens and Borchardt, 1989: 302).

The Commission used relatively small amounts of research funding to influence the early emergence of policy issues and policy ideas. For example, the research commissioned by the Council of Science Ministers and the PREST working group prepared the ground for the establishment of the PREST programme and the COST initiative in 1971.[17] Both allowed the Commission to coordinate a series of loosely related projects in the ICT field. In practice, however, COST was never a solely EU project; although centred on the EU it included seven non-member countries (Sharp and Shearman, 1989: 28).[18] Even at this early stage, the impossibility of maintaining a purely EU-based ICT policy was evident. The realities of the scientific research process dictated wider participation. Although COST was more of an inter-governmental programme than the CEU had initially desired, it proved to be a successful forum for pan-European cooperation in applied scientific research thus reinforcing the benefits of European-level cooperation. Meanwhile, in 1974, the Council of Ministers finally agreed to the transformation of the PREST working group into a joint committee of the Council and Commission to be known as

CREST (Committee for Research into European Science and Technology) (Nau, 1975: 631). In the summer of 1973, recognising the impossibility of gaining agreement from the Council for the establishment of EU-centred institutions in the R&D field, the new Commissioner for Science, Research and Education, Ralf Dahrendorf, had suggested an alternative approach. CREST was to coordinate national R&D policies rather than promoting a harmonised EU R&D strategy (Nau, 1975: 638). The clever 'trick', in the cases of both COST and CREST, was that the Commission ensured a key role for itself in these rather loose, predominantly intergovernmental, networks of actors in an area in which there was no formal legal basis for CEU action at all.

While few binding ICT policy measures were implemented in the 1970s, this was not for want of Commission efforts. In the context of the oil crisis and recession, with slow growth rates and high unemployment, national governments defended their national industries in traditional protectionist style. In this context, it has been argued that the support of the Heads of State and Government of the member states, through their Summit statements, was crucial for the development of EU ICT policy (Nau, 1975: 632). Indeed, at The Hague Summit (1969) the Heads of State and Government declared:

> As regards the technological activity of the Community, they reaffirmed their readiness to continue more intensively the activities of the Community with a view to coordinating and promoting industrial research and development in the principal pacemaking sectors, in particular by means of common programmes, and to supply the financial means for the purpose.
>
> (Bull. EC 1/1970: 15)

Further, the Heads of State and Government committed themselves to ensuring the 'most effective use of the Joint Research Centre' (Bull. EC 1/1970: 15). This led to a reorganisation of the work of the EU laboratories. The reorganisation of the management of the Joint Research Centre (JRC) in the summer of 1973 increased its autonomy. It also, however, curtailed the leadership role which the Commission staff had enjoyed over JRC activities (Nau, 1975: 637). As so often, Commission progress in the ICT field is a tale of one step forward followed by two steps back.

Undoubtedly, however, the Paris Summit on 24 October 1972 provided an important boost to CEU activities in the ICT field. Heads of State and Government declared that they felt that there was a need to try and provide a uniform foundation for industry throughout the Community. . . .

This policy implies coordination of national policies within the Community Institutions and the joint carrying out of action in the Community interest.

(Bull. EC 10/1972: 19–20)

To this end the CEU was asked to submit an action programme with a 'precise schedule backed by appropriate means' by 1 January 1974. As so often, however, the statement from the member states did not come as a bolt from the blue. In March 1970, for example, the CEU, under the supervision of Altiero Spinelli had produced a memorandum on 'Community Industrial Policy' (Bull. EU, Supplement 4/ 1970). The report declared the Commission's aim of a more concerted approach to industrial policy: including the removal of technical barriers; the opening of public procurement to competition and the promotion of research into advanced technologies as well as into the application of the technologies. Crucially, the report identified the lack of a 'satisfactory structure for the study and preparation of decisions and for their implementation in the field of research'. In many respects the CEU report echoed the fifteen recommendations identified by Christopher Layton (1969). Further, in 1972, in preparation for the Paris Summit, the Commission had issued a statement on the 'objectives and instruments of a common policy for scientific research and technological development' (Nau, 1975: 637). The document, which requested the recognition by the Council of the powers of the EU in all fields of R&D, the development of the institutional basis for EU intervention in the ICT field and an annual budget of 120 million units of account, went well beyond what the member states were willing to accept (Nau, 1975: 638). However, as the Paris communiqué demonstrates, the CEU strategy met with at least some success.

The details of the Paris Summit statement, in large part, reflected the priorities identified in the CEU's earlier reports. The CEU, nevertheless, stressed that its action programme, based on a memorandum submitted to the Council on 7 May 1973,[19] reflected the priorities laid down by the Council at the Paris Summit:

the Commission's memorandum was therefore drawn up on the basis of general guidelines set out in the Final communiqué of the Paris Summit Conference, which provided for the elimination of technical barriers to trade, the elimination of barriers (in particular, fiscal and legal) to closer relations and mergers between undertakings, the rapid adoption of a European company statute and the progressive and effective liberalisation of public contracts.

(7th General Report, 1973: 288)

It is undoubtedly the case that

summit decisions have been critical in sustaining discussions of R&D cooperation over the opposition or, at least, indifference of many subnational actors in the scientific and industrial sectors.

(Nau, 1975: 632)

At the very least such statements and declarations provided a potent legitimation for continued CEU action in the ICT field.

Although by mid-1974 the Commission had managed to secure only one statement of intent for a common policy in data processing (Nau, 1975: 639), gradual, incremental progress towards the development of an EU ICT policy continued. The 1974 commitment on data processing allowed the CEU a role in coordinating national policies in this area and was followed up, in 1976, by a Council decision allowing the allocation of some limited funding for joint R&D research projects on data processing (OJ L 223, 16.8.76: 11). This, in turn, was followed up by a Council Decision on 22 July 1976 setting up an Advisory Committee on the Joint Data projects (OJ L 223, 16.8.76: 16). During this period, Christopher Layton admitted that 'proposing new institutions [in the present period] does not go down well' (cited in Nau, 1975: 619). However, although proposals for a European R&D Committee (CERD) and for a European R&D Agency (ERDA), issued in parallel with the COST initiative in 1971, had met with little response (Sharp and Shearman, 1989: 28), the Commission was gradually building up its institutional framework for action in the ICT field and importantly was beginning to draw industrial actors into this emerging framework. The Commission continued to encourage the participation of industry in this area and discussions with leading component companies led to a Council Resolution (OJ C 231, 13.09.79: 1) on EU Action promoting microelectronics technology. However, the Commission's proposal for a Regulation on microelectronics technology (COM (80) 421 Final), based on the earlier Resolution, met with strong opposition on the part of the member states.

Already, by the late 1960s and early 1970s, the top-down, and somewhat heavy-handed, approach by the Commission to the development of an EU ICT policy, in an ever worsening economic climate, and in an area in which there was no consensus that there was even a role for the EU, merely had the effect of reinforcing member states' opposition to EU activity in the ICT sector.

> If anything, the Commission's tactics backfired. Mistrust of its motives meant that few important EU collaborative projects outside of energy R&D were launched until the 1980s.
>
> (Peterson, 1991: 275)

While most CEU initiatives for binding legislative advances in the ICT field were either impossible or failed, the slow build-up of ICT research continued. In 1978, for example, the FAST 1 (Forecasting and Assessment in the Field of Science and Technology) programme (OJ L 225, 16.8.78) was set up to analyse the implications of scientific and technological changes for Community R&D and other policies. In 1979 a four-year research programme on informatics applications was established and in 1981 a microelectronics research project was set up (Sharp and Shearman, 1989: 47). These activities were important if rather subtle steps towards the eventual creation of an EU ICT policy. Assisting research with EU funds served a number of functions. It established a precedent for Commission action in the ICT sector, despite the lack of a legal basis for action, it was an important aspect in the softening up process, and it has been a vital element of the Commission's efforts to create a role for itself in this important policy area.

Crucially during this period there was no clear administrative infrastructure within the Commission for pursuing a coherent policy in the ICT field. The efficacy of Commission activities was constantly hindered by this fact. For example, as the Commission had no legal basis for initiating activities in the field of R&D, which were not defined in the Treaty of Rome, the Committee of Permanent Representatives (COREPER), for a period, insisted that all PREST proposals should be submitted to the Council of Ministers only after consideration by a COREPER working group (Nau, 1975: 637).

> Buried within the Commission bureaucracy, PREST had only a limited mandate to *define* new fields of cooperation. It had no authority to work out the substantive or administrative details of such cooperation. ... The bureaucratic struggle between the Council and the Commission (not limited to the field of R&D) called for new guidelines clarifying the organizational and statutory authority of Community institutions in R&D.
>
> (Nau, 1975: 637)

The majority of CEU proposals for EU action in the ICT field initially emerged from DGIII (Directorate-General for Industrial Affairs), in particular from Etienne Davignon and Christopher Layton (Hills, 1991: 132). However, this Directorate-General was relatively young and was established only in 1967 (Sharp and Shearman, 1989: 26). Hence in the late 1960s and early 1970s, this DG was still establishing its role both within the Commission and *vis-à-vis* the Council and the key industrial actors.

Meanwhile, DGIV (Competition) enjoyed the strongest powers of any Commission unit, including the power to act without the support of member state governments in certain areas. However, during this early period DGIII and DGIV adopted conflicting approaches to the ICT sector. Thus, the concentration and merger activity, encouraged by DGIII, in the ICT field, came under the close scrutiny of the Competition Directorate (Sharp and Shearman, 1989: 27). Moreover, at this early stage in this contentious policy area, even the relatively stronger powers enjoyed by DGIV were not able to be fully applied:

> hostility from the PTTs and the telecommunications sector's exclusion from GATT provisions caused telecommunications to be omitted from the 1976 Directive on the liberalisation of large scale public procurement contracts.
>
> (Hills, 1991: 132)

It was not until the mid-1980s that it was possible for the full extent of the Commission's competition powers in the ICT field to be realised.[20] In DGXII (Science, Research and Development), meanwhile, the promotion of R&D and scientific research continued throughout the 1970s. For example, DGXII issued a major blueprint for action in the ICT field in 1973: 'Scientific and Technological Policy Programme (Parts 1 and 2)' (Bull. EC S14/73). This was followed by a communication, in 1975, detailing the 'Objectives, Priorities and Resources for a Common Research and Development Policy' (Bull. EC S4/76) and a call for a 'Common Policy in the Field of Science and Technology' in 1977 (Bull. EC S3/77).

DG XIII, which was ultimately to become the Directorate-General responsible for ICT policy, was initially a Euratom Directorate-General (Dissemination of Information). DGXIII was one of only five Euratom administrative units to be retained intact after the merger of the three European Communities in 1967. Thus, when the definitive list of new Directorates-General appeared, after much controversy, in July 1968, DGXIII emerged as a unit of the new single Commission (Coombes, 1970: 269).

In the late 1960s and 1970s, a disparate set of policy initiatives emerged from the Commission from a range of administrative units, which had not yet learned to cooperate and which occasionally found themselves in direct conflict. It was, thus, hardly surprising that the Commission should have had difficulty establishing a coherent EU ICT policy and a central role for itself in this policy area.[21] In this organisational context, and in the face of opposition from many member states and from key industrial actors, the failure to develop a centralised EU ICT policy at this time was, perhaps, only to be expected.

4 DEVELOPING AN INSTITUTIONAL IDENTITY: FROM TASK FORCE TO DIRECTORATE GENERAL

During the 1980s the Commission began to develop a clear institutional identity in the ICT field. In 1983 the Commission set up a Task Force for Information and Communications Technologies. Located in DGIII, under the directorship of Michel Carpentier, the new Task Force was staffed with high-level civil servants (mainly from DGIII) along with experts from PTTs and industry. The Task Force had a wide remit. As well as two general units concerned with 'Programme Administration' and 'Strategy of Information Technology and Telecommunications ' (specifically standardisation and type approval and inter-institutional relations and non-governmental organisations), the Task Force had two separate divisions: Directorate A (Information Technology and ESPRIT) and Directorate B (Telecommunications).[22] The Task Force also enjoyed a degree of autonomy within the Commission bureaucracy as it reported not to a Director-General but directly to the Industry Commissioner (Sandholtz, 1992b: 255).

In 1986 the ICT Task Force was merged with the existing DGXIII (Information Market and Innovation) to become the new DGXIII (Telecommunications, Information Industry and Innovation) (Bull. EC 4/1986: 119). Michel Carpentier, previously Head of the Task Force, was appointed Director-General of the new DGXIII. Thus, since 1986, the work of the Task Force has been largely taken over by the new Directorate-General XIII. This, of course, follows well-known patterns of bureaucratic development. At a certain point, the policies and programmes launched by a small part of an existing bureaucracy reach critical mass and this leads to further organisational specialisation. At some point the functions become sufficiently well organised, for a new division, department, or indeed agency, to be created. Just as technological innovation creates whole new industries (for example, video recorders), then so policy innovation creates new agendas, budgets and clients.

A characteristic of the EU ICT sector is its extreme complexity and the involvement of a wide range of powerful actors. The frequent reshuffles and restructuring of responsibilities between the various relevant DGs, for example, is in part an indication of the inherent fluidity of the ICT sector, which constantly demands new bureaucratic and governmental responses to technological developments. However, it is also a reflection of the difficulty which member states and the Commission have had in agreeing the extent to which policies developed for Information and Communication Technology (the responsibility of DGXIII) can be isolated from a more general industrial policy (the responsibility of DGIII). Likewise, to what extent can R&D in the ICT field be treated separately from the broader research programme of the Union (the responsibility of DGXII)? Even within DGXIII itself, relations are not always harmonious with each Directorate seeking a higher profile for its work and, of course, an increased share of scarce resources. The most recent reorganisation of responsibilities in the ICT sector, thus, saw shifts in the division of responsibility between the relevant Directorates-General (in particular DGXII, DGXIII and DGIII) in an attempt to rationalise their activities, to avoid conflicting priorities, and the duplication of work (Innovation and Technology Transfer 2/92: 3).

Given the constantly shifting priorities of the influential actors involved in ICT policy, however, any compromise is likely to remain in a precarious, and temporary, balance. The ICT sector has undergone many important changes since the 1970s when the Commission was able to treat Telecommunications as a subsector of the IT sector (Fuchs, 1994: 181). While at this early stage it had proved necessary to 'link policy on telecommunications networks to the more politically salient market of information-technology products' (Hills, 1991: 132), already by the 1980s the CEU had begun to pursue parallel actions in IT and Telecomms (COM (80) 422 Final). By the early 1990s Telecommunications policy had, meanwhile, come to account for most of the regulatory policy emerging from CEU.[23] With the current convergence of technologies in the ICT field, and with increasing progress towards the information society, the old DGXIII (Information Market and Innovation) and the new DGXIII (Telecommunications, Information Industry and Innovation) have almost come full circle as technological advances have required new institutional responses.

However, in the 1990s, the central institutional role of the Commission in ICT policy is no longer in doubt. ICT policy is now seen as a central aspect of the transformation of the European economy rather than as a separate policy sector (Ungerer, 1990: 101). Indeed the position of ICT policy in the Commission is now rather similar to the role attributed to ICT policy at the national level in the 1970s.

5   ESPRIT AND RACE: TOWARDS A EUROPEAN TECHNOLOGY COMMUNITY

Having been well prepared, through its support of R&D activities, to respond to the emerging environment in the early 1980s, the Commission was able to produce timely proposals for European level solutions to common European problems:

> cooperation does not emerge self-created out of the soup of failed unilateral strategies. Some political actor (or actors) must propose cooperation and sell the idea to potential partners.
>
> (Sandholtz, 1992a: 3)

By the early 1980s the time was ripe for a more experienced, and coordinated, Commission unit to initiate a European offensive on the ICT sector, this time taking great care not to alienate national administrations without at least ensuring that it had the back up of the powerful industrial interests of the Community.

5.1   Innovator of selective incentives: the case of ESPRIT

It was in this climate, then, that the Commission made its first attempts to harness support from European industry for the launch of the EU ESPRIT programme. In encouraging cooperation between EU companies, the Commission's role was substantial and not only in financial terms (participants in ESPRIT receive up to 50 per cent subsidies of collaborative R&D ventures from Community resources). Aware that ICT firms had already accepted that cooperation between European firms in the ICT field was necessary, but that the facilitating infrastructure was lacking in Europe, the Commission brought together the twelve leading ICT companies in the EU to form the 'European IT Round Table'.[24] Importantly, until the first formal proposal was presented to the Council of Ministers in May 1982, Commission efforts completely bypassed national governments (Sandholtz, 1992b: 15).

Inspired by Japanese success in incorporating private enterprise into public policy making (for example, through the Very Large Scale Integration (VLSI) programme), Etienne Davignon, then European

Commissioner for Industry, invited the heads of the 'Big Twelve' companies to draw up a set of proposals for new collaborative projects (Sharp, 1990: 106). The first initiative came from Davignon in 1979 and by 1983 the pilot phase of ESPRIT, a pre-competitive research programme, was already underway. ESPRIT put into action the proposals generated by the leaders of European industry. The most important client groups had been identified, mobilised and had played a leading role in designing the policies. With the support of industry secured, and in the prevailing climate of dissatisfaction with national policies (with the added factor that the pilot phase cost only £8.5 million and additional costs were met by industry), the agreement of national governments was not difficult to achieve.[25] Indeed, the Commission was so confident that support would be forthcoming from the Council that it published an advance notice for participation in the pilot project in the *Official Journal* on 18 October 1982 (Sandholtz, 1992a: 171). ESPRIT 1 also passed through the Council with relative ease and was held up only by minor budgetary disputes:

> The key to Commission success in winning approval for ESPRIT was that it did not try to do the job itself. It got industry to sell the program to national governments. Quite simply, the Commission recruited industry, industry became committed to the cause, and industry took the cause to the national capitals.
>
> (Sandholtz, 1992a: 173)

The Task Force for Information Technology took the major responsibility for the administration of ESPRIT, thus maintaining the vital contribution of industry to the management of the programme. Since 1986, of course, this role has largely been taken over by Directorate A of the new DGXIII. The close relationship between administrators and industry has, however, been maintained within the ESPRIT unit. There is close involvement of the industrial partners at all stages of policy-making in DGXIII, although this varies in intensity from sector to sector. Essentially, DGXIII has an interest in maintaining and developing policies and industry has an interest in securing public funds to facilitate necessary collaboration. Thus, that EU ICT policy has been characterised by the almost symbiotic relationship between officials in DGXIII and the powerful ICT industries is not surprising. While the Commission could not have operated in the face of overt opposition from industry or from national governments, by acting as 'innovator of selective incentives' (Olson, 1971), the Commission has, however, managed to influence the direction in which ICT policy has developed in the EU.

It is clear that 'ESPRIT acts against the natural tendency for collaboration to diminish in a completed market' (Kay, 1990: 267). Indeed, the attitude of industry to ESPRIT has not remained static and support for ESPRIT has begun to dwindle among the big twelve as the non-tariff barriers in Europe have continued to fall. In the game of providing incentives, the efficacy of the incentives has to be constantly reassessed. Industry has always advocated a shift towards more market-oriented research with an emphasis upon research application and has long urged both national governments and the Commission to speed up their efforts to bring EU R&D closer to the market.

> In the EU R&D Framework Programme and in the standards arena, the European vendors have worked together and have set precedents for the ways in which the internal market should function. We look to our national governments and the Commission of the European Communities to follow our lead by evolving policies on a Europe-wide basis in consultation with the industry.
>
> (Bonfield, Deputy Chief Executive, STC, and
> Chairman of ICL, 1988: iii)

This position was reinforced in the Report of the Information and Communication Technologies Review Board (July 1992) which was drawn up with considerable high-level industrial input. The early emphasis in ESPRIT 1 on 'pre-competitive' research allowed a clash with EU competition policy to be avoided. This approach caused, however, some problems for the credibility and future viability of ESPRIT. As George McNeil, Managing Director and Chief Executive Officer, Bull HN Information Systems, observed, 'R&D on its own is not enough. To be useful the technology it produces has to be adopted and sold into the market place' (1991: 17). In the event, the later ESPRIT programmes moved towards more market-oriented research.

While ESPRIT is the most substantial of the Community research programmes, when looked at in terms of resources it constitutes only a tiny percentage of state expenditure in the R&D field.[26] Whatever the actual effects of ESPRIT, however, it has been important to establish a major project in an area where there was no established legal competence for Community intervention. The ESPRIT programme has now entered its fourth phase and has formed the prototype for innumerable subsequent EU programmes in the ICT field. As a model policy innovation it has proved potent (Sharp, 1990: 116). Arguably too, it was the consensus generated over the ESPRIT initiative which allowed the Commission to introduce the idea of a Framework Programme as a medium term planning device for R&D programmes. The 1st Framework Programme (1984–87), adopted in July 1983 (OJ C 208, 25.7.83: 1), was a means of giving a conceptual structure to the various R&D programmes which were emerging (Findlay, 1991: 296). There have since been three further Framework Programmes (1987–91), (1990–94) and (1994–98). As is often the case, programmes develop a life of their own.

> ESPRIT has proved a turning point in policies towards advanced technologies in more than one sense . . . it marked a new departure in style for EC policies with the collaborative, decentralised, project-based programme replacing the top-down style of earlier years. It also . . . provided a model for a whole new range of Commission-based policies latterly brought under the aegis of the Framework Programme. It even, arguably, stimulated the setting up of a competitor programme – EUREKA [European Research Coordinating Agency] – which was fairly rapidly tamed and has become a complement rather than a competitor.
>
> (Sharp, 1990: 116)

Although close links exist between the Commission and the ICT industry, this does not mean that the Commission has followed industry slavishly. Thus, although industry would prefer a more market-led approach to R&D, the Commission, aware of the threat this might pose to intra-EU competition, initially steered cooperation toward pre-competitive research. Equally, the ESPRIT unit has, on occasion, been willing to unsettle the big twelve ICT producers. In drawing up its 1992 work programme, for example, the ESPRIT unit invited representatives from 380 companies to participate, and provided travel expenses. Previously, the practice of consultation through traditional mechanisms had favoured the larger companies and it caused considerable upset among the large ICT companies when the new method was introduced. In a sense, the way that ESPRIT has worked has itself prompted the emergence and mobilisation of a new constituency: the smaller firms. However, given the dwindling interest of the major ICT companies, in anything other than receiving subsidies via ESPRIT, the close involvement of a wider range of participants is arguably a vital means of maintaining a constituency of support for EU-based R&D. If the big firms lose interest, the Commission loses its main constituency. Once again, the Commission has responded to the prevailing environment, this time by appealing to the needs of small and medium size enterprises (SMEs), now as politically salient as was ICT in the 1980s. Similarly, DGXIII has begun to appeal to the large industrial users of ICTs.

5.2 RACE: courting the PTTs

Although based on the same principles as the ESPRIT programme (fifty/fifty funding and cross-national collaboration), in practice, RACE displays more differences from than similarities with ESPRIT. Far from being captured by the major industries in its field (as it could be argued that ESPRIT has been), RACE was originally viewed by national PTTs as the Trojan Horse of EU policies. In the telecommunications field: 'manufacturers and operators were satisfied with the status quo, and there was no political constitutency supporting change' (Hills, 1991: 132). Being particularly wary of the Commission's activities in the area of competition policy, the PTTs were initially unwilling to get too involved in any of the Commission's activities.

To a large extent RACE 'rode the wave of the collaborative enthusiasm generated by the Commission's ESPRIT program' (Sandholtz, 1992b: 258). The original programme was initiated by the Commission and drawn up in cooperation with the Roundtable companies with the aim of introducing 'Integrated Broadband Communications (IBC)' throughout the EU by 1995. The RACE definition phase was approved by the Council of Ministers in July 1985. A fundamental difference between ESPRIT and RACE has been the attitude of the PTTs compared to that of the major producers. Whereas the big twelve were closely involved in all stages of ESPRIT, and indeed of RACE, PTTs have been much more reluctant partners. In response to early requests from the CEU for discussions on cooperation: 'telecoms administrations were extremely reluctant and ended up sending only low level representatives' (Sandholtz, 1992a: 239). Consequently, Commission incentives also had to be directed towards those other actors with an interest in the development of a collaborative EU telecommunications policy such as manufacturers and users of telecommunications equipment and users of services. These groups have been closely drawn into the development of the RACE programme at all levels.

Because of the initial behaviour of the PTTs, Commission officials were forced to develop early policy initiatives without the enthusiastic participation of one key set of actors, the PTTs. This also worked to the disadvantage of the PTTs as in the early stages policy development took place without their full involvement. Ultimately both sides recognised the logic of cooperation: 'in the end the PTTs approved of RACE after reshaping it somewhat to their liking' (Sandholtz, 1992a: 209). The PTTs have, to some extent, been courted by the Commission and significant progress has been made 'by extending its technology push from manufacturers to operators, by focusing on infrastructure via [Integrated Services Digital Network] ISDN, on R&D into new technologies and broadband, and on standardization of terminal equipment, the EC program became nonthreatening to PTTS' (Hills, 1991: 136). Similarly, as the PTTs' monopoly position has been increasingly undermined, they have recognised that there is no other cooperative environment to compare with RACE. As PTTs also faced increasing problems in bringing together services and applications in the market place, they began to turn towards the Commission and RACE .

Of course, in the face of initial opposition from the PTTs, RACE had a battle to survive and ESPRIT, enjoying the support of a broad coalition of powerful industrial backers, has consistently gained a larger slice of EU funding. While there has been a real increase in cooperative R&D in the telecommunications sector, and what could be described as the creation of a new breed of people in R&D who are now used to working in a cooperative environment, RACE still faces the problem of the non-implementation of results which largely depends upon the cooperation of the PTTs.

Thus, RACE is a good example of the Pressman and Wildavsky (1973) observation that the implementor decides and of the so-called 'logic of negotiation' suggested by Jordan and Richardson (1987). If policies are formulated in the absence of active and enthusiastic participation by those whose cooperation is essential at the implementation stage, then implementation failure is much more likely. Although PTTs participate in RACE, they are not, of course, obliged to implement the results of the programme. If the results do not fit into their business strategy then they have no reason to invest in expensive and risky enterprises. This problem has, of course, been exacerbated by the liberalisation of telecommunications markets and the privatisation of some of the PTTs. Under growing competitive pressure, PTTs increasingly focus on their short-term commercial needs rather than on long-term investments for which the demand is unclear.

However, the Commission has undoubtedly had a significant effect by encouraging the creation of a European research community in the field of telecommunications and by creating a vision for the future of EU telecommunications. It is largely the Commission, for example, which can claim credit for pushing forward the Global System for Mobile Communication (GSM) digital communications standard. Peter Radley, director of Alcatel's Mobile Communications division, has described the system as 'a great European Marketing success' which has helped to give European manufacturers an important edge over their international competitors (FT 15.10.92: 2). RACE has had a significant impact upon the environment in which new developments take place. It is unlikely that, even with the demise of RACE, EU-level cooperative R&D in the field of telecommunications would disappear altogether. Having established a precedent for action, the Commission rarely lets it slip away. Equally, the large number of producers, manufacturers and users of telecommunications services and equipment who have been mobilised through their participation in RACE are unlikely to return completely to old behaviour patterns.

6 REVITALISING EU ICT POLICY IN THE 1980s

Throughout the 1980s the Commission continued to press for a revitalisation of EU ICT policy and for an increased role for the CEU in the development of this policy. In 1985 the CEU presented a Memorandum to the Milan Council entitled *Towards a European Technology Community* (COM (85) 350 final). At the Milan Council the Heads of State and Government in turn renewed their commitment to the development of EU ICT policy:

> The European Council noted a collective effort to master new technology was a condition for maintaining European competitiveness. It therefore decided to give the Community a new technological dimension.
>
> (Bull. EC 6/1985: 15)

In particular the Council concluded that there was a need to 'establish a close link between technological development and the effort to unify the internal market' (Bull. EC 6/1985: 15). In a communication, submitted to the Council on 1 October 1985, the Commission set out a detailed plan for the implementation of the European Technology Community. In many respects this story reads rather like that of the late 1960s and early 1970s, following The Hague and Paris Summits. The ICT environment was again facing difficult times, national governments were faced with the need for policy adaptation in response to liberalisation, changing technology and globalisation in the ICT field. Yet in the 1990s, the CEU has come to occupy a pivotal position in the EU ICT field. A crucial question is what changed in the 1980s and 1990s.

First, the ICT sector had undergone a prolonged period of softening up at the EU level, the Commission had mobilised the key industrial actors in the ICT field and even warmed some of the member states to its project. Second, the Commission had developed a clear institutional identity in the ICT field and was capable of capitalising on the legitimising concept of the Single Market and 1992 project. In practice,

> while the importance of telecommunications was recognised in the 1985 White Paper on the Internal Market, the previous neglect of this sector meant that it did not feature explicitly in the White Paper's 300 measures except under the heading of integrating public procurement.
>
> (Holmes, 1990: 21)

There were few specific new powers in the ICT field and the Single European Act, in effect, only 'made *de jure* what was already *de facto*' (Sharp, 1990: 101). Nevertheless, the symbolic importance of the new legitimation for CEU action and the drive to establish the Single European Market (SEM) cannot be understimated. It is no coincidence that, in June 1987, when the Commission presented its Green Paper, *Towards a Dynamic European Economy: On the Development of the Common Market for Telecommunications Services and Equipment* (COM (87) 290), it chose the completion date for its telecommunications project as 1992.

6.1   Institutionalising EU ICT policy: from *de facto* to *de jure*

As has become clear, the Commission has proved to be particularly successful in the initiation of collaborative R&D programmes in the ICT field. The establishment of these programmes has served a number of important purposes. First, it is difficult for governments not to approve a programme which is designated as concerning solely precompetitive research and which has the support of industry and for which 50 per cent of the funding comes from the EU and 50 per cent directly from industry. Where any mention of industrial policy might raise the hackles of at least some national governments, the potential benefits of external support for R&D efforts are hard to ignore. Second, the offer of 50 per cent funding provides a powerful incentive to industry to take the first step toward cooperative research. The programmes tend to develop a dynamic of their own. While a programme may originally apply to only a narrow policy area, it is often used as a model for future programmes in broader areas. In this way, the ESPRIT programme has, for example, served as an initial model for the BRITE (Basic Research in Industrial Technologies for Europe) and RACE programmes.

> The basis for these policies is now provided by the SEA which, given that ESPRIT I was well underway in 1985 when the Act was first mooted, effectively made legal what was already happening in practice.
>
> (Sharp, 1990: 112)

Likewise, the first framework programme (1987–91) adopted in 1987 (OJ L 302 28.9.87) was also given a legal basis in the SEA but had been under discussion for two years previously. Importantly, however, interviews with those involved in R&D in the European ICT industry indicate that, through participation in EU R&D programmes, they have learned how to work together and have become more mutually responsive. Indeed, it could be argued that a common business identity is emerging in Europe in the area of ICT. Finally, by encouraging the rapid development of new technologies in Europe, and ultimately their transmission to the market-place, these programmes facilitate the emergence of gaps in national legislation (for example in safety standards) into which EU legislation can most easily insinuate itself. Indeed, following the success of the ESPRIT 1 programme the Commission, in consultation with the 'Big twelve' ICT firms, declared:

> the rapid implementation of a Community-wide coordinated strategy for standards is essential in view of the urgency and importance of this issue for the future of IT in the Community.
>
> (SEC (84) 796: 2)

It is easy to argue that the firms have simply gone where the money is and that standards may be elaborated with little intention on the part of the industry to implement them. However, the spill-over effects of drawing powerful industrial interests into the policy process at the EU level have had important implications for the extension of EU activities in the ICT field. Industry has been an important force in promoting the Single Market programme and in promoting the reduction of non-tariff barriers throughout the EU (Cowles, 1995). Thus, encouraging industry to cooperate at the EU level in the ICT field has been an important achievement for the Commission. As the 'deregulatory' thrust of the SEM continues, it increasingly generates regulatory vacuums in areas which then require 'reregulation' at the EU level (Majone, 1990). It becomes much easier for the Commission to justify the introduction of minimum standards at EU level and hence an increase in EU competence in the ICT field having established precedent for Commission intervention in the field, having developed a coherent overview of the sector, and having convinced industry and national governments of the logic of EU level collaboration.[27]

It is clear that 'international organisations register the greatest impact on interstate cooperation during periods of policy adaptation' (Sandholtz, 1992b: 252). DGXIII has not, however, managed merely to respond to transitional policy vacuums at the national level but by encouraging the speedy development of new technology and new applications of technology and, since the mid-1980s, the active enforcement of competition rules the CEU has played an active role in promoting policy adaptation at the national level and thus in creating policy vacuums in the ICT field.

6.2 The Single European Market: liberalisation, deregulation and reregulation

Altering the environment in which the development of ICT policy takes place has perhaps been one of the most significant achievements of the Commission, yet one to which little attention is paid (but see Thatcher, 1994). Until the 1980s, Commission achievements in the ICT field had been fairly minor. Since then, however, there has been rapid policy innovation at EU level in the ICT field, which has enabled the Commission to establish itself as a key actor in the ICT field. A number of developments, not all completely external to the Commission, have contributed to this development.

First, the liberal, competitive ethos promoted by the Single Market programme has allowed the Commission both to encourage the deregulatory momentum occurring throughout its member states and to an extent to jump on the bandwagon of this movement. As Karl Van Miert, European Commissioner with responsibility for competition argued, liberalisation does not mean deregulation:

> In fact liberalisation will probably increase not reduce the role of competition policy in telecommunications with the Commission acting as referee to ensure fair play.
>
> (Agence Europe, 22.4.93, 1832: 6)

The ethos of deregulation and liberalisation in the member states has, in effect, presented a regulatory vacuum which has allowed the

Commission to reregulate in order to guarantee a competitive environment throughout the Community (Majone, 1990).

> To ensure that uniform prices prevail for goods and services some form of intervention will be required of the CEC. Deregulation and liberalisation need to be accompanied by an active competition policy to reap the benefits of the single market.
>
> (Locksley, 1990: 12)

The rise of the deregulatory ethos, has moreover, facilitated increased cooperation between the Directorate-General for Competition (DGIV) and DGXIII. Indeed, those responsible for setting standards in DGXIII often threaten recalcitrant companies with the 'competition sheriffs' in DGIV. Firms are encouraged to participate in cooperative, voluntary, standard setting and thus to pre-empt any accusations of anti-competitive behaviour through the establishment of discriminatory proprietary standards. The application of competitive principles to the field of ICTs, particularly in the area of telecommunications, has also been an important means of creating a role for the Commission even against the will of the PTTs. Moreover, the prohibition on anti-competitive behaviour in the area of ICTs has undermined the capacity of member states to steer their own industries via public procurement practices.[28] Similarly, under Directive 83/189, national governments are obliged to inform the Commission of any new standards they intend to introduce. The Commission is, therefore, given advance notification of any standards which are emerging and is able to introduce a European standard in the same area:

> this procedure will have to be applied forcefully enough to ensure that any planned initiative is rapidly followed by the mobilisation of the Community standardisation procedures.
>
> (SEC (84) 796: 13)

Commission encouragement, via its R&D programmes, of rapid advances in ICT technology provides another means by which the destabilisation of the national ICT environment can be encouraged. As new technologies develop, generating new gaps in national legislation, the Commission, armed with the knowledge gained from consultation and research at the EU level and backed by its constituency of supporters, is able to respond quickly with new EU proposals for action. The autonomy of industry has also been circumscribed as the Commission has employed a *de facto* merger policy in the field of telecommunications. In the 1980s firms increasingly began to notify the Commission, and effectively to seek clearance, prior to enacting cross-border mergers. This gave companies the chance to ensure that they were not contravening Articles 85 and 86 of the Rome Treaty's competition provisions. In effect 'the power of the Commission to threaten to disrupt mergers is as good as the power to ban them!' (Holmes, 1990: 24).

The 'new approach', adopted by the Commission since 1985, advocating less harmonisation and more mutual recognition initially appears to contradict this analysis of the Commission's attempts to maximise its scope of action. This would not, however, be an accurate interpretation of the Commission's activities (see Majone, 1989a). While mutual recognition has become an increasingly important part of the Commission's approach to ICT policy, this does not mean that the Commission has become willing to play a lesser role. Mutual recognition is intended to speed up progress towards the Single Market and to lead to a greater demand for the reduction of non-tariff barriers to trade. This, in turn, is likely to lead to the emergence of a regulatory vacuum in the ICT sector and, ultimately, to the 'reregulation' of the sector at the EU level. There are also cross-sectoral implications of regulation in such key sectors as ICT. Central regulation of telecommunications, for example, requires central regulation of data protection, copyright, trading standards and consumer protection. Furthermore, mutual recognition itself requires the setting of certain minimum standards. Increasingly it is Commission regulations which guarantee these standards. The central role of the Commission in ICT policy is, therefore, reinforced by the trends towards liberalisation and deregulation in the ICT sector. Although the preference for mutual recognition and voluntary standards is presented by the Commission as a 'hands-off' non-interventionist approach, in practice the transformation in approach is largely symbolic.

6.3   Post SEA: the rise of EU telecommunications policy

The symbolic importance of the 1992 project and the ethos of liberalisation and deregulation which it promoted have been central to the revitalisation of EU activities in the ICT field. First, the Commission was able to rationalise its activities in the field of telecommunications in relation to the Single Market project although, in practice, the Commission's 1987 Green Paper was not formally connected with the 1985 White Paper on the Single Market (Hills, 1991: 126). Second, the focus on deregulation and liberalisation allowed the CEU to make use of its very powerful, hence highly controversial, competition-based powers.

The Commission's Green Paper on Telecommunications (COM (87) 290) was firmly couched in the language of free and open competition. Yet, in the 1970s:

> the decision to exclude telecommunications from the public procurement rules was a political decision by member states not to apply the rules of the Treaty.
>
> (Holmes, 1990: 24)

Given the rather difficult relationship between the Commission and the PTTs and the relationship between these and their national governments it would have been very difficult for the CEU to adopt a 'head on' approach in the ICT field without some very powerful support for its action. Crucial to the strategy of the Commission in the 1980s was, therefore, the involvement and mobilisation of a wide range of actors concerned with developments in the ICT field. In November 1983, for example, the CEU set up the Senior Officials Group for Telecommunications (SOGT). Discussion between SOGT and the Commission centred on six 'lines of action' in the telecommunications field which had already been identified by the Commission (COM (83) 573 Final). Following SOGT agreement on these points, the six 'lines of action' in turn formed the core of the CEU's telecommunications strategy (Sandholtz, 1992b: 257).

Meanwhile, supported by two key rulings of the Court of Justice, the CEU began in the 1980s to develop its use of the procedures provided for in Article 90 of the Treaty.[29] Importantly, Article 90 empowers the Commission to issue Directives without seeking the approval of the Council of Ministers, thus limiting the power of national governments to curb the activities of the Commission in this area. Article 90 allows the Commission to take action to prevent member states from introducing or maintaining measures for 'public enterprises' which conflict with the other Articles of the Treaty (such as Articles 85 and 86 on competition). In the new era of liberalisation, deregulation and competition, it was difficult for the member states to dispute the principles upon which the Commission's actions were based (although there have been a number of legal challenges to the Commission's approach). Indeed, it is rather ironic that the UK has been the least vigorous opponent of the use of Article 90, presumably because the powers have been used in a pro-competitive manner (Holmes, 1990: 26). On the basis of the new approach, laid out in the 1987 Green Paper, the Commission has thus been able to introduce a number of Directives which now play a key role in regulating the ICT sector.[30]

The Green Paper also provided for the further institutionalisation of the CEU's central role in the ICT field. In March 1988, the European Telecommunications Standards Institute was established to create standards in the area of telecommunications which had traditionally been the domain of the European Conference of Postal and Telecommunications Administrations. In many respects, CEPT was considered to be too heavily dominated by the PTTs. In contrast, ETSI involves representatives from national administrations, public network operators, manufacturers, users, private service providers and research bodies (Besen, 1990: 522). The Commission, in contrast to its relationship with the CEPT, has a number of important roles with respect to the operation of ETSI:

> first, it can urge, and provide the needed resources for, the adoption of standards that it believes are needed to make markets more competitive ... Second, it can encourage the use of European standards by requiring their employment in public procurement and by telecommunications administrations, which increases the importance of standards developed by organisations like ETSI. Third, it can prevent the adoption of standards that may be desired by some members if it believes that those standards will inhibit the flow of trade.
>
> (Besen, 1990: 529–530)

Meanwhile, the Commission continued to ensure the involvement of a wide range of actors in its attempt to develop EU ICT policy. This has sometimes helped to push the process even further than the CEU had hoped. For example, in October 1992, the Commission issued a request for views on its tentative proposals for the future of telecommunication networks in the EU which heralded the start of a rigorous and prolonged process of consultation. By bringing together the various opposing interests in the area of telecommunications, the Commission was able to test the waters before producing its proposal for the liberalisation of telephone services. Significantly, the results of the consultation allowed the Commission to present a considerably more radical proposal (for parallel liberalisation of national and intra-EU services rather than the more restricted liberalisation of solely intra-Community services) than the Commission had originally considered feasible. The proposal, presented to the Telecoms Council on 10 May 1993, emerged following five general hearings, consultation with 130 organisations, and the examination of 180 written communications

(Agence Europe, 29.4.93, 5970: 5). A general consensus emerged that liberalisation is inevitable.

Predictably, the interests could be divided into 'hawks' and 'doves'. For example, the large industrial users pressed for early liberalisation, whereas at least some of the PTTs and several national governments pressed for a slower rate of change. Even among the PTTs, however, there has been a growing realisation that their own self-interest should lead them to support eventual liberalisation, as the evidence suggests that this is the best way to expand the total market for telecommunications services. The Commission's competition Directorate (DGIV) is reported as calculating that the rate of growth following deregulation as likely to be twice that without further deregulation (*The Economist*, 13.3.93: 14). A compromise proposal eventually emerged which gave something to both the innovators and the laggards, as a five-year transitional period was proposed, with full liberalisation to be achieved by 1998.

The Commission strategy, pursued in the 1987 Green Paper, proved to be rather successful. This was followed up, on 25 October 1994, when the European Commission adopted Part 1 of a Green Paper on the liberalisation of telecommunications infrastructure and cable television networks (COM (94) 440 Final). This in turn was followed up by Part II on 25 January 1995. Part II specifically aims to launch

> a broad discussion with all interested parties of the major issues involved in the future regulation of network infrastructure. This will allow the development of a common approach to infrastructure provision in the European Union. This approach must be fully integrated with the range of Union policies designed to support the Information Society.
>
> (COM (94) 682 Final: iii)

Not only has the CEU recognised the benefits of consultation for mobilisation in the ICT field, but the Commission has now latched its proposals on to a new legitimising concept in the form of the Information Society.

7   MAASTRICHT AND THE INFORMATION SOCIETY

The Maastricht Treaty brought about a number of significant changes in the legal basis for EU action in the ICT field. In Title XII on Trans-European Networks (TENS), for example, Article 129b(i) specifically includes telecommunications as one of the sectors in which TENS should be promoted, while Article 129b(ii) identifies the importance of promoting 'interconnection and interoperability'. To this end, Article 129c(i) states that the EU must establish a series of policy guidelines identifying common projects which may be pursued and 'shall implement any measures that may prove necessary to ensure the interoperability of the networks, particularly in the field of technical standardization'.[31]

Once again, the Treaty provisions introduce little which was not happening in practice already. However, a firm legal basis undoubtedly allows the Commission greater scope for action. Perhaps, the most important development in the post-Maastricht era, however, has been the growing importance attached to the concept of the 'Information Society' by member states, industry and the Commission. The Commission's White Paper on Growth, Competitiveness and Employment (COM (93) 700 Final) and the report drawn up by a group of leading industrialists,[32] chaired by Commissioner Bangemann (Bangemann Report), for example, have been important milestones in the post-Maastricht development of the EU ICT Sector.[33] Both documents emphasise

> the need within Europe for an efficient and effective communications infrastructure, capable of supporting the emerging information society.
>
> (COM (94) 682 Final: ii)

As the development of the information society progresses, the importance of the softening up process becomes clear. Thus, for example, the Bangemann Report recommended moves toward the application of technologies in ten areas which were to build upon the existing R&D programmes of the EU.[34] Meanwhile, the Bangemann Report also recommended further institutional development at the EU level in the ICT field:

> Given the urgency and the importance of the tasks ahead, there must be at Union level, one Council capable of dealing with the full range of issues associated with the information society.
>
> (Bangemann Report, 1994: 35)

It was not specified whether this Council was to be intergovernmental or supranational in nature; however, the Report specifically recommended further institutionalisation of the Commission's role in the ICT sector:

> A board composed of eminent figures from all sectors concerned, including the social partners, should be established by the Commis-

sion to work on the framework for implementing the information society.

(Bangemann Report, 1994: 35)

On 19 July 1994, the Commission presented the Council with a Communication, *Europe's Way to the Information Society: An Action Plan* (COM (94) 347 Final). The institutionalisation of the EU ICT sector has continued apace. By the end of 1994, the Information Society Project Office (ISPO) had been established as a joint project by DGIII and DGXIII. A one-stop-shop, ISPO is charged with promoting awareness of the information society, stimulating partnerships and launching international cooperation initiatives. Meanwhile, in September 1995, the European standards organisations responded to the push towards the information society and the increasing convergence of high technologies by establishing the ICT Standards Board. The aim of the board is to match preparation of standards and specifications to the needs of the information society:

> the new Board will consider standardization requirements from any relevant source, notably industry's High Level Strategy Group and the European Commission.

(Electrotechnical Standards Europe, 6/96: 3)

In July 1994, the G7 countries (Canada, France, Germany, Italy, Japan, UK and USA) agreed to allow the European Commission to host the 'G7 Ministerial Conference on the Information Society'. The Conference, held 25–26 February 1995, gave important international recognition to the key role which the Commission has come to play in the ICT field. There is little doubt that, while the Commission occupied a peripheral position in the ICT field in the 1960s and 1970s, in the 1990s the CEU has emerged as a pivotal player at the centre of a network of powerful actors in the ICT field.

8 CONCLUSION

The ICT policy area was, to a certain extent, ripe for the timely intervention of a central body which could develop an overall view of the sector. The very nature of technological development is inherently unstable and is continually presenting new issues for governments to deal with. The new fashion of liberalisation, occurring throughout the countries of the EU, was added in the 1980s to the long-term trends towards sectoral instability. The combination of structural   weaknesses   and   liberalisation   presented   changed opportunities in the 1980s and 1990s to which the Commission has responded. However, there is no inherent logic requiring the development of an EU, rather than an international, ICT policy, other than a generalised belief in aiding or protecting European industries (which is not formally espoused by the EU). Indeed, this reality is reflected in the fact that few of the Commission's activities in the ICT sector are limited only to the member states of the EU. Moreover, neither of these explanations accounts for the failure to develop an EU ICT policy, in the rather similar environment which prevailed in the late 1960s and early 1970s.

National governments have not been keen to relinquish their control over firms despite their recognition of the need for a new strategic approach in this area. An important element of the Commission's activities in the ICT field has thus been its ability to capitalise on the fluidity and inherent instability of the ICT environment, on the inability of national governments to devise new solutions to the old problem of European competitiveness, and on the problems which large and competitive industries experience in trying to sustain collective action (Olson, 1971).

Getting national governments to condone the development of an EU policy was not an easy task and the support of national governments often comes at the risk of running counter to other entrenched EU policies, for example, competition policy. By justifying its intervention in terms of bolstering the competitive position of *European* industry *vis-à-vis* Japan and the USA, the Commission has, to an extent, succeeded in selling intra-EU collaboration to reluctant EU governments. Defending and promoting European industry has become, therefore, the EU equivalent of national protectionism at the level of the nation-state. As such, the policy instruments were relatively familiar and acting collectively in the European interest provided a legitimising concept. The promotion of this type of protectionist policy, albeit largely symbolic, however, runs the constant risk of being shot down by the 'competition police' in DGIV. Thus, again, a careful balance has to be struck between getting national governments onside while avoiding inter-institutional conflicts with DGIV. Of course, inter-institutional relationships are not always conflictual. For example, the same 'competition police' can provide an important bolster for those in DGXIII trying to convince industries not to adopt their preferred proprietary standards but to support the development of a common European standard. Similarly, proponents of the Information Society have increasingly emphasised the vital importance of CEU competition instruments for its realisation.

The prioritisation of a particular approach to ICT policy is further complicated by the critical role which industry plays at almost every step in the policy process. Whether as individual actors, in committees or consultation groups, or as group members in industry federations and national and European standards bodies, industry is an omnipresent force in the ICT field.[35] DGXIII enjoys a rather symbiotic relationship with industry which is involved at almost every stage of policy deliberation in the area. Yet, this did not come about without some effort on the part of the Commission. As rational actors, firms might have been expected to seek out the strategic and tactical alliances which best serve their technological, market, and R&D requirements, irrespective of national or regional boundaries. These alliances would, of course, have included trans-European collaboration in any case, but would more likely have been predominantly global in orientation.[36] DGXIII has, however, managed to 'massage' the direction which this cooperation has taken and has encouraged significant increases in the extent of intra-EU cooperation between firms.

The Commission cannot afford to alienate either the many powerful global actors which operate in the sector or important national governments. The Commission has, however, learned to operate a rather successful two-fold approach in the ICT sector. On the one hand, as demonstrated in this chapter, it has provided incentives for industry to cooperate at the EU level and stemmed government opposition by providing funding and by justifying this activity in terms of supporting a European industry. On the other hand, the CEU has learned to select the appropriate policy types and policy instruments for application in the ICT field very carefully (see Chapter 4).

4 Policy types and policy instruments in the European Union policy process

1 INTRODUCTION

One crucial aspect of the European Commission's work is to determine the extent to which EU intervention in a particular policy area is likely to prove acceptable. As will emerge in this chapter, the Commission's power to propose a particular policy type as well as the preferred instrument for its implementation is not insignificant.

In the following sections, the various types of policies emerging from the two policy areas under examination (social policy and ICT policy) are disaggregated. While a number of attempts have been made to distinguish between policy types at the national level (Froman, 1968; Hayes, 1978; Lowi, 1964; Ripley and Franklin, 1986), there has been little attention paid to the significance of various types of policies evident in EU legislation (but see Bulmer, 1994a; Cram 1993; Majone, 1992a, 1993; and Pollack, 1995a). There has, it emerges in this chapter, been a clear trend towards the use of regulatory policy at the EU level in both of the policy areas under examination. Thus, the question to be tackled is why this legislative pattern has emerged.

The choice of policy instrument is a highly politicised activity (Dahl and Lindblom, 1976; Hood, 1983; Kirschen, 1964). Indeed, 'very commonly it is the instrument selected for realising a policy aim that is far more contentious than the aim itself' (Hood, 1983: 136). Yet the choices involved in the selection of policy instruments for the delivery of public policies at the EU level have been given insufficient attention:

> implementation must involve a process of interaction between organizations, the members of which may have different values, perspectives, and priorities from one another and from those advocating the policy.
>
> (Hogwood and Gunn, 1984: 208)

In the case of the European Union, this diversity of influences is, of course, heightened by the divergent national traditions of policy-making and implementation and the key role of important sectoral actors in implementing EU legislation. In this context, the power to select particular non-binding policy instruments (for example, soft law provisions such as Recommendations or Opinions), or to delegate rule-making responsibility to the European standards organisations (CEN, CENELEC and ETSI), often allows the Commission to gain a toe-hold in contentious policy areas. Meanwhile, the early use of binding legal measures (for example, Directives, Regulations, Decisions), which may antagonise national governments or important sectoral actors, is avoided until the policy area has been softened up. Increasingly, awareness of the important role of sectoral actors in the implementation of EU level measures has, for example, led to an active attempt on behalf of the Commission to discern the acceptability of particular measures with affected interests before a formal policy proposal emerges.[1] The selection of policy instruments in the Commission is, thus, a complicated political process, involving detailed research, complex interactions with other EU institutions and with national administrations, with businesses and interest groups, as well as with multinational companies and aspirant member states of the EU.

2 EU LEGISLATION: CATEGORIES AND PROBLEMS OF DEFINITION

The first problem encountered in the analysis of EU legislation is that of categorising policies. This is a problem familiar to analysts attempting to operationalise, for example, Lowi's (1964) classification of public policies. Policies rarely fit neatly into the boxes required. For the purposes of this chapter, and building upon Lowi's categories of redistributive,[2] distributive, regulatory and constituent policies, the following four categories have been developed which usefully illustrate the pattern of policy development in the EU:

- *Process* establishing rules and procedures at the EU level, setting up committees and organisations.
- *EU action/direct expenditure* requiring direct EU expenditure and intervention, for example, through the European Social Fund or the Framework Programme.
- *Regulatory* setting standards, establishing rules of conduct with which national governments, businesses and individuals must comply.

- *Soft Law*   non-binding legislation which nevertheless has political significance.[3]

The second problem which arises when attempting to analyse EU legislation is one of definition. Thus, for example, what is referred to as social policy in the context of the EU does not necessarily comply with general conceptions of what constitutes social policy. Public health, education and housing policy are, for example, virtually non-existent at the EU level.[4] Here, rather than adopting any single definition of what constitutes social policy that adopted by the EU has been followed. The legislation analysed is that contained in the section entitled 'Social Policy' in the *Directory of Community Legislation in Force and Other Acts of the Community Institutions* (as at June 1995: see Figures 2–5). Similarly, as developments in EU ICT policy have traditionally been subsumed under the general heading of 'Industrial Policy and Internal Market' it has been necessary to select from within this general category those sections which relate specifically to the ICT sector. Thus, the legislation analysed is drawn from the two sections entitled 'Information Technology, Telecommunications and Data-Processing' and 'Research and Technological Development' in the *Directory of Community Legislation in Force and Other Acts of the Community Institutions* (as at June 1995: see Figures 6–9). Analysing only the legislation of the EU fails to illustrate the extent of regulatory activity in which the CEU is involved, through its cooperation with the European standards bodies. Thus, a separate Table, detailing the numbers of European standards emerging from these institutions is also presented (see Table 2). These are not, of course, ideal categorisations.[5] However, they give a general picture of existing trends in EU social and ICT legislation.

3   EU SOCIAL POLICY: THE LEGISLATIVE PATTERN

The results of the analysis of EU social legislation are shown in Figures 2 to 5.[6] As can be seen in Figure 2, most EU legislation in the social field is process legislation. This legislation establishes the procedures within which the Commission operates in the area of social policy. Process legislation establishes, for example, joint committees and advisory groups at the EU level. However, process legislation does not, in itself, directly affect individuals in Europe. Rather it establishes the general framework and machinery within which EU social policy may be developed. As will be explored, however, current

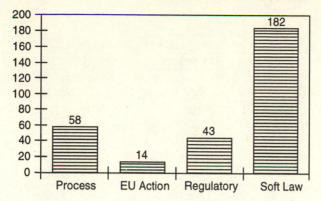

Figure 2 Social policy: relative incidence of the four policy types
Source: *Directory of Community Legislation in Force and Other Acts of the Community Institutions* (as at June 1995)

process legislation may prove to be a significant step towards the establishment of a future regulatory framework.

Only two of the policy categories employed have a direct impact on European citizens and on national activities in the social field: regulatory policies through the setting of standards which must be adhered to, and EU social programmes through direct EU expenditure. Of

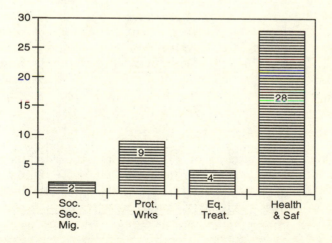

Figure 3 Social policy: regulatory policy by policy area
Source: *Directory of Community Legislation in Force and Other Acts of the Community Institutions* (as at June 1995)

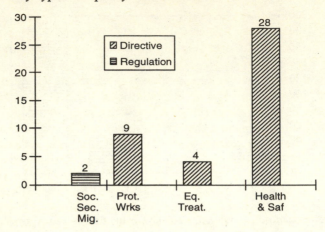

Figure 4 Social policy: regulatory policy by policy area and instrument of enactment
Source: *Directory of Community Legislation in Force and Other Acts of the Community Institutions* (as at June 1995)

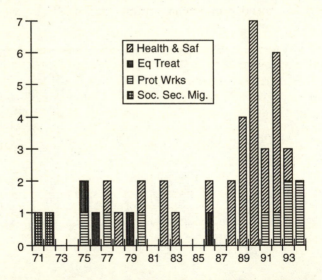

Figure 5 Social policy: regulatory policy by policy area over time
Source: *Directory of Community Legislation in Force and Other Acts of the Community Institutions* (as at June 1995)

these two policy types, regulatory policies are clearly greater in number. Notably, policies involving direct EU action and expenditure are numerically the least significant of the four categories employed. The fourth category of policy, soft law, while non-binding in nature, is clearly, in terms of volume, a significant category. As will emerge, this type of policy may also be an important element in the Commission's approach to the development of future EU social policy.

As regulatory policy is the principal category of EU social policy affecting European citizens and national practice, the characteristics of EU social policy regulation are explored in more detail. As is clear from Figure 3, EU social policy regulation occurs only in a limited number of areas. Regulatory policy is evident most conspicuously in the area of Health and Safety for Workers (Health & Saf) but also appears in the areas of Equal Treatment of Men and Women (Eq Treat), Protection of Workers (Prot Wrks), and Social Security for Migrant Workers (Soc Sec Mig). These policies have been implemented mainly by means of Directives. Only in the area of Social Security for Migrant Workers have EU Regulations been applied (Figure 4).[7] Even in this area, EU Regulations leave national systems intact while performing a purely coordinating function, universalising entitlements to already existing benefits. Finally, as Figure 5 shows, the first regulatory policies in the social field were those concerned with Social Security for Migrant Workers in 1971 and 1972. The other areas of regulation did not take off until the mid-1970s, and even then proceeded at a minimal rate. Since the late 1980s, however, there has been a significant increase in the output of social policy regulation by the EU. This increase comes most obviously in the area of Health and Safety which, in 1990, constituted the total output of EU social policy regulation. This increase would seem to be directly related to the introduction of Article 118a of the Single European Act which provided for qualified majority voting by the Council on matters concerning the Health and Safety of Workers.

Thus, regulatory policy appears to be the principal form of EU social legislation affecting European citizens, in terms of both volume and of impact, but not of scope. While there is an increasing output of regulatory policy in the field of EU social policy, this output has been strictly limited to specific policy areas.

3.1 EU social legislation: the puzzle

It is clear from the preceding analysis that, while the legislative output of the EU in the field of social policy is limited, EU policies affecting national practice in the social field are predominantly and increasingly regulatory policies. To understand this pattern, the following questions need to be addressed: Why regulatory policy? Why in these specific areas? Why at these particular times?

Majone (1991c: 11–12) has emphasised the Commission's desire to increase 'its influence as measured by the scope of its competences'. The financial constraints under which the Commission must operate mean, he states, that 'the only way for the Commission to increase its role is to expand the scope of its regulatory activities'. Peters (1992: 16) has also noted 'the importance of regulation and lawmaking, as opposed to large taxing and spending programs, in the process of the Community'. Viewing the EU policy process from the perspective of bureaucratic politics, Peters notes both the desire of the Commission to increase its power and the EU's limited budgetary base. He also points out that regulations do not require any great financial resources from the EU itself for their implementation. In particular, he emphasises the important function performed by regulations in disguising the overall winners and losers in policy areas which would normally be subject to redistributive policies. Policies involving taxation and expenditure, on the other hand, make redistributive issues immediately obvious to national participants. As such, he argues, the use of regulatory policies should help to make progress towards 1992 somewhat less divisive.

The benefits to the Commission of a regulatory approach seem clear. Regulatory policy, being virtually costless to the regulator, allows the Commission to increase the scope of its competence without making massive inroads into its limited resources. Moreover, smoothing the path towards the completion of the Single Market can only enhance the position of the European Commission. However, the Commission does not have a free rein over the development of EU policy. While the power implicit in Commission control over the policy-making machinery should not be underestimated, it nevertheless operates within an environment in which national governments formally have the final word on policy decisions. Although the right to initiate policy gives the Commission far greater power over the policy environment than has generally been attributed to it, the Commission may act only within the parameters allowed to it by the member states. Despite this ultimate constraint however, the Commission has become an adept strategist in the field of social policy. Learning from past experience, the Commission has developed a variety of techniques designed to expand its influence in the social field without alienating national governments. Promoting and facilitating the growth of EU regulatory policy has been central to its approach. The actual policies which emerge from this process are, however, necessarily mediated by the environment in which they are developed. These environmental influences have meant that policy development has been neither random nor universal. EU social regulations have, in practice, been restricted to four specific areas: Health and Safety for Workers; Equal Treatment of Men and Women; Protection of Workers; and Social Security for Migrant Workers.

Majone (1991c) has also argued that the interests of multinational, export-oriented companies have been important in supporting European-wide regulation in the social field. Certainly, the evidence from the recent European Works Councils Directive does indicate a preference on the part of multinationals for coherent EU-wide regulation.[8] Given the option not to implement EWCs in the UK, multinationals have chosen not to capitalise on this opportunity.[9] It is difficult, however, to explain restriction of the regulations to four narrow policy areas in terms of the role of multinationals. Why should multinationals advocate the equalisation of standards in only some areas of social policy and not in others which equally present themselves as costs to their firms? Why should they be more concerned, for example, with harmonising health and safety standards across Europe than with harmonising contributions to benefits or wage levels?

One of the most obvious explanations for the expansion of EU regulatory policies in these four particular areas is that they all have a basis in the Treaty of Rome: Social Security for Migrant Workers (Article 51); Equal Treatment of Men and Women (Article 119); Protection of Workers (Article 118) and Health and Safety of Workers (Article 118 of the Treaty; Article 118a of SEA). This is, however, too simplistic. EU social policies have rarely flowed directly from the Treaty. Even in the area of Equal Treatment, where the Treaty basis for action is least ambiguous, action was only reluctantly accepted by the member states and no policies were implemented until 1975. Yet in this area, the policies finally implemented actually expand the scope of the Treaty. Certain other areas also mentioned in the Treaty have, on the other hand, to a large extent been neglected. Why, for example, was health and safety policy developed from the basis of Article 118 and not employment policy or social security policy? Until the SEA they all existed on the same basis in the Treaty in Article 118 yet they have developed at an extraordinarily different pace.[10] Clearly, the Treaty basis has not had a systematic impact on the development of EU regulatory policy. While all of the areas in which regulatory policies have been implemented do have a basis in the Treaty, not all areas mentioned in the Treaty have evolved into regulatory policies. Equally, the Treaty does not explain the timing of the introduction of these policies. If the Treaty were the sole basis for action then the extent of, for example, Equal Treatment legislation which exists now might have been expected in the 1960s. Clearly there were other factors at play.

A second possible explanation is that all four areas are closely linked to the functioning of the internal market. This is however a highly controversial issue. Since the very inception of the European Union there has been an ongoing debate as to the nature and significance of the links between economic and social policy. In 1975 a report compiled for the International Labour Organization by a group of experts concluded that there were no clear grounds for advocating the harmonisation of social security costs throughout the European Union. It was considered that social security costs could not be viewed as distinct from other social costs in their effect on competition as they were only one among a number of factors, such as taxation systems and wage levels, which affect employers' costs. Following the same logic, why should it now be considered that differential rates of pay for men and women or divergent health and safety standards, in isolation, can significantly alter the balance of competition in Europe?

Both of these explanations might, however, be important in so far as they are used by the Commission as justifications for EU action in the social field. Arguably, the language of justification is of interest, even if it does not imply causality. The stated Commission policy, of introducing social measures only in so far as they aid the implementation of economic integration, may be a sensible way of avoiding provoking national opposition and of avoiding the accusation that the Commission is invading national policy space. EU regulation in all four of the policy areas examined here can be justified in these terms, is virtually costless to the EU and, of course, was actually accepted by the Council of Ministers. Of central importance in gaining this acceptance, the costs of these regulations tend to fall on employers and individuals rather than on national governments, as would have been the case, for example, if social security payments were to be harmonised. The locus of financial responsibility might also partly explain the reluctance of many governments to allow any expansion of EU activities in the field of 'education', generally considered to be a state responsibility, while allowing some scope for EU action in the field of vocational training which is often considered to be the responsibility of employers.

Thus a significant factor determining the policy areas which have been subject to regulation by the EU may be the extent to which they involve expenditure by national governments. If costs can be deflected to businesses or individuals, the member states may be less reluctant to endorse common European standards (see also Majone, 1993). The member states still have the final word on policy decisions. However, the fact that these issues reach the policy agenda in the form of proposals for regulations, at the particular times that they do, might best be understood by examining the particular dynamics of the Commission's approach to social policy.

The Commission has, it appears, been able to exert some influence over the pattern of social policy development in the EU. While the actual regulatory policies which get through the Council must be approved by the member states, and this necessarily affects their content, the increase in the number of regulatory policies and the timing of these policies may well be explained by the bureaucratic processes and timely opportunism of the Commission. Below, some possible indications that the Commission may be preparing the way for further regulatory action in this field are briefly explored. In the cases of Health and Safety, Protection of Workers and Equal Treatment, existing EU regulations expand the scope of the Treaty and were first introduced shortly after the first Social Action Programme in 1974. The Commission's rapid response to the political impetus generated by this programme may have been significant in accounting for the policies which were finally implemented.

3.2 Preparing the ground for further regulation: rhetoric, soft law and symbolic politics

Providing a declaration of political commitment to certain goals, soft law is often used by the Commission as a precursor to subsequent legally binding decisions (Wellens and Borchardt, 1989: 302). The rhetoric of member states has, likewise, come to be an important resource for the CEU to draw upon in the social policy process. The rhetoric of the member states may, for example, be used as a rationalisation for Commission action. For example, a senior Commission official argued that Council Conclusions, 'give you a knock out blow in negotiations. If you can cite a European Council conclusion in a debate you're away' (cited in Peterson, 1995: 72). By holding the member states to ransom over their stated commitment to the social dimension, the Commission has often claimed that it has legitimacy to act in the social field. European Summit or Council conclusions often, at least, provide the justification for the introduction of a research project or an action programme or may help to obtain agreement to a recommendation, an opinion, or a resolution from the Council of Ministers.

In turn, these small steps, often implemented via soft law provisions, play an important role in establishing institutional norms and precedent for future action in the social field. Armstrong and Bulmer (1997) have, for example, discussed the contribution of Commission research and action programmes, implemented in the 1970s, to the creation of issue-specific governance regimes in the areas of Health and Safety and Equal Opportunities policy, two areas in which there is now a significant body of binding EU legislation. Indeed, the fact that the Commission, having already commissioned relevant research, has been prepared and ready to act at politically opportune moments has been highly important. Prior to the Social Action Programme in 1974, for example, the Commission had already carried out research into, for example, the issues of Health and Safety and into Equal Treatment. It was thus technically equipped to present considered proposals rather quickly.

The Commmission practice of establishing action programmes and non-binding guidelines for action in the social field goes back as far as 1962. Indeed, the effectiveness of this incremental approach was established in the early years of the Coal and Steel Community:

> as the High Authority has demonstrated in the social field, the power to enquire, to collect facts, and to make proposals, is often a most effective way of promoting action.
>
> (Commission cited in Collins, 1975: 189–190)

The establishment of action programmes in sensitive policy areas has often been used as a means for claiming that the Commission now has some competence in the particular field. For example, although there is clearly no agreement as to what the EU role ought to be in social matters, and the field of social security has been particularly controversial, the Commission managed to justify its interest in the area of social protection on the grounds that it had already established a role for itself in this field through its actions in the Poverty Programme. Thus, the Commission argued that:

> Solidarity with the disadvantaged sections of the population is primarily a matter for the Member States.
> *However, since the mid-1970's, the Community has become involved in these matters too.* The two Poverty programmes

1975–1980 and 1984–1988 were joined by the Council Decision of 18 July 1989 establishing a new Community programme for the economic and social integration of the least privileged (1989–1994).
(COM (91) 511 Final, emphasis added)

Two recommendations in the field of social protection were subsequently passed by the Council of Ministers in July 1992 (92/441/EEC & 92/442/EEC). The Council of Ministers refused, however, to sanction the latest phase of the Poverty Programme, in part on the grounds raised by the German presidency that 'by choosing Article 235 as legal basis for its proposal, the European Commission itself clearly showed that there is no Community competency in the fight against poverty' (Agence Europe, 31/10/94, 6348: 14). After almost twenty years of EU action in the field of poverty this was a rather interesting discovery. Nevertheless, on the basis of the two recommendations on social protection, and 'of the conclusions of the *informal* meeting of the Social Security Ministers of 2 February 1995' (Medium-Term Social Action Programme 1995–97, 1995: 23, emphasis added), a common framework for the analysis of problems and solutions in the field of social protection is to be established by the Commission. Thus, although the initial legitimation for action in this field has been removed, the momentum continues.

Drake (1995: 157) has argued that one consequence of Jacques Delors's dynamic presidency of the EU Commission, in that it alerted 'public concern about the shaky political legitimacy of the EC's institutions, foremost among them the Commission', may, paradoxically, have been to spell 'the end of the style of Commission leadership which he so successfully embodied, and [to usher] in its antithesis'. Similarly, in the field of EU social policy, it appears that the very success of the Commission's strategy in the 1980s may have alerted member states to the potential costs incurred by 'cheap talk' (Lange, 1992: 242) and to the possible significance of apparently innocuous soft law measures. In particular, the Commission action programme of 1989 demonstrated how the relatively small Treaty advances in the SEA, backed up by a non-binding declaration signed by only eleven member states, could be manipulated by the CEU to develop a core of binding directives based on qualified majority voting which would apply to all twelve member states, including the UK.

An important element in explaining the UK opt-out from the social agreement of the Maastricht Treaty may be that it was the result of learning from past 'mistakes'. The UK government, when negotiating the SEA, was unable to anticipate fully the implications of its actions in signing up to apparently minor reforms concerned with 'efficiency' issues in the area of health and safety regulation. Presented, however, with the evidence of a flurry of legislative proposals based on this provision, which would ultimately extend its scope, and with a new action programme, which the Commission explicitly sought to base on the new provisions of the SEA, the UK government adopted a much firmer stance in the Maastricht negotiations. To some extent, the opt-out can be interpreted as the veto of the 1990s.[11] Previously, unanimity allowed member states to indulge in symbolic politics while assured of their ability to veto unwelcome proposals in the Council of Ministers. With the increased use of QMV, however, the Commission's ability to hold the member states to ransom over their public statements was enhanced. The option now exercised by the UK in its use of the opt-out clearly reduces the scope for CEU action once again. The UK opt-out limited the opportunities for other member states 'to hide behind its coat-tails' (Rhodes, 1991: 260) and may, in fact, encourage the UK's fellow member states to be slightly more cautious when tempted to indulge in 'cheap talk'. To this extent then, the Commission may have become a victim of its own success.

A further potential brake on the Commission strategy, of securing a toe-hold in various sensitive policy areas by securing agreement from the Council to a soft law measure, may result from the increasingly maximalist interpretations of soft law emanating from the European Court of Justice. One of the most important developments in the EU policy process, generally, has been the development by the ECJ of a teleological approach to legal interpretation (Wincott, 1995b). From very early on in the field of social policy the ECJ took the opportunity, during the Defrenne cases, to underline clearly the social goals of the EU on the basis of the original Treaty provisions:

> these are not limited to economic activity, but must at the same time ensure, through common action, social progress and pursue the continuous improvement of living and working conditions of the European peoples, as is stressed in the preamble to the Treaty.
>
> (ECJ, 8 April 1976, Case 43/75, Defrenne II)

As the Court has increasingly used the statements of the national governments, their declarations, or the preambles to Treaty revisions, as indications of the spirit in which EU legislation should be interpreted, it has become more and more difficult to dismiss these statements as merely symbolic or as empty rhetoric. As soon as the ECJ uses rules of conduct, or 'soft law' as a legal foundation or '*ratio decidendi*' for a judgment, these rules become 'hard law': that is they provide legally enforceable rights and obligations (Wellens and Borch-ardt, 1989: 291). As Klabbers (1994: 1023) argues, the Court has 'consistently favoured contents over form, an attitude which, it is submitted, can ultimately only be explained methodologically by starting from the presumption that agreement creates legally binding rights and obligations, unless the opposite can clearly be shown'. It may be that the Council, in questioning the legal basis of existing agreements on, for example, the Poverty Programme, is beginning to wake up to the potential consequences of apparently symbolic acts.[12]

4   EU ICT POLICY: THE LEGISLATIVE PATTERN

The results of the analysis of EU ICT legislation are shown in Figures 6 to 9. Standards emerging from the key European standards organisations are, meanwhile, illustrated in Table 2. As can be seen in Figure 6, of the four categories of legislation employed here, those which figure least often in the ICT field are process legislation and soft law. However, in the case of process legislation it is important to recall that ICT legislation has traditionally been subsumed under the broader category of 'Industrial Policy and Internal Market', thus those committees and organisations which have been set up at the EU level and deal with issues in the ICT field may appear somewhat fewer than is actually the case.

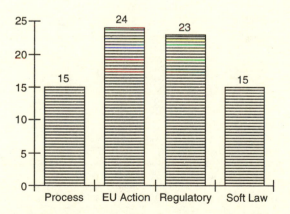

Figure 6   ICT policy: relative incidence of the four policy types
Source: Directory of Community Legislation in Force and Other Acts of the Community Institutions (as at June 1995)

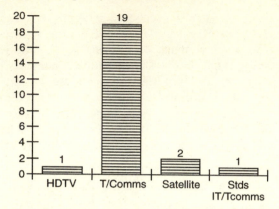

Figure 7 ICT policy: regulatory policy by policy area
Source: *Directory of Community Legislation in Force and Other Acts of the Community Institutions* (as at June 1995)

In Chapter 3 it became clear that there is now a comprehensive institutional framework at the EU level for the development of EU ICT policy. Likewise, although the number of pieces of soft law in the

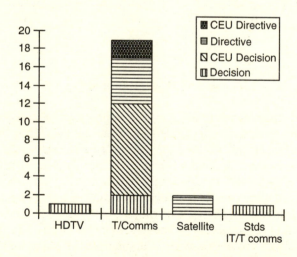

Figure 8 ICT policy: regulatory policy by policy area and instrument of enactment
Source: *Directory of Community Legislation in Force and Other Acts of the Community Institutions* (as at June 1995)

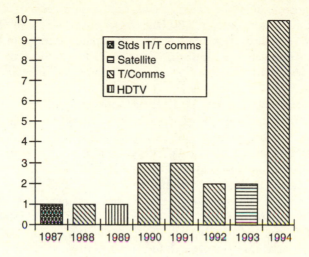

Figure 9   ICT policy: regulatory policy by policy area over time
Source: Directory of Community Legislation in Force and Other Acts of the Community Institutions (as at June 1995)

Table 2   Standards emerging from European standards organisations by year

Organisation	1984	1989	1994
CEN	33	116	471
CENELEC	36	176	370
ETSI	0	0	270

Source: Correspondence with CEN, CENELEC and ETSI

ICT field appears relatively low, the importance of this category of legislation should not be underestimated. In the 1960s and 1970s, particularly, soft law allowed the Commission to establish a precedent for action in the ICT field when it could not gain approval from the Council of Ministers for binding legislation.[13] EU action emerges, in Figure 6, as numerically the most significant of the four categories of EU legislation in the ICT field. Indeed, in Chapter 3, the crucial role of EU R&D programmes in the development of the EU ICT policy became clear. However, when the number of standards emerging annually from the European standards organisations (see Table 2)[14] is viewed in conjunction with the EU regulatory legislation (Figure 6), it becomes clear that a comprehensive regulatory regime has emerged at the EU level in the ICT field. Meanwhile, as is clear from Figure 7, ICT regulatory legislation occurs only in a specific limited number of policy areas: High Definition Television (HDTV); Satellite; Standardisation of ICT; and, most significantly, in the area of Telecommunications. Indeed, nineteen of the twenty-three regulatory policies in force in the ICT apply to the area of telecommunications.

A detailed examination of EU regulatory legislation in the field of telecommunications reveals some interesting characteristics of EU activity in this policy area. In Figure 8, for example, it becomes clear that most of the regulatory legislation in the telecommunications field has been implemented by Commission rather than Council legislation. Indeed, twelve of the nineteen pieces of regulatory legislation in the area of telecommunications were implemented either by a Commission Directive (two) or by a Commission Decision (ten). Thus regulatory legislation in the area of telecommunications has largely been enacted without the need for the approval of the Council of Ministers. An important question is, thus, how this situation could have emerged in a traditionally controversial policy area in which member states remain divided over the role of the EU. A further striking feature of EU regulatory legislation in the area of telecommunications emerges in Figure 9. Until 1990 there was no EU regulatory legislation in the telecommunications field. Yet, of the ten pieces of regulatory legislation in the ICT field enacted in 1994, all were Commission Decisions providing for the development of 'Technical Regulations' (or standards) in the area of telecommunications.

The Commission has emerged as a key actor in a complex nexus of regulatory legislation and standards in the ICT field. First, as the CEU has achieved increased credibility and legitimacy as an actor in the ICT field, it has learned to capitalise on the diverse institutional roots of EU ICT policy and to make use of the powerful competition instruments at its disposal to produce Directives and Decisions for which it does not require the support of the member states. Second, the Commission has managed to develop a central role for itself in a complex standard-setting process. This serves the dual purposes of not requiring national government approval (as voluntary standards are set by industry) and of allowing the Commission some input into a process from which it would otherwise be almost entirely excluded. Both the timing of policy developments in the area of telecommunications and the pattern of policy instruments selected for the implementation of regulatory policy at the EU level needs to be explained.

4.1 Competition and telecommunications: applying existing powers in a new context

The Commission's progress in the area of telecommunications regulation can largely be attributed to an incremental process of intervention and its subtle application of the competition provisions of the Rome Treaty to the area of telecommunications:

> Intensified use of its existing powers on competition is an ingenious way of both ensuring genuine integration of the EC market and of enhancing the status of the EC Commission. Thus, although there has been no new attribution of powers to the EC in the domain of telecommunications services, the Commission has seized on the notion of deregulation as a way to get in on the act!
>
> (Holmes, 1990: 24)

The support of key judgments of the European Court of Justice has been crucial in allowing the Commission to develop and apply its competition-based powers to the field of telecommunications. In 1982, the Commission made its first attempt to apply competition provisions to national telecommunications monopolies. The Commission (OJ L 360 1982: 36) argued that British Telecom's decision, to prohibit private message-forwarding agents from relaying messages between two foreign countries, constituted an abuse of dominant position under Article 86 of the Treaty (Darnton and Wuersch, 1992: 112). This, the Commission argued, allowed for the appplication of the Treaty's competition provisions to telecommunications monopolies. The Commission's controversial interpretation of Article 90(2) allowed it to establish a general principle without establishing a precedent which would require case-by-case battles with PTTs concerning the applicability of Article 86. The BT decision

> cut right to the heart of the matter and established the principle that state telecommunications monopolies were subject to full application of the Treaty's competition rules for all of their operations.
>
> (Darnton and Wuersch, 1992: 114)

Importantly, Article 90 empowers the Commission to enact binding measures without requiring the assent of the Council of Ministers. Thus the use of Article 90 as a basis for action limits the power of national governments to curb the activities of the Commission in the area of telecommunications regulation (see Chapter 3). Although the Commission's approach was challenged, the European Court of Justice found largely in the Commission's favour.[15] The Commission was quick to capitalise on its success. Meanwhile, subsequent decisions of the Court have helped to strengthen the position of the Commission in the area of telecommunications regulation.

The decision to include telecommunications in the context of EU competition policy had a fundamental impact on the role of the Commission in the ICT sector. The Green Paper on Telecommunications (COM (87) 290), issued in 1987, incorporated the new, competition-based approach into the Commission's telecommunications strategy. This, combined with an emphasis on the changing requirements of new technology in the telecommunications field (as a result of the growing convergence of computer and telecommunications technologies), formed the basis of the Green Paper's proposals for competition in the area of 'value-added services':

> The Commission's use of the B.T. case together with the market analysis of the Green Paper, created a new perspective from which the Commission reconsidered the structure of the telecommunications sector within the European Community.
>
> (Darnton and Wuersch, 1992: 124)

Rather than enter into interminable controversy as to what 'value-added services' actually meant, the Commission made the rather smart move of defining a very minimal conception of the 'reserved services' which were not to be subject to competition (Ungerer, 1990). The conclusion of the Green Paper was that only the basic operation of the telecommunications network should be reserved from competition rulings. No sooner, however, had consensus been achieved on the liberalisation of telecommunications services and a timetable agreed,[16] than the European Commission adopted, on 25 October 1994, Part 1 of a Green Paper on the liberalisation of telecommunications infrastructure and cable television networks (COM (94) 440 Final), rapidly followed up by Part II on 25 January 1995 (COM (94) 682 Final). With reference to the liberalisation of telecommunications infrastructure Commissioner Van Miert had, moreover, stated his 'personal' commmitment to the use of Article 90 for its realisation (Agence Europe, 30.9.94, 6326: 6).

On the basis of the new approach, laid out in the 1987 Green Paper, the Commission introduced a number of Directives, two of which – telecommunications equipment (1988 OJ L 131 73) and services (1990 OJ L 192 10) – were based on Article 90. Although these were challenged by the member states,[17] the Directives survived largely intact and the Court has, in the main, ruled favourably on the Commission's actions. Having established a precedent for autonomous action, the

Commission was not slow to act and these Commission Directives were followed up by a series of Commission Decisions determining the need for common technical regulations (i.e. standards) in the field of telecommunications.[18] Commission action in the field of telecommunications continues at a rapid pace. Since those Directives and Decisions (identified in Figure 8) were implemented, the CEU has adopted or proposed a number of new measures in the field of telecommunications. Thus, in February 1995 the Open Network Provision Interconnection Directive (OJ C 197/95) was adopted and three more directives have been proposed for consultation purposes on the basis of Article 90: in December 1994, Cable TV (Dir 95/51 L 256/95) and, on 19 July 1995, Mobile Telephony (OJ C 197/75 draft) and a General Article 90 Directive (OJ C 263/95 draft).

> the sudden reinvigoration of Competition Policy owes nothing to changes in the formal rules but everything to the new political climate. In telecommunications DG IV makes no secret of the fact that it is looking for cases to allow it to demonstrate that no developments may take place without reference being made to EC Competition Policy.
>
> (Holmes, 1990: 23)

In September 1991 the Commission published its own 'Guidelines on the Application of EEC Competition Rules in the Telecommunications Sector' (OJ C 233 6.9.1991). Telecommunications is thus the only sector for which the CEU competition services have delivered specific guidelines and competition rules are vigorously enforced in this area. Meanwhile, as promotion of the information society (by both the Commission and the ICT industry) intensifies, the distinction between ICT policy, industrial policy and competition policy has increasingly become blurred. As Martin Bangemann, Commissioner for Industrial Policy, has argued,

> the development of the 'information society' is one of the major challenges of industrial policy... because the state which neglects developments in this area will have no chance of remaining an industrial nation in the future.... It is time to stop thinking that [the abolition of telecommunications monopolies] is for me or the Commission a question of principle or even philosophy. It results very simply from an absolute necessity, because I can live perfectly well with a public telecommunications company, but on one condition: that it can compete.
>
> (Agence Europe, 9.9.94, 6353: 11)

The Commission has learned how best to capitalise on the prevailing ethos of deregulation and liberalisation, and to make use of the powers available to it. Interestingly, not only did the use of competition rules revitalise the telecommunications sector but also since the 1987 Green Paper, the number of complaints to the Commission's competition services has increased dramatically. Thus the initial intervention of the CEU, justified in terms of the prevailing trend towards deregulation and liberalisation, has created a demand for further CEU intervention in the ICT field:

> it is correct to say that the number and the importance of cases concerning the sector has gone hand in hand with the pace of the current liberalization and deregulation in the Union.
>
> (*Competition Policy Newsletter*, spring 1995, 1/4: 1)

4.2   Setting EU ICT standards: 'hands off' intervention?

In the area of standards setting the Commission has also been able to influence the ICT environment while sustaining a 'hands off' approach consistent with the current climate of liberalisation and deregulation. The Commission has been involved in the standards-setting process for many years. Working with the European standards bodies, CEN, CENELEC and, more recently, ETSI (and increasingly through smaller workshops, such as the European Workshop for Open Systems (EWOS), which enjoy direct input from commercial organisations rather than via the national standards bodies which constitute the membership of CEN and CENELEC) the Commission has had considerable influence on the standards which have been set in Europe. Although the standards bodies are formally independent organisations, the Commission can issue them with a mandate and with the financial backing to carry out the necessary work to develop a European standard in conjunction with a Commission Directive. The standards remain voluntary but all member states must allow access to their national markets for products conforming with the standard referred to in the Directive:

> Rather than waiting to see what standards emerge, the EC has committed itself to determining which telecommunications and infomation technology standards it wishes to have developed and to commissioning the work necessary to produce those standards.
>
> (Besen, 1990: 529)

CEU involvement in the standards process serves a number of purposes. First, as the Commission could never hope to force industry's hand, issuing a mandate via the standards process provides a good early testing ground for a Commission proposal. If the request for a standard falls on deaf ears then it can be put onto the back burner for a more opportune moment. Second, the fact that national standards bodies must inform the European bodies of any new standards which they are considering adopting gives the Commission important information on areas which might be conducive to European standardisation (in the area covered by CENELEC, for example, there are now almost no national standards issued). The voluntary nature of standards encourages the cooperation of industry which might be averse to legally binding EU regulations in this area. Equally, as there is almost no involvement of national governments in this process, the Commission is able to bypass, to some extent, the resistance of certain member states. Finally, and perhaps most importantly, the existence of European standards reinforces the central role of the EU in the ICT field, even when international standards might appear more logical (the vast majority of European standards come directly from existing international standards).

In the early 1980s, industry and national governments had begun, once again, to rail against what they perceived as an overly impositional approach from the Commission to the regulation of the IT sector. Industry, in particular, was against the inflexibility of European standards. It was felt that they were often arbitrary and the standards-setting process was lengthy in an area in which product life-cycles might last only two years. The Commission's relationship with the standards bodies has thus been modified and since the introduction of the 'new approach' in 1985, Commission directives contain only the overall goal to be achieved and essential requirements to be met. The detailed technical specifications are then left to be drawn up by the standards bodies. The rapid increase in the number of standards emerging since the mid-1980s (see Table 2) can, in part at least, be attributed to the succes of this strategy. Meanwhile, standards bodies are increasingly aiming to reduce their financial dependence on the Commission. Interviews with CENELEC, for example, indicate that while it is dependent for about 30 per cent of its financing on the Commission in 1996, it is actively seeking to reduce this to 18 per cent by 1999.

The Commission will always have to modify its approach to standardisation according to the demands of industry but it has proved successful so far in maintaining its distance while simultaneously increasing its influence. It has, thus, sidestepped the tag of meddling 'Eurocrat'. The 1992 project, meanwhile, revealed thousands of areas which required standardisation. For the Commission, setting the agenda via vague and rather broad specifications, while allowing the controversial and politically delicate details to be drawn up in the standards boards, has obvious advantages. Likewise, there has been a considerable growth in the demand for European standards as the results of European collaborative research programmes reach the applications stage. Thus, in a world of limited resources, that standards bodies are trying to increase their financial autonomy might come as something of a relief to the Commission.

5   CONCLUSION: REGULATORY POLICY IN THE EU

There has been a growing interest in the significance of the regulatory dimension of the EU policy process (Majone, 1989a, 1991a, 1991b, 1991c, 1992a, 1992b, 1993; Bulmer, 1994a). The analysis of the legislative pattern in the fields of social policy and ICT policy has, moreover, confirmed the significance of this aspect of policy-making in the EU. Not only, however, have the policy types selected by the Commission proved to be important, but also the policy instruments chosen for their implementation may have been as significant.

As is clear from the analysis presented in this chapter, viewing the policy output of the European Union as if the only significant actors were national governments fails to explain the expansion of EU policies even in highly controversial policy areas. The state-centred approach cannot explain, for example, the significant increase in EU regulatory policies in the area of EU social policy, a sector usually characterised by the predominance of redistributive policies. Nor can the state-centred approach explain the major increase in regulatory legislation in the ICT field, where major multinational firms and member states are divided as to the utility of EU level action. National governments have, generally, been reluctant to expand the scope of the Commission's influence on EU policy in these areas, and it might be argued that countries with lower standards would not vote for the imposition of higher EU standards which could prove costly for them to meet. Thus, if national governments were the only important actors in the EU policy process then the growth of EU regulatory policy in the two policy areas observed would have been unlikely to have taken place.

Yet in the social field it emerges that the use of regulatory policy increasingly allows the European Commission to take on the role of 'calling the tune without paying the piper'.[19] EU social policy is still, of course, extremely limited in scope. However, by making use of regulatory policies in the area of social policy rather than those involving direct EU expenditure, EU social policy, in a number of specific areas, increasingly sets the standards to be adhered to in the member states while incurring minimum EU costs. The unpopular task of collecting taxes to pay for social welfare is left to national governments while the actual costs of most EU regulatory policies in the social field tend to rest with individual employers. When the development of EU social policy is examined over time, moreover, it becomes clear that, while initially this pattern of policy-making may have come about more by accident than by design, the Commission has learned from its experience and has begun to prepare the ground for further regulatory action in this field. Thus, to understand the significant growth in EU regulatory policies in the social field, it is important to take into account both the desire of the European Commission to expand its sphere of competence, and the relatively costless (to the Commission) nature of regulatory policy-making (Majone, 1993).

Another factor which may, however, help to explain the continued growth of EU regulation is the interest of multinational, export-oriented firms in supporting European-wide regulation (Majone, 1991c). This 'pre-emptive federalism' is seen as a means of eliminating inconsistencies between national standards while avoiding the potential knock-on effect of increasingly more stringent national legislation. The adoption of a single European standard will, the companies hope, prevent the continued upwards escalation of national standards. The case of the European Works Councils Directive supports this thesis to some extent. However, the role of multinational companies has proved to be particularly relevant in promoting EU regulatory legislation in the ICT field.

In particular, multinationals (for example British Telecom) and the High Level Group of Industrialists which drew up the Bangemann Report (1994) on the information society, have declared their support for centralised regulation of the ICT sector at the EU level. The reasons behind industrial support for EU level action are many: centralised legislation is more coherent and easier for industry to incorporate into their long-term plans than competing national regulations; centralised European standards and regulations may help to lock European consumers into the purchase of European goods which would provide a competitive advantage for European businesses; finally, as standards are voluntary firms are aware that they are not obliged to implement the results.[20]

From the Commission's perspective, standards allow the CEU to appear non-interventionist while exerting considerable influence over the output of the standards organisations and promoting the development of standards with a quasi-legal basis which member states are increasingly obliged to implement. The use of regulatory policy, moreover, allows the Commission to draw up rules and to set deadlines which allow the ICT firms time to adjust and hence to sign up to policies for which they might not otherwise be able or willing to implement in the short term. Finally, the deregulatory thrust promoted by some member states and by industry increasingly creates a demand for reregulation at the EU level. Whether it is deregulation or reregulation, EU legislation ensures a central role for the CEU in the ICT sector in Europe.

5 Collective action at the EU level
Implications for the integration process

1 INTRODUCTION

There is increasing evidence of the involvement of a wide range of actors at the EU level and of a growth in new collective forums through which these actors may concert their activities. Cross-sectoral studies, highlighting the critical role which Euro-interests play in the EU policy process (Greenwood *et al.*, 1992; Mazey and Richardson, 1993a; Van Schendelen, 1993),[1] have provided a welcome antidote to the focus on national governments as the dominant actors in EU policy-making which prevailed throughout the 1980s. Yet conceptualisation of the role of Euro-interests in the integration process is still proving problematic. The dominant theoretical approaches to understanding European integration are unable to explain the precise role which Euro-interests play. For example, case studies of the pharmaceutical industry (Greenwood and Ronit, 1992) and the car industry (McLaughlin *et al.*, 1993) have shown that Euro-interests (whether acting as groups or as direct 'policy participants') are far more important actors in the integration process than most intergovernmentalist theories allow. Yet Euro-interests have not performed quite the role predicted for them by neo-functionalists either. The activities of Euro-interests have been neither as spontaneous, nor as effective, in influencing policy developments as Ernst Haas (1958) had anticipated. Indeed, Euro-groups are criticised for being 'so numerous and so weak' (McLaughlin and Jordan, 1993) and it is argued that 'Euro-groups, far from being the dynamic agents of integration, have tended to be rather ineffective bodies unable to engage in constructive policy dialogue with the Commission' (McLaughlin *et al.*, 1993: 192).

There is an implicit assumption in much of the literature on European integration that Euro-interests automatically come together to influence those with power. When issues regarding the logic of collective action are addressed they tend to be framed in terms of whether an organisation may influence the policy process more or less effectively, through one form of collective action or another, or whether individual action might be more effective. It is asked, for example, what types of collective forums are most efficient. Thus, in Olson's (1971) terms, the selective incentives which encourage cooperative action are largely assumed to be the opportunities offered to influence the policy process and to shape policy developments. Rarely is it asked if the organisation ever set out to influence EU policy in the first place.[2] Clearly, there has been a rapid increase in the number of interest groups seeking to influence the European policy process: 'changes in the distribution of power between the Member states and the European Community have prompted a proliferation of interest group lobbying at the EC level' (Mazey and Richardson 1993a: 3). However, as Mazey and Richardson (1994a: 178) also note, much of the 'pressure' exerted by Euro-interests is, in practice, pushing at an open door.

As became clear in Chapter 3, the involvement of major ICT firms in EU research programmes and ultimately in the administrative infrastructure for the development of EU ICT policy was, in part, a response to the 'selective incentives' offered by the European Commission. Crucially, at this stage power could not be said to lie in Brussels in the ICT sector. The example of the activities of Euro-interests in the area of EU social policy, likewise, showed a close relationship between the activities of the European Commission and other European institutions and the pattern of collective action. Once again, the challenge is to explain why interests are mobilising around an institution with relatively little power in the policy area. Thus, why are groups apparently shooting where the ducks are not?

As the example of the symbiotic relationship which has developed between industry and the EU in the ICT field makes clear, it is also important to ask whether the participation of Euro-interests in the EU policy process, or in Euro-groups, has affected the activities and interests of those participants. Indeed, 'if interest groups shape policies, policies can shape interest groups. The organisational structure and political goals of groups may change in response to the nature of the programmes they confront or hope to sustain or modify' (Pierson, 1993: 598). Thus, collective action in a EU context may have important spill-over effects or unintended consequences (for example on the part of ICT firms). These may lead to the development of a shared set of assumptions, to a growing sense of Europeanness among the actors involved, to the development of a common identity or, at least, to an increased propensity to act collectively in the future. As power has increasingly transferred to Brussels in the ICT field, for example, ICT firms have now formed an impressive range of collective forums aimed at influencing the EU policy process.

2   EU SOCIAL POLICY: THE COMMISSION AS CATALYST TO COLLECTIVE ACTION

In this section the case of Euro-interests in EU social policy is examined, paying particular attention to the important role which the EU institutions play as 'innovators with selective incentives' for collective action (Olson, 1971: 177). It is argued that even fairly ineffective Euro-groups (in terms of their power or influence in policy-making terms) may have some impact on the integration process.

2.1   Collective action in EU social policy: influencing the seats of power?

The 'mechanical link between the influence of the EC and the mobilisation of interests' has also been questioned by McLaughlin and Jordan (1993: 122). In part, this is because national responses to shifts in power need not automatically be in the form of transnational groupings, and in part because, as Olson claimed, the natural tendency of rational interests is not to join collective forums but to 'free ride' whenever possible (McLaughlin and Jordan, 1993: 123). However, in the case of EU social policy it is not only the automaticity of the change in focus of the relevant actors which must be questioned. Indeed, it must be asked whether power actually has shifted to the EU in the area of social policy and whether all Euro-interests, in fact, set out with the explicit aim of influencing the policy process. As will become evident, the case of Euro-interests and EU social policy calls these traditional assumptions into question.

First, it is not clear that there has really been such a major shift in power to the EU in the area of social policy as this approach would imply. While the EU is becoming an increasingly important legislative force in the area of social policy, its regulatory power has been strictly circumscribed.[3] There is no binding EU legislation in the areas of homelessness, poverty, family policy, old age or disability – to name just a few of the areas in which a proliferation of Euro-groups has emerged. Yet, in 1992 more than 100 networks of voluntary or community organisations were identified in Europe (Harvey, 1992: 277). Many of these operate in areas in which the EU could hardly be said to wield power. Indeeed, these have often been the very areas in which national governments have jealously guarded their national prerogatives.

Even, however, if it could be argued that there has been a significant transfer of power to the EU in the social field, the question remains as to whether the EU is now perceived by the relevant actors as an important locus of power. As yet it is not clear that awareness of the EU as anything more than a source of funding has filtered through to many of the national non-governmental organisations (NGOs) in the social field. This has certainly been one of the problems cited by those concerned with building, for example, the European Anti-Poverty Network (EAPN):

> for some members it can be difficult to see the relevance of a European network and of EU legislation and policies. It is difficult to explain how the EU impacts upon their daily work.
>
> (Interview)

While some actors may be acutely aware of the significance of the EU, for them and for their members, perhaps it is more important to ask how this awareness developed than to assume that this is an automatic response to a shift in power to the EU level.

Second, there is only limited evidence of the spontaneous development of Euro-groups and of Euro-interest activity in EU social policy, without funding or support from the EU institutions. The problems involved in developing collective action between Euro-interests in the area of EU social policy have been immense. The costs of working at the European level, reliance on national sources of funding, diverse traditions, different mentalities and language difficulties are just some of the many factors which are cited as making cooperation at the European level extremely difficult. Although the problems faced by NGOs in the social field may be becoming more similar, there remains an enormous diversity in the tradition of voluntary sector activities in the twelve member states (Robbins, 1991). Not least, the same issues are often dealt with by quite different types of organisations in the different member states. The Confederation of Family Organisations in the EC (COFACE), for example, found that in the UK, Ireland, Denmark and, to some extent Italy and the Netherlands, general family organisations, as such, simply did not exist.

Indeed, the experiences of those attempting to set up European level collective forums have not always been easy. NGOs in the social field often do not have an effective national organisation. For example, as administrators setting up the European Forum for Disabled People as part of the EU HELIOS II Programme discovered,[4] when seeking to represent the twelve national councils for disabled people on this forum, only Denmark had a truly representative national council incorporating all aspects of disability. While the Netherlands did have a national body concerned with disability, it did not include organisations for mentally ill and mentally handicapped people. Meanwhile, in other countries, such as France and the UK, no overarching structure for disabled people's organisations existed at the national level. Likewise, when initial attempts were made to set up the EAPN, intended to be a European network of national networks concerned with the fight against poverty, a working group was set up to find groups in the member states willing to constitute national networks. Although it is usually fairly easy to find networks in the making, this is not always the case. In some countries, such as Spain and Italy, where there is little tradition of national organisations in the anti-poverty field, the establishment of a network proved quite difficult. Likewise, in Greece, where there is only a limited tradition of NGO activity, the establishment of a national network was difficult. Far from displaying the automatic coming together of interested parties, the establishment of such networks has required sustained effort on the part of some dedicated individuals.

Third, it is not clear that the sole, or most important, motivating factor, encouraging Euro-interests to act collectively, is the desire to influence the EU social policy process. Few evaluations have been carried out into the reasons that various actors join or support the development of a Euro-forum. However, two examples of surveys by quite different organisations show that the primary interest of their members was in obtaining help in finding EU funding. The EU IRIS network, for example, conducted an evaluation in 1990 to establish what benefits participants had gained from IRIS services and to find out what IRIS participants wished to see the network do in the future. In terms of benefits from existing membership, the benefits of gaining information on EU programmes (i.e. other sources of EU funding) featured highest (57 per cent), closely followed by the 'facilitation of European contacts' (54 per cent) and the benefits of IRIS grants came fairly low (19 per cent). Meanwhile, in terms of what the network should aim for in the future, help in finding EU funding came a clear first (78%), while promoting the issue of women's training in the EU came fourth, though with 71% support (IRIS, 1990: 21). Before the European Citizen Action Service (ECAS) was established in 1989, as an independent lobbying and information service for voluntary sector NGOs in Europe, a survey was carried out amongst prospective members of the service to establish where ECAS should focus its efforts. Once again, top of the priority list was 'assisting organisations with fundraising at the EC level'. In fourth place came 'regular briefings about EC activities' and in seventh place 'monitoring work of the EC institutions' (*Euro-Citizen*, 1990: 1). In both surveys the need for information was evident, as was the desire to foster contacts (third on the priority list for ECAS respondents and third in terms of future priorities for the IRIS network (72 per cent)). While one of the priorities of the IRIS network is to act as a lobby on the issue of women's training in Europe, and while ECAS was set up specifically 'to correct the imbalance between lobbying on behalf of business and lobbying in the public interest' (*Euro-Citizen*, 1990: 1), this was not the only driving force encouraging their members to act collectively at the European level. Indeed, some European level collaborative projects, such as the European Association for Creativity by Disabled People (EUCREA), are already noticing the diminishing willingness of their members to cooperate at EU level. As CEU funding is being reduced, and as EU funding criteria become more stringent, many organisations are finding it more cost-effective to seek funding at the national level.

This is not to say that there have been no examples of a collaboration of interested parties from different member states in response to changing EU powers in the area of EU social policy. Likewise, the main aim of many actors joining Euro-groups may be to influence EU social policy. The argument is simply that this is not always, nor even perhaps predominantly, the case. There are many different types of Euro-interests in EU social policy and many different reasons for collective action. Significantly, for example, the EU institutions have provided an important catalyst for collective action in the area of EU social policy. In the next section, some of the ways in which the collective action of Euro-interests has been spurred on by EU initiatives are examined. Incentives have been offered not only to encourage collaboration between national actors at the European level but also between the various Euro-groups at EU level.

2.2   EU institutions providing the catalyst for collective action?

There are a wide variety of collective forums in which Euro-interests in EU social policy are active. These range from organisations completely independent of the EU to independent networks sponsored by the European Commission (CEU), such as the EAPN, and to networks initiated by the CEU, but coordinated by other organisations, such as the networks on older people in poverty and the network on older workers and age discrimination which are coordinated for the CEU by Eurolink Age. Independent organisations established on the initiative of the CEU also exist. These include, for example, the European Women's Lobby (EWL) and the Migrants Forum. Likewise, a number of organisations have developed which were initially sparked off by CEU funded initiatives. FEANTSA (European Federation of National Organisations Working with the Homeless), for example, initially emerged from a CEU-funded conference on homelessness held in Dublin in 1985 (Harvey, 1992: 181). Meanwhile, there are a number of social programmes which the CEU operates, such as HELIOS II, IRIS II and the Poverty Programme, in which participating Euro-interests (i.e. those which meet the funding criteria) are often awarded up to 50 per cent of the operational costs of their transnational collaborative activities. The CEU also funds a number of 'observatories' to investigate the issues of, for example, social exclusion, ageing, homelessness and unemployment in the fourteen member states. Often coordination of these observatories is a crucial source of funding for the Euro-groups. FEANTSA's principal project, for example, is the European Observatory on Homelessness (FEANTSA, 1993). In all of these bodies, national organisations work collectively at the European level. However, the incentives for collective action do not stop there. The CEU has also established a number of forums in which Euro-groups may jointly participate in the EU policy process. Thus, in the liaison groups concerned, for example, with social exclusion, older people and education, representatives from the various Euro-groups concerned with the issue in question are gathered together.

Importantly, it is not only the CEU which has encouraged the development of collective action at the EU level. Euro-interests are actively involved with the European Parliament (EP) and, for example, the intergroups on public health, elderly people and the family and consumers are coordinated by the European Public Health Alliance (EPHA), Eurolink Age, COFACE and the European Bureau of Consumers' Unions (BEUC) respectively. The EWL, meanwhile, has close links with the women's committee in the EP. Euro-interests are also involved, of course, in the relevant committees of the Economic and Social Committee (ECOSOC) (although to a lesser degree) and participate, for example, in the conferences initiated by ECOSOC. Meanwhile, a number of collective activities are also undertaken on the initiative of the Council Presidency. Thus, for example, the UK hosted the 'Ageing Well' conference run by Eurolink Age in 1992.

The Belgian Presidency launched a conference on 'The Young European Consumer', (held in 1993) and in September 1994, the German Presidency hosted a conference on the 'Future of the Family' in which COFACE was closely involved.

There are, of course, many organisations which predate the establishment of complex EU-funded networks or which were established without active EU support. COFACE, for example, has a relatively long history in terms of a Euro-interest in EU social policy. Initially established as the European Action Committee of the International Union of Family Organisations (IUFO), COFACE has gradually gained autonomy. It was established in response to a growing awareness of the importance of EU legislation and with the explicit aim of encouraging the EU institutions to view their policy developments with 'family eyes'. Since 1979 it has formally operated as an independent organisation and has capitalised on a long history of lobbying on family issues developed within the IUFO. Of course there are many other similar examples. However, few would deny that the existence of the new collective forums in the CEU and the EP, initiatives by the Council Presidency or, indeed, the availability of European funding, have fundamentally altered the environment in which they work. For example, although the Centre for Research into European Women (CREW) was established as a women's cooperative in 1980 by European women primarily concerned about the lack of information on women's issues in Europe (and without EU support). CREW is now closely involved in a wide range of EU projects which account for a large proportion of its funding. It was responsible for the coordination of the IRIS network from 1988 to 1993, and is now in charge of a group of coordinating organisations for the IRIS II network (1994–98). CREW also has projects running under the EU TACIS and FORCE programmes and has carried out research for the European Social Fund.[5] Meanwhile, the European Network of Women (ENOW), established in 1983 as an independent initiative, has found the environment in which it operates radically altered since the establishment of the EWL, on the initiative of the women's information unit of the CEU, in September 1990. The EWL receives considerable support from the CEU to act as the umbrella organisation of the women's movement and ENOW has since joined this network (Meehan, 1993: 143). Some organisations are, of course, more closely involved with the EU institutions than others. However, few Euro-interests remain completely untouched by EU priorities. At the very least, the agenda of many NGOs since 1993 has been focused on preparing their responses to the CEU's Green Paper on Social Policy

(COM (93) 551) and subsequently on adapting to the new Commission White Paper.

The path towards cooperation has not always been easy, however. Indeed, EU policies have sometimes rather complicated the work of European organisations. COFACE, for example, insists on maintaining a global approach to family issues in the EU and denounces the increasing sectoralisation of issues which the CEU is perceived to be pressing. The availability of funding may, indeed, alter the incentives for members to join an organisation. For the majority of COFACE members, for example, funding has not been a driving force in stimulating membership. However, since the organisation became co-coordinator, in alternation with Eurolink Age, of the HELIOS II sector 'Families and Elderly People', this has had some impact upon the incidence of prospective members interested in participating in the HELIOS programme.

EU financial support does not always, however, provide an incentive but may in fact prove to be a disincentive for collective action. When the EAPN was established, for example, Germany initially refused to join on the grounds that a network supported by the CEU could not possibly be independent in its battle against social exclusion (interview). Cooperation has not always been easy to establish. Significant differences in mentality and tradition still persist. COFACE, for example, has found it difficult to establish transnational family exchanges. The approach to such exchanges varies so considerably from country to country that coordination has often proved impossible. Even within the CEU liaison groups cooperation is often no easier to establish. The liaison group, for example, concerned with older people's issues is currently re-evaluating the role of the liaison group in an attempt to improve the effectiveness of this body.

The EU institutions, and particularly the CEU, have clearly played an important role in encouraging collective action between the various Euro-interests. This has not, however, been a uni-directional force and sometimes cooperation has been, at best, half-hearted. The CEU could not have forced unwilling actors to collaborate. It has merely provided additional incentives for Euro-interests to act in a collective manner. Indeed, many of the Euro-interests interviewed described this collaboration as the result of a confluence of demands: of an interest on the part of their members to exchange information and experience at the European level and of an interest, on the part of the CEU, to find a consultative partner in the field. In the case of the EWL, for example, disappointment with national legislation on equality for women, despite years of hard lobbying at the national level, encouraged women to turn to Europe in an attempt to force member states to change their national legislation in line with EU equality legislation. Even organisations completely independent of the EU institutions have increasingly been drawn into a variety of EU sponsored activities. Meanwhile, some organisations, such as the EAPN, simply would not exist without CEU funding. Few HELIOS or IRIS projects would have had a European dimension if this was not a criterion for funding and some, such as the project on disability and creativity (EUCREA), may simply fade away at the European level and fail to continue their work at the national level if CEU funding continues to diminish. As will be argued, however, the impact of this collective action may have a lasting effect upon the policy environment in the EU.

3   COLLECTIVE ACTION AND THE POLICY ENVIRONMENT

Clearly, the range of Euro-interests operating in the area of EU social policy is extremely diverse and, while the EU institutions have provided a number of important catalysts for collective action, the role which Euro-interests play, and the reasons that they collaborate at EU level, vary significantly. To conceptualise these diverse relationships, and their significance for the process of integration, is problematic. Recently, the concept of policy networks has begun to be applied at the EU level in an attempt to explain the complexities of interest involvement in the EU policy process, to describe the complicated interactions between policy-makers and Euro-interests in the policy process, and to take account of the evident sectoral variations in this process (Bomberg, 1994; Altenstetter, 1994; Peterson, 1991, 1992, 1995). However, this approach fails to tackle the problem of accounting for why Euro-interests come together in the first place. Rarely has the question of the logic of collective action been directly addressed. More seriously, perhaps, those focusing on policy networks pay little attention to how participation within those networks or communities has affected the participants. It is rarely asked, for example, if the initial interests of the participants have been altered through their involvement in a policy network. This is a significant lacuna in the literature. Existing work on epistemic communities (see Haas, 1992) also assumes the rather automatic emergence of an epistemic community concerned with a particular issue. Once again, the actual impetus for the coming together of a particular group of experts is seldom questioned although the constitution of the group will inevitably have a fundamental impact on the ideas which are generated by the epistemic community. However, by seeking to illuminate the reasons behind 'the creation of collective interpretation and choice' (Adler and Haas, 1992: 368), and by shifting the focus in studies of the policy process from who gets what to 'who learns what, when, to whose benefit and why?' (Adler and Haas, 1992: 370), this approach may offer a more appropriate standpoint from which to assess the importance of Euro-interests in the EU social policy process than those which focus solely on the concepts of relative power and influence.

As has become clear, a community of experts can quite consciously be created by an interested actor. The case of the EU observatories on, for example, social exclusion, unemployment, the family and old age, provide excellent examples of how networks of national experts have been encouraged to establish epistemic communities at the European level. Through participation in such collaborative research, the researchers themselves will develop and change, as new approaches are shared and the researchers are presented with new perspectives on the issues at hand. In the case of the observatories, the experience gained and the contacts made would not easily be lost: 'the effects of epistemic community involvement are not easily reversed' (Adler and Haas, 1992: 373). Once a particular approach to an issue is adopted, it tends to persist in the work of policy-makers. As will be demonstrated, working with other Euro-interests, and with the EU institutions in the area of EU social policy, has had a significant impact upon the interests and activities not only of the Euro-groups, but also of their national member organisations and even of national policy-makers.

3.1 The European level

A number of tangible effects on the work of Euro-interests at the EU level can be discerned as a result of their participation in the EU policy process and in various collective forums. The funding which an organisation receives, and the forum on which it is represented, for example, affect the direction of the work undertaken by the organisation. COFACE, for example, although primarily a family organisation, was initially recognised by the CEU as a consumer body. In the 1970s, COFACE was awarded a small CEU grant as a consumer organisation and was one of the four European organisations to sit on the Consumer Consultative Committee of the CEU. As a result, the working group on consumer affairs was one of the first working groups to be set up within COFACE and consumer issues undoubtedly take up more space on the agenda of COFACE than they might do in some of the national family organisations.[6] Cooperation between Euro-groups also impacts, of course, upon their policy priorities. For example, collaboration between Eurolink Age and COFACE, on the HELIOS II 'Families and Elderly People' sector, has clearly encouraged the two organisations to work closely in developing their priorities themes for the next three years (*Eurolink Age Bulletin,* November 1993: 10). This type of interaction gives both organisations, and all of the participants in the sector, a new perspective on their own interests. The outcome of this particular collaboration is that priority will be given by both organisations to the issue of intergenerational solidarity in 1996.

Many organisations have noted the knock-on effects of participation in collective forums. For example, there are numerous examples of actors from different countries having met through participation in a CEU-funded forum, such as HELIOS or IRIS, which have then put together applications for future collaborative projects, either within these programmes, or in other CEU programmes. Many participants in the HELIOS network have, for example, applied jointly to the HORIZON programme to extend their collaborative activities. Those involved in the IRIS network have described IRIS-funded training exchanges as providing the 'motor' for collaboration. IRIS partnerships often feed into joint participation in, for example, the NOW, EUROFORM and HORIZON programmes (IRIS, 1992: 15).[7] Participation in the exchanges has a number of effects, from increasing the self-confidence of the women involved to stimulating the development of new ideas through the exchange of different national experiences. This has profoundly altered the propensity of many of the women involved in the IRIS network to undertake cross-national collaborative projects (interview). Meanwhile, as these networks gain greater credibility, an increasing range of actors become involved in the programmes.

In HELIOS, the involvement of NGOs has gradually evolved and expanded, ultimately resulting in the establishment of the European Forum for Disabled People as part of the HELIOS II programme. Likewise, the IRIS programme has seen a growing involvement of a broader range of actors and IRIS II now makes specific provision, for example, for the establishment of a closer working relationship with the social partners. Other effects of collaborative action have included the development of off-shoot organisations to deal with specialist issues. The European Public Health Alliance (established in March 1993), initially developed as a sector within the European Citizen Action Service and continues to be affiliated to ECAS. Yet in the initial survey undertaken by ECAS, the desire of the members that ECAS should encourage the establishment of new European public interest groups came only eleventh on the list of priorities (*Euro-Citizen*, 1990: 1). Clearly, close collaboration in the area of public health has convinced those actors involved that there is sufficient support for a specific body concerned with public health in Europe.

3.2   The national level

National organisations

Involvement in collective forums at the EU level also has a significant impact upon the activities and interests of national organisations. Not only, for example, has recognition of COFACE as a consumer body impacted upon its work at the EU level, but also an increasing number of its national members have begun to highlight family consumer affairs on their national agenda. Likewise, one-fifth of respondents to the IRIS evaluation questionnaires stated that their curriculum and training materials had been influenced by IRIS contacts (IRIS, 1992: 4). The coordination of national campaigns at EU level also, of course, impacts upon the contents of those national campaigns. The EWL, for example, has been coordinating a joint campaign to promote an increase in women's participation in the EP and has received financial support for the publication of the *European Women's Lobby Election Newsletter* (EWL, 1994b):

> The EWL campaign strategies have been integrated already into the national strategies of women's NGOs. These include consultation, cooperation, networking, research, information, advice, pressure, lobbying and publicity.
>
> (EWL, 1994a:1)

Eurolink Age has also expressed an interest in coordinating a similar campaign to promote the interests of older people in the Euro-elections.

Participation in EU-level activities may also affect the very structures in place at the national level. The case of the Netherlands, France and the UK altering or establishing new national forums in the area of disability, in response to the HELIOS initiative, is a clear example of this. The establishment of the EAPN also had a significant impact upon the national environment in which the fight against social exclusion takes place. Not least, because national networks simply did not exist before EAPN was set up. In Germany the EAPN network has had some effect upon the domestic environment by encouraging changes in the national pattern of organisation. Smaller organisations have sprung up alongside the traditional large private organisations, which have dominated service provision in the area of social exclusion, and have been allowed to join the network. EU-sponsored activities may also encourage national counterparts to come together at the national level. For example, at the Eurolink Age 'Ageing Well' conference (held in December 1992), delegates were organised into working groups by country to discuss how an EU Action Plan for older people could best be adapted for their own countries (Eurolink Age, 1993: 3–4). This provided both a forum for collaboration between national counterparts and a means of allowing ideas, generated in a European context, to filter through to the national level. Likewise, the development in the European observatories of common research methodologies and evaluation criteria will have a significant impact on the work of those involved.

National policy-makers

As the interests and activities of national organisations in the social field are modified in response to their experience of collective action at the EU level, so too will the demands made by these organisations upon national administrations change. If consumer policy comes to be seen as a significant family issue, then pressure to act on European consumer issues will be brought to bear from new sources in the policy process. New issues may also come to light as a result of cooperation at the EU level. For example, while the term 'social exclusion' did not exist in many European countries prior to the initiation of EU activities in this field, it has now become common currency among policy-makers concerned with the issue of poverty. In turn, by incorporating groups not usually considered to be poor in the traditional sense, but who may well be socially excluded for a variety of reasons, such as older people, women, and people with disabilities, the issue in question has itself been altered.

There are also tangible examples of cases in which the results of cooperation by Euro-interests at the EU level have had a significant impact upon the actions of national policy-makers. Two, for example, have resulted from activities within the HELIOS framework. In 1987, a conference was held in Greece to investigate the educational needs of deaf people. A direct offshoot of this activity was the decision to set up a university department in Patra, Greece, to carry out research into the particular needs of deaf people in relation to education. A further conference was later held in Portugal to examine the issues of training and employment with regard to the specific needs of deaf people. Once again, the host country gained considerable benefit from the proceedings and the conference has had a significant impact on the training and employment policies for deaf people in Portugal as well as paving the way for a subsequent application for collaborative action under the HORIZON programme (interview). In the case of the IRIS network, four countries (the Netherlands, France, Italy and Germany) have, in fact, funded their own national offices to promote IRIS nationally (IRIS, 1992: 1).

4 COLLECTIVE ACTION IN EU SOCIAL POLICY: TOWARDS A SENSE OF EUROPEANNESS

The main thrust of this chapter has been to challenge the assumption that Euro-interests spontaneously come together in order to influence the EU in which power is increasingly concentrated. The situation in EU social policy is clearly much more complex than this approach would lead us to believe. A range of powerful incentives have been offered by the EU institutions, and by the CEU in particular, to encourage the participation of Euro-interests at the EU level and the development of transnational cooperation. The concern of this chapter is not with the extent to which the EU is now a locus of power in the EU or with which actor is able to influence EU policy-making most effectively. Rather, it is asked whether the participation of Euro-interests at the EU level, in the variety of collective forums which have emerged, may actually encourage and consolidate the transfer of power to the EU, and thus have an important impact on the integration process, regardless of the 'effectiveness' of the organisations in question. Clearly, through participation at the European level, the activities and interests of Euro-interests are modified. The priorities of national organisations may alter in a variety of ways, national agendas may change and, on occasion, perhaps, even the perceptions held by national policy-makers of their own interests may be altered as new perspectives on old issues, or altogether new issues for the national context, come to light (cf. Hall, 1989).

There are a number of obvious factors which encourage the EU institutions to offer incentives to Euro-interests in addition to their interest in developing a dialogue at the European level. Indeed, the commitment of the EU institutions to developing a true dialogue with the various Euro-interests in the social field can be questioned. COFACE, for example, has criticised the fact that although the Green

Paper on Education (COM (93) 457) issued by the CEU, asked for responses by the end of December 1993, the CEU proposal for a new educational programme, SOCRATES, was issued by 4 January 1994. To what extent could the comments requested really have been taken into account (COFACE, 1994: 10)? The various directorates within the CEU also, however, need a constituency of support for their activities. In the environmental field, for example, it has been noted that DGXI has both created and, indeed, mobilised this type of constituency to defend its involvement in the environmental sphere when challenged by national governments (Mazey and Richardson, 1993c). In the case of social affairs, this type of constituency is no less necessary or obvious. Indeed, when the Women's Information Unit in DGX threatened to disappear under the heading of 'General Public' and to cease to exist as a separate unit, the EWL immediately mobilised to defend this body (EWL, 1993–4: 6). On the other hand, collaboration with the EP similarly provided an important ally for the EWL when it was announced that the EWL subvention from the CEU was to be reduced by 65 per cent for 1994. The Women's Rights Committee of the EP objected strongly and argued for at least a reinstatement of the amount received in 1993. Concerted lobbying efforts paid off and the 1993 budget was ultimately reinstated (EWL, 1993–4: 5). The involvement of Euro-interests in the EU policy process also helps the institutions to push for an expansion of their competences. As Euro-groups push for new issues to be addressed at the EU level, officials, for example, in DGV are often more than happy to take these issues on board. Allowed to operate within only a limited sphere of legitimate action, officials may openly welcome any attempt to expand the scope of their competences. This is especially the case in areas where the CEU has only limited legal competence and when the organisations can claim wider support from other Euro-interests. Thus, it is also to the advantage of the Euro-interests to cooperate with other interested parties.

The collaborative activities encouraged by the EU institutions are not, however, solely concerned with creating a consultative partner, establishing a constituency of support or with a piecemeal expansion of competences. Nor, as has become clear, is this their only effect. A less tangible outcome may be equally important. The general rules concerning the co-financing of activities organised by NGOs in the Framework of HELIOS II state, for example, that

> during the activity, the Commission contribution and the European Dimension should be highlighted in the opening and closing

addresses. The EC flag should also be used as well as the European anthem when appropriate.

(HELIOS II, 1993: 4)

This symbolic aspect of EU activities may be critically important in the sense of establishing some sense of a European identity. The close collaboration of Euro-interests may contribute to a changing policy environment in the EU. Indeed, many of those interviewed had observed a growing sense of Europeanness among their members or, at least, a growing propensity to adopt a European approach to problem solving and a greater willingness to work together with their European counterparts. Others, such as the EWL, were consciously trying to create a separate identity for the movement. As one interviewee observed:

> Certainly when I talk about this European Disability movement, it was very evident, as you might imagine, at the European Day of Disabled People at the European Parliament. That's a very tangible example. Not necessarily in a militant way but in a way that is linked to a sense of identity and a sense of pride as well, a certain pride in being part of a specific culture or group.

5   BUSINESS ALLIANCES IN THE EU ICT SECTOR

5.1   Industry and the EU policy process

ICT firms are closely involved at all levels of the policy process in Europe. In an environment in which 'technology is now dominated by international collaboration and multi-national companies' (Sharp and Pavitt, 1993: 129), major ICT multinationals are able to exert pressure on the EU policy process as a result of both their important position in the global economy and through the vestiges of their status as national champion industries at the national level.[8] ICT firms are heavily involved in the policy process from the level of broad industrial policy debates, to the setting of standards and the allocation of resources within specific EU research and development programmes such as ESPRIT and RACE. Indeed, 'Esprit is as much managed by industry as the Commission itself' (Peterson, 1991: 277; see also Peterson 1992). Several officials in DGXIII (Directorate-General for Telecommunications, Information Industries and Innovation) have, for example, commented that they are in such close contact with industrial representatives from the ICT sector that they could hardly consider this lobbying – there is an ongoing process of consultation between industry and the policy-makers.[9]

Since the mid-1980s there has been an explosion of collective activity between major ICT companies (both European and non-European owned) at the EU level. Clearly the companies are managing to some extent to overcome some of the thorny problems of collective action identified by Olson (1971). Existing studies examine the nature of technological collaboration in the ICT sector (Sharp and Shearman, 1989) and the incentives for collective action between member states in the area of ICT (Sandholtz, 1992a, 1992b, 1992c). In this chapter, an overview of the major collective forums in which businesses participate in the ICT sector at the European level is presented and some of the factors promoting or inhibiting alliances in the ICT field for political ends are examined.

5.2   Participation by the ICT industry in collective forums at the European level

General industry associations: formal direct membership

ICT firms not only are influential within the ICT sector but also include some of the most influential industrial actors in the EU policy process. The European Roundtable of Industrialists (ERT), for example, is an association of about forty-five of Europe's largest corporations from both EU and non-EU countries. Formed in 1983, under the chairmanship of Pehr Gyllenhammar of Volvo, this invitation-only group includes such major ICT producers and users as Philips, Siemens, Olivetti, Daimler Benz, Volvo, Fiat and Bosch (Sandholtz, 1992a: 234). Concentrating predominantly on broad strategic issues such as industrial competitiveness, rather than on the nitty-gritty of individual policies (Grant, 1995: 27), the ERT has become a powerful lobby. Indeed, it has been argued that the ERT played a significant role in launching the Single European Market programme and that, in particular, a major role was played by Wisse Decker (then ERT chair from Philips: Green, 1993: 46; Sandholtz and Zysman, 1989: 117).

An analysis of the membership of the ERT gives some indication of the level at which many of the major ICT companies participate in the EU policy process. Inevitably ERT discussions are not centred on solely ICT related issues, and much more specialist organisations have evolved to deal with these. However, the direct access to the Commission President, to other Commissioners and to national governments, which membership of the ERT affords (Grant, 1995: 27), provides a powerful incentive to participate. Likewise, an analysis of the ERT warns against an exaggerated view of the role of ICT users in the policy process. Recent attempts by national governments and the European Commission to encourage a greater role for users provide a seductive prospect and may appear to indicate a greater democratisation of the policy process: perhaps a shift away from the domination of multinational companies. It should, however, be remembered that the users of information technology products are a very diverse group and many of the most powerful multinationals are heavy users of ICT. As the membership of the ERT indicates, many of the users of ICT products may be just as influential as the producers and equally enjoy privileged access to decision-makers. Contacts at this level undoubtedly also help the producers to learn at the very highest level what the major users require from their products.

General industry associations: federations of federations

A myriad of federations of national industrial federations exist at the European level. These organisations exist at various degrees of specifity. The major information technology firms are, of course, broadly represented within UNICE. Most, however, express frustration with the enforced blandness of UNICE positions (an inevitable consequence of the need to incorporate the views of a wide range if industries and businesses) and rarely would a company depend on this as a sole channel of representation on any particular issue. In this respect, the ICT industry is in line with most other industrial sectors – particularly those dominated by multinational companies (Collie, 1993). Firms prefer to retain recourse to a range of strategies in an attempt to maximise their impact on any given issue (see studies in Greenwood *et al.*, 1992; Mazey and Richardson, 1993a). Thus a preference for 'multiple strategies' (McLaughlin *et al.*, 1993) prevails. In the ICT field a trend towards the establishment of ever more specialist groupings with carefully selected memberships is evident.

General industry associations: informal direct membership[10]

A number of highly selective informal organisations of industrial elites have also begun to emerge at a working level. While the representatives from major multinationals, which participate in these groups, do not directly represent the policies of any of the companies concerned, these meetings have come to represent an important point of contact for senior industrialists. One such group, for example, comprises a select number of representatives from a number of important multinationals in Europe and the US (as yet there has been no member admitted from Japan although there have been discussions on this subject). The group is a purely private organisation with no representative from the EU institutions. The organisation has no formal structure and no budget; a temporary chair rotates on a six-monthly basis between the various member companies. The usual format is that members are invited in turn by the various member companies, who will host a lunch. The host is entitled to introduce a topic for debate and members are asked for a spontaneous reaction to the issue on the agenda. The second half of the meeting is devoted to the discussion of 'current rumours'. In this way members keep themselves informed of up-to-the-minute developments in European industry.

While the organisation is in no way a lobbying organisation, membership of the group is considered to be very important by its members. Meanwhile, a similar organisation has emerged alongside which includes some representatives from major Japanese multinationals. However, this group is very informal and highly dependent on the personalities involved. The exchange of information in these less structured groups is of prime concern to their members. While the groups themselves are not involved in the lobbying process, those armed with the information derived from participation in such forums are better able to target the relevant policy-makers and to identify suitable partners for future alliance.

Sectoral organisations: federations of federations

At a more sectorally specific level, many of the major ICT companies are represented at the European level through the Liaison Organisation for the European Mechanical, Electrical and Electronic Engineering and Metalworking Industries (ORGALIME), established in 1954. This organisation, while encompassing many of the interests of ICT companies is once again, however, often considered rather too broad to deal with specific issues related to the ICT industry. The more specialist sectoral federation which claims to gather together almost all of European manufacturers in the field of business machines, information technology and telecommunications terminal equipment is the European Association of Manufacturers of Business Machines and Information Technology (EUROBIT), established in 1974. The equivalent organisation in the telecommunications sector is the Association of the European Telecommunications and Professional Electronics Industry (ECTEL), established in 1985.[11] Meanwhile, associations of electrical components manufacturers are represented via the European Electrical Components Manufacturers' Association (EECA), established in 1973 and national consumer electronics associations have a European platform via the European Association of Consumer Electronics Manufacturers (EACEM), established in 1983.[12]

Overlapping membership of organisations is a persistent feature of business organisation in the ICT sector but as Schneider (1992: 65) observed with regard to the organisation of industrial interests in the telecommunications sector, 'the relationship between these associations is essentially non-competitive'. Indeed, in the ICT sector, close consultation between the organisations will frequently lead to mutually supportive policy positions. These often over-worked and under-staffed organisations are sometimes happy to avoid covering the same ground.[13] Indeed, as a representative from ORGALIME said, 'ORGALIME is very pleased when a strong sectoral body exists, such as ECTEL or EUROBIT, and tends to let them get on with it.' As well as cooperating with their European counterparts, these organisations are often in close contact with their equivalent international organisations, particularly in Japan and the US.

There are a number of incentives which encourage participation in the EUROBIT framework. First, as the European Commission generally prefers to communicate with sectoral organisations rather than with individual firms (Grant, 1995) membership of EUROBIT is important to all firms in the ICT sector. EUROBIT does not have a Brussels office, although it has a permanent secretariat in the offices of VDMA in Germany. Schneider (1992: 59) has argued that these modest administrative facilities may indicate a 'letter-head status' or that of a 'listening post'. The organisation is, however, in constant communication with the EU institutions and is not short of contacts in Brussels. The president of EUROBIT, Dr Bruno Lamborghini, is from the Italian multinational Olivetti which has its own offices in Brussels. The secretary-general, Günther Möller, meanwhile, is from the German VDMA, which also has its own liaison office in Brussels. Likewise, many of the major member ICT firms such as Olivetti, IBM, Bull, Philips and Siemens-Nixdorf have their own premises in Brussels. EUROBIT also uses the VDMA offices in Brussels as a base where EUROBIT members can meet.

Many of those firms interviewed claimed that EUROBIT suffers from the usual problems of a broad-based organisations, encompassing conflicting views, which result in a watering down of policy positions. The large ICT firms frequently choose to go it alone or to form small *ad-hoc* groupings when an issue is of particular concern to them.

This, perhaps, lends weight to the image of EUROBIT as a rather ineffectual 'letterhead' organisation. There is, however, a further important feature of the EUROBIT organisation. EUROBIT incorporates firms in the ICT field regardless of their country of origin. Thus non-European owned ICT firms may participate via their national federations in the work of EUROBIT. This is of particular significance to US-owned, and to an even greater extent to Japanese-owned, firms. All the more so as the prevalence of 'invitation-only forums' which regularly exclude these (particularly the Japanese-owned) firms from participation continues.[14] Following the acquisition of the controlling shares in ICL by Fujitsu in 1990, for example, and the effective debarring of ICL from the European IT Round Table, EUROBIT became an important platform for ICL and the firm allocated considerable resources to EUROBIT participation. Hence, whether the logic of influence or the logic of membership prevails, in providing the incentive for collective action, largely depends on the alternative channels of influence which are open to the firm in question. Not all firms in the ICT sector enjoy equal direct access to the ears of the policy-makers. It is also, of course, important for indigenous European-owned firms to remain in close contact with their international counterparts.

Sectoral organisations: direct membership associations

Direct membership associations increasingly play an important role in a number of industrial sectors – for example, in the areas of biotechnology (Greenwood and Ronit, 1992) and in the automobile industry (McLaughlin *et al.*, 1993). Grant (1995: 16) has argued that certain sectoral conditions favour the formation of these organisations. In particular, the industry should have a strong international orientation, the decisions of the EU should have an important impact on the sector and the industry should be dominated by a relatively small number of major firms. These features clearly exist in the area of ICT. In the information technology sector major European firms have long enjoyed the ear of the EU policy-makers via their direct participation in the European IT Round Table. Established in 1979–80 on the initiative of Etienne Davignon, then European Commissioner for Industry, the European IT Round Table brought together the twelve leading ICT companies in the EU (Sharp and Shearman, 1989: 49),[15] and played a critical role in the establishment of the EU ESPRIT programme.[16]

The IT Round Table has since undergone a number of changes in membership, reflecting essentially the pattern of take-over and merger in the ICT sector as well as the changing nature of new technologies.[17] It continues, however, to provide an important forum for the discussion of ICT-related matters. This group, rather like the ERT, tends to provide a more useful forum for discussing strategic policy issues (in this case related to the ICT sector) than details of specific policies. The broad nature of representation within the IT Round Table, while reflecting the complex diversity of the ICT sector (i.e. ranging from equipment manufacturers and service providers to the innovators in technology), encompasses too many conflicting interests to generate clear policy outcomes. In particular, there is often direct conflict between the interests of the ICT companies – for example, Olivetti, Bull, SNI – and the interests of the telecom equipment manufacturers – such as Alcatel, Philips and the 'main' branch of Siemens. There is a tendency to water down policy positions in an attempt to generate consensus between the various actors. Once again, however, membership of this group provides an important point of contact and source of information. As one representative from a major ICT multinational said of his firm's participation in the IT Round Table, 'we listen more than we talk'.

Sectoral organisations: participation in standards institutions

The ICT industry is involved voluntarily at all stages in the standards-setting process, either through the participation of firms in national standards bodies or through their direct participation in European standards bodies. Particularly since the launch of the Single European Market programme, the pace of standardisation in the EU has been stepped up and the direct involvement of ICT firms in the standards process has increased. The formal European bodies concerned with standards in the ICT field have traditionally been CEN (established 1961) and CENELEC (established 1958). Both institutions were formed as an umbrella for the regional cooperation of West European national standards institutions. However, in March 1988 the European Telecommunications Standards Institute, which allows for the direct participation of manufacturers, users, public service providers, research bodies and national administrations on equal terms, was created (Besen, 1990). The institute has so far proved to be rather effective and, despite generating some highly controversial debates (most recently, for example, over intellectual property rights), it is generally considered to be the most important of the standards institutes. There is little doubt that the formal direct participation of ICT firms and of ICT users in standard setting is only likely to continue.

Within the CEN/CENELEC framework, for example, EWOS was established in December 1987. EWOS was created by a number of the most representative European federations of ICT producer and user organisations (see EWOS, 1993) to aid progress on the drafting of standards in the area of open systems interconnection (OSI).[18] Meanwhile, in 1992, the executive structure of CEN was reorganised and the organisation now makes provision for greater participation of economic interests (not merely through the national standards organisations) in the standardisation process (CEN, 1993).

Formal channels of direct access are clearly opening up for ICT firms in the standards process. However, the ICT firms have always played a major role even at an informal level. On the one hand (as we have seen), they have formed a number of organisations concerned with the promotion of standards. On the other hand, major ICT multinationals may attempt to influence the output of the various standards bodies by utilising their multiple access points at the national level. Thus, firms often use their participation in national standards bodies – for example, DIN in Germany and BSI in the UK – as a means of influencing European-level standards. All of the European standards bodies stress that they are simply a structure to facilitate the work of their members. The organisations themselves have only small staffs and standards are made in committees made up of representatives from member organisations (national standards bodies) who are, of course, members of the affected firms. Examining the structure of the European Association of Consumer Electronics Manufacturers, Cawson (1992: 108) argued that Philips and Thomson have been able to play a dominant role in the organisation as a result of their heavy presence in the various national member associations. In similar fashion, it is not uncommon for one major multinational company or an alliance of companies, represented in several of the national standards bodies, to weight standards committees in their favour by sending multiple representatives.

Participation in the standards process is important for ICT firms – in a rapidly changing technological environment, the output of the organisations cannot be left to chance. On the one hand, there is the possibility that the firm may be able to push its own proprietary standard to the forefront. On the other hand, it is important that a standard is not passed which is contrary to the interests of the particular firm. As McLaughlin and Jordan (1993: 30) argue, 'a free rider cannot expect to steer the vehicle'. However, the voluntary nature of most industrial standards further complicates the scenario. As one interviewee from a standards body stated, there is a complex game played by industry – they send people to standards meetings but then don't implement the standards. Or they get involved only at the point where something interests them in particular. Generally, consensus is achieved early but on the basis of an underlying non-intention to implement.

Clearly, the incentives to participate in the standards process are not solely connected to the output of the organisations. Rather, the standards bodies also provide an important collective forum for the ICT firms. Participation in the various technical committees can provide an important early warning system for the ICT firms – both on the priorities for standardisation which the European Commission is identifying and, of course, on the priorities of their competitors.

Sectoral organisations: participation in collective forums connected to the EU institutions

The close involvement of ICT firms with their counterparts and with the EU institutions has emerged not only as a result of the establishment of lobbying alliances but also as a result of their participation in a myriad of collective forums attached to the EU institutions. The involvement of the ICT industry occurs at every level of the formal policy process in the EU institutions.[19] Many of the critical contacts which ICT firms have established with each other have been formed as a result of their participation in a whole range of EU research programmes.[20] Each directorate within the Commission has a range of advisory committees and the ICT industry is heavily represented in all the relevant committees. The most recent example of ICT industrial participation at the very highest levels of EU policy formulation has been the participation of the ICT industry in the so-called Bangemann Group – the high-level group charged with the task of formulating the series of recommendations to the European Council on *Europe and the Global Information Society* (26 May 1994), which prepared the ground for the Commission's action plan, *Europe's Way to the Information Society* (COM (94) 347 Final). The action plan particularly stresses the need to maximise the involvement of the private sector in the realisation of the global information society.

Sectoral organisations: specialist ad-hoc *groupings*

Increasingly ICT companies indicate a preference for action through *ad-hoc* specialist groups. Sometimes this type of grouping arises simply because no existing organisation quite encompasses the particular alliance of interests. Thus in the early 1990s, when the debate over the EU software directive effectively split the ICT industry, the major US and European ICT companies (essentially the owners of large portfolios of intellectual property) formed SAGE which set up in opposition to the organisation of Japanese companies and the smaller ICT firms.

Specialist *ad-hoc* groupings serve a number of purposes. On the one hand, an alliance lends weight to the lone voice of a single company. On the other hand, small groupings are more likely to be able to reach a workable, while still meaningful, consensus. As most of these groups are intended to die off the vine when the issue in question has subsided or been resolved, they can also provide a rather cost-effective means of addressing an issue without the administrative costs associated with more permanent associations. Not least, the problem of the free-rider is largely avoided as each member is forced to pull its weight within the group. The ultimate sanction, of course, is that dissatisfied partners will not seek out a persistent free-rider for future alliance.

However, the scenario is not quite this simple and it appears that, to a certain extent at least, firms remain keen to maximise the degree of certainty within these initially *ad-hoc* arrangements. Thus, in August 1993, Bull, Olivetti and Siemens, for example, signed a memorandum of agreement which formalised their hitherto *ad-hoc* cooperation in a number of areas (FT, 16.9.93). While the agreement (commonly known as the BOS alliance) clearly has a technical purpose (namely the collaboration of the three firms on a European-wide computer network) it also important political goals – not least, the need to convince the Commission of the worth of their scheme.

6   THE RATIONALITY OF COLLECTIVE ACTION IN THE ICT SECTOR: HORSES FOR COURSES

> There is a horses for courses approach in Euro-lobbying and companies must keep open a number of options when entering the policy process.
>
> (McLaughlin, 1994: 12)

This statement about Euro-lobbying applies specifically within the ICT sector. Firms are constantly weighing up the costs and benefits of the various possible routes of influence and of the potential alliances which may be built. To pursue the race-course analogy a little further – the question for the firms is not only which horse to back, but also which role to play in the consortium of race-horse owners.

ICT firms have a number of routes of influence available to them beyond those collective European associations presented here. For example, no company is foolhardy enough to forget the importance of the national route of influence and most pursue simultaneous strategies of lobbying at the member-state level as well as at the European level. Meanwhile, at the European level, a number of major ICT firms have opened their own offices in Brussels. The offices are beginning to prove their worth by facilitating contacts not only with the EU institutions but also with potential partners in strategic alliances. Philips' headquarters in Eindhoven is, for example, within commuting distance of Brussels. Yet the director of the Philips' EU Liaison Office stresses the importance of a base in Brussels and the need to be where things are happening. Not least, the semi-social aspects of business life in Brussels are a critical means of keeping up to date with important events.

Another option open to ICT firms is the employment of political lobbyists or consultants. Few of the major ICT companies, however, employ lobbyists. On the one hand, lobbyists are rarely well received in the Commission. On the other hand, few lobbyists enjoy the privileged access to EU institutions enjoyed by these powerful industrial actors themselves. On the use of consultants, however, there is less consensus. Many firms use these for information purposes if not for lobbying. However, as one representative from a major multinational stated, 'we are sometimes in a better position to sell information to consultants and lobbyists than to buy it' (interview). There may be some evidence that Japanese ICT firms are more inclined to make use of consultants (McLaughlin, 1994). However, again this is not uniform: the head of the Hitachi office in Brussels, for example, almost never employs consultants as he claims that they rarely have enough understanding of the Japanese ICT industry to provide a useful service.

There are no cut and dried explanations of how or why a specific alliance or route of influence is chosen. As has been argued elsewhere, firms operating in the European policy process reflect more closely Simon's (1976) characterisation of the firm as acting with a 'bounded' rationality than Olson's (1971) image of the 'purely' rational firm (McLaughlin and Jordan, 1993: 3). In an uncertain world, firms do not have perfect information on which to take rational decisions. The ICT sector, in particular, characterised by a highly diverse and changing group of participants, constant technological innovation and changing public policy approaches, is fraught with uncertainties. Thus, the alliance strategies which firms operate can be viewed as a process of trial and error. As the process is iterated, however, the firms are beginning to learn the types of alliances which are most effective and which best suit their particular needs.

There are certain conditions which firms identify as inclining them towards one alliance strategy rather than another. The factor which most firms identify as paramount is the nature of the issue. Hence, on an issue which relates to industry in general, they are likely to choose the channel through which they exert most influence at the general industry level (thus for ERT members, this may be the obvious choice). On an issue which is likely to have a specific impact on an individual firm, few firms would hesitate to take unilateral action. This has particular advantages in terms of speed of action, often critical in this fast-moving environment. However, if allies can be found swiftly, a joint position from a number of affected firms may well have more impact than a single voice which may be accused of 'special pleading'. The need for rapid responses from this type of specialist grouping may, to some extent, explain the increasing formalisation of *ad-hoc* specialist groups (for example, the BOS alliance). Close, repeated, contact allows for greater certainty as to the likely positions to be adopted by potential partners and for a speedy reaction to the issue at hand. A rough sliding scale of preferred channels of action, according the degree to which an issue affects an individual firm, can be identified as follows: individual action, specialist *ad-hoc* alliance, the IT Round Table, EUROBIT and, at the most general level, the ERT. Most firms will, however, pursue a number of these options simultaneously while also lobbying at the national level.

The level at which the issue in question is administered and the attitude of public policy-makers to the issue may also impact on the decision of a firm to go it alone or to seek out some form of alliance. For example, if an ICT multinational is seeking to encourage the EU to launch a cross-border initiative, it will stress its presence in a number of countries and its close alliances with important industrial partners in yet other member states. On the other hand, if the same company is seeking support for a project under the structural funds (administered solely through national channels) it will seek to stress its national roots and its critical position in the national economy. Likewise, while the support of other major multinationals often lends important support to an individual company's position, if the priority of the public policy-makers is to increase the role of small and medium size enterprises or of ICT users, multinationals may choose to forge an alliance with representatives from these groups rather than to stress their close links with the other dominant actors in the field.

Critically, it must be remembered that not all European associations are equally open to all participants in the ICT field. Hence, the alliances chosen and the collective forums on which companies are represented may differ significantly (see Section 5.2 on ICL's attitude to EUROBIT membership). Many Japanese-owned ICT companies, in particular, have been excluded from the various collective forums in the ICT field. Likewise, many Japanese firms are well aware that their voices carry little weight in EU policy circles. For many of these firms, strategic *ad-hoc* alliances with European-owned firms allow them some voice in the policy debate.[21] Although US ICT firms have been incorporated to a much greater extent than Japanese companies into the European collective forums, a number of US ICT firms also stress that they will often seek out alliances with European firms to enhance their position in the European policy debate. On the other hand, US firms have also made use of their access to the US channels of influence when necessary. For example, during the controversy over intellectual property rights generated in ETSI, a number of US companies, including IBM, Motorola and Digital, chose to lobby through a US organisation, the Computer and Business Manufacturers' Association (CBEMA). Lobbying on this issue in the US resulted, ultimately, in a formal complaint from the US government to the European Commission. Thus, on occasion, a rather precarious position on the sidelines can have its advantages.

The clear trend in the ICT sector is for ICT firms to be increasingly involved directly in the policy process – at the broadest strategic level of EU industrial debate, when dealing with specific ICT industry concerns, in the standards-setting process and when dealing with the specific details of particular policies. There is less and less willingness to be represented through third parties, whether these be industry associations or professional lobbyists. The complex nature of strategic alliances in the ICT sector reflects the rather promiscuous nature of an industry, in which a constant balance is being sought between collaboration and competition. The evident trend towards the establishment of *ad-hoc* specialist groups reflects, to some extent, a response to constantly changing market needs. As new technology is developed, new issues are generated and new alliances may be required to press their case. Likewise, changes in alliance patterns reflect quite clearly changes in the overall structure of the industry. Hence, the increasing involvement of ICT users in strategic alliances is rather unsurprising when the general shift in the ICT industry towards a concentration on ICT services is taken into account. ICT producers are, of course, keen to hear precisely what their users require.

Overall, however, it appears that in the ICT field cooperation in itself breeds further cooperation. Firms collaborating in EU funded programmes, such as ESPRIT, in the work of the standards bodies, or in the various federations and direct membership associations, are increasingly in an informed position to make strategic decisions about their choice of allies on particular political issues. Likewise, the growing trend towards establishing a base in Brussels appears to be encouraging closer contact between the various actors. Those established so far appear to be rather successful and others seem likely to follow. In part too, the alliance strategies of the various firms reflect the impact of EU institutional incentives. Apart from the knock-on effect of programmes such as ESPRIT, and the critical role which the EU played in establishing the ERT and the IT Round Table, the importance of participation in the various collective forums connected with the EU, in generating a technological community of individuals who know and trust one another, cannot be underestimated (Sharp, 1990).

7   CONCLUSION

Euro-interests have not played quite the role predicted for them by the neo-functionalists. Yet the role which they play may be significant, not simply in terms of influencing the policy process, but also, on the one hand, by gradually altering the policy environment in the EU, and on the other hand, in facilitating the growth of the 'common sense of Europeanness' which Deutsch (1968) argued would result from increasing levels of transactions between actors in the different member states and would, ultimately, play an important role in the integration process. It appears that the effect of the catalytic role played by the EU interests may have contributed to some extent towards the development of a set of 'shared assumptions and expectations' (Vickers, 1965: 15) on the part of those actors drawn into participating at the EU level. This, in turn, appears to have had some impact upon the interests and activities of not only the Euro-groups, but also their national member organisations and even of national policy-makers. As it has long been argued that domestic pressures are key determinants of member state preferences in EU negotiations (Bulmer, 1983; Moravcsik, 1993), any alterations brought about in the pattern of domestic interests, as a result of CEU or EP sponsored activities, may have a significant effect on the emerging opportunities to which the CEU must respond and, ultimately, upon the direction of the integration process more generally.

As Vickers (1965: 29) has argued, 'policy-making assumes, expresses and helps to create a whole system of human values'. More and more policies are emerging at EU level and various interests are increasingly being drawn into the Community policy process (Mazey and Richardson, 1993b). Those involved in this process, and thus in constant interaction with one another and with the Commission, are increasingly likely to develop a shared set of assumptions and values, even a common set of aspirations and, most importantly perhaps, a common belief in the importance of the EU as a forum through which to press their demands. Thus, in Haas' (1958: 19) terms the 'complex interaction of belief systems' required for the development of a political community appears to be taking place. As demands are increasingly articulated and negotiated at the EU level, and as the number of bodies whose sole *raison d'être* is to press for European responses to national or sectoral problems continues to proliferate, it becomes more and more difficult to envisage a reversion to previous nation-state-centred behaviour patterns. Ironically, however, it is not only support for EU action which ensures the centrality of the EU in the minds of policy-makers and affected interests. As Galtung (1973: 25) argued, opposition to the EU in itself only reinforces its position as an important actor. The central importance of the EU in policy debates is likely to be strengthened further as opposing interests begin to organise on a transnational basis. The implications of these policy developments for the integration process cannot be ignored easily.

6 The institutional dimension of EU policy-making

Breaking down the monolith

1 INTRODUCTION

> Those who become engaged in a course of decision-making soon
> become aware that each decision is conditioned not only by the
> concrete situation in which it is taken but also by the sequence of
> past decisions; and that their new decisions in their turn will influ-
> ence future decisions not only by their effect on the history of
> event but also by the precedents which they set and the changes
> which they make in the way decision-makers in the future will see,
> interpret and respond to event....
> ...judgement and decision, though mental activities of individuals,
> are also part of a social process. They are taken within and depend
> on a net of communication, which is meaningful only through a
> vast, partly organised accumulation of largely shared assumptions
> and expectations, a structure constantly being developed and
> changed by the activities which it mediates.
>
> (Vickers, 1965: 15)

While there are a variety of ways in which the Commission might
influence the policy process, the constraints upon and opportunities
for Commission action vary between policy sectors. In this chapter
some of the pitfalls inherent in treating the Commission as a monolithic entity, alluded to throughout this book, are elaborated. It is
argued that both the Commission as a whole, and its individual
directorates, are constantly engaged in a strategy of 'purposeful opportunism' in their attempts to expand the scope of their competence and
to get their preferred issues onto the policy agenda.[1] Using the analysis of the two Directorates-General – DGV (Employment, Industrial
Relations and Social Affairs) and DGXIII (Telecommunications,
Information Industry and Innovation) – developed in this book, some
of the differences and similarities in the ways that Directorates-

General may operate are pointed out. It is concluded that treating the Commission as a multi-organisation is crucial for attempts to understand the process of European integration.

2 'PURPOSEFUL OPPORTUNISM' AND POLICY ENTREPRENEURSHIP IN THE EUROPEAN COMMISSION

In both the ICT and the social policy field, the European Commission has had a significant impact upon the environment in which policies are developed and in mobilising support for future activities. In both of these policy sectors, national governments have been unable to achieve consensus on the extension of EU competence. Thus, traditional state-centred approaches to EU policy-making offer little insight into the reasons for the evident progress which has been made in these policy areas. In the case of EU social policy, national governments have traditionally opposed any attempt to upset the carefully established 'truces' which have evolved at the national level. In ICT, meanwhile, the policy of European governments has historically been one of protecting and promoting their national champion industries. The two policy areas have attracted very different constellations of influential actors (for or against EU action). Yet in both sectors European Union legislation is having an increasing impact.

It is, of course, difficult to discuss the role of the 'Commission' in EU policy-making. Confusion arises, in the first instance, because the term 'Commission' is used to refer to both the Commission as an administrative body and to the Commission as an executive college. This confusion is compounded by the fact that the Commission, as an administrative unit, is composed currently of twenty-four Directorates-General and a whole range of policy divisions, task forces and policy units. Policy negotiation in the Commission takes place at a variety of levels between the division or directorate, where a proposal is drafted, and the executive Commission, from which proposals formally emerge.[2] Each of these features makes it difficult to discuss 'the Commission' as a single entity, or to attribute any characteristics to 'the Commission', unless it is made explicit to which aspect of the Commission's activities one is referring. In the areas of ICT and social policy, the relevant DG has been well prepared, through its support of R&D and small-scale catalytic programmes, to identify common European problems and to produce timely proposals for European Union solutions. Ultimately, however, it is the Commission as an executive body which is responsible for the final phrasing and timing of the publication of policy initiatives, for establishing the opportune moment for action, and for the final selection of the instruments with which policies should be implemented. Thus, to this extent it may be possible to offer an overall characterisation of the role of the Commission.

Like most bureaucracies, the ultimate aim of the Commission is to expand its powers or at least to avoid having its powers curtailed. However, there are a variety of factors which inhibit the abilility of bureaucracies to pursue their expansionist goals. Not least of these is the level of resources available to the agency, whether human or financial. While the Commission has extremely high calibre staff and, perhaps more importantly, a staff highly committed to the development of the Union, its access to financial resources is extremely limited. In the case of the European Commission, the aim is to 'maximise, not its budget but its influence as measured by the scope of its competence... the utility function of the Commission is positively related to the scope rather than to the scale of the services provided' (Majone, 1992b: 138).

While the European Commission is often characterised by opponents of its activities as a monstrous bureaucracy with ever lengthening tentacles (for example, Spicer, 1992: 40–43), the Commission is, in fact, relatively small and is not well resourced. That the Commission would be able to ride roughshod over the interests of its opponents, (which invariably include at least one member state) or manage to impose its own priorities in an impositional style, is unlikely. Indeed, the Commission has encountered serious difficulties in the past when it has tried to adopt an overly impositional approach. Requiring the support of its member states for most actions, and lacking the range of policy instruments which national governments have traditionally employed as incentives or as sanctions against interests, the Commission has learned to make adept use of its crucial role in the policy-making process. It has learned to respond to opportunities for action as they present themselves and even to facilitate the emergence of these opportunities. Much of the activity of the European Commission might well be interpreted as an attempt to expand the scope of EU competence gradually and without alienating national governments or powerful sectoral interests. The Commission, acting as a purposeful opportunist, has employed a variety of techniques aimed at expanding the scope of EU competence, and the extent of its own scope for action.

Importantly, however, purposeful opportunism as an organisational strategy is played out not only at the level of the Commission *vis-à-vis* the other Union institutions and the member states, but also within the Commission itself. This characterisation of overall Commission behaviour should simply be a starting point for analysis. Each individual directorate has to battle to get its proposal onto the official Commission agenda. Thus, proposals which finally emerge from the European Commission are the product of a complex series of inter-actions between the various directorates and policy units within the Commission, important sectoral actors, and national governments. Concentrating solely on the role of the Commission as a whole pre-vents us from looking further into the factors which influence the behaviour of this institution.

3   BREAKING DOWN THE MONOLITH

The importance of bureaucratic politics in European Union policy-making has begun to be recognised, and there have been a number of atttempts to examine the influence of the Commission in particular policy sectors (Majone, 1989a; 1991; 1992b; 1993; Cram, 1993; Pol-lack, 1995). It is now increasingly accepted that much of the move-ment towards integration has resulted from gradual bureaucratic pressure from the Commission:

> day by day, drafting regulation after regulation, the Commission and its Eurocrats have been constructing a public policy founda-tion for the integration envisaged by those political acts. Likewise, their seemingly incremental and bureaucratic activities interpret and ramify the meanings of political actions and may at times push integration even further than intended (or would be possible) by the more politicized Council.
>
> (Peters, 1992: 23)

This shift in the focus of research has presented an important chal-lenge to the traditional international relations theories of European integration. By emphasising the crucial role of the Commission in EU policy-making, these studies offer a new perspective on what may be important features of the integration process. As yet, however, there has been little attempt to break down the image of the Commission as a monolithic unit, and to examine the political dynamics of the policy process within the Commission itself.

It has become something of a truism that when looked at closely 'an agency that appears to be a single organisation with a single will turns out to be several suborganisations with different wills' (Pressman and Wildavsky, 1973: 92). The European Commission is no exception to this rule and indeed is a particularly complex case. This raises a number of important questions. How do the various levels of the

Commission, and divisions within the Commission, interact with one another? What is the relationship between the Commission as an administrative body and the Commission as the executive college? Finally, and this is the question to be tackled here, if it is accepted that the Commission as a whole has developed some degree of autonomy within the policy process, have individual Directorates-General within the Commission not also developed a degree of autonomy within the Commission? Concentrating only on the overall role of the Commission *vis-à-vis* the other EU institutions and the member states neglects the important fact that:

> the various Directorates General of the Commission, broadly equivalent to national ministries, function with considerable internal autonomy. The wide range of executive, supervisory and legislative functions carried out by the different services inevitably lead to differing administrative styles.
>
> (Donnelly, 1993: 5)

Different Directorates-General within the Commission have developed very different working practices and have, on occasion, established quite opposite relationships with important sectoral actors. The relative influence which Commission Directorates exert on the policy process may differ in nature and in effect, from sector to sector according, not least, to the range of other interests involved, to the structural instruments available to it, and to the extent to which its actions are supported or even extended by the activities of the Court of Justice. Equally, there may be fierce in-fighting between different Directorates-General or indeed between the President of the Commission and a particular Directorate.[3] The process by which issues get accepted onto the agenda of the executive Commission is itself complex and requires a significant degree of policy entrepreneurship on the part of those within the Directorates-General. Observing the activities within different Directorates of the Commission, moreover, enables us to gain a better insight into the way in which different bodies within the Commission can learn from one another and may transfer models of policy innovation from sector to sector, or adopt similar justificatory rationales, albeit in a modified form.

4   ICT POLICY: DANGLING THE CARROT

While the activities of the Commission are necessarily circumscribed by the important role which national governments and industrial actors play in the ICT sector, the Commission acting as a purposeful opportunist has employed a variety of techniques aimed to increase its competence in the area of ICT policy. There is no question that the European Union now plays an important role in the ICT policy sector, and that the Commission has come to occupy a central position in the development of EU ICT policy. This has been achieved through a variety of means. While progress has not always been smooth not least because conflicts within DGXIII and between DGXIII and the other relevant DGs are not unusual. Industry cannot be guaranteed to implement the standards which it accepts and national governments continue to be the thorn in the side of any emergent industrial policy at EU level. The spill-over effects of creating a role for the EU in ICT policy have, however, been highly significant.

The European Commission could not possibly survive a clash with the major industrial interests of the Community without the firm support of its member states or where action is based on firm legal principles enforceable by the Court of Justice. Thus, there is no suggestion in this book that the Commission has ridden roughshod over industry or managed to impose its own priorities in an impositional policy style (Richardson *et al.*, 1982). Rather, it is suggested that the Commission, as a body with expertise and some general overview of the sector, has managed to develop a policy-making role for itself and has in turn had some practical impact upon the development of the ICT sector in Europe.

The Commission, acting as a purposeful opportunist, has employed a variety of methods aimed to create a role for itself in ICT policy. A long process of softening up the policy sector, by sponsoring research, a gradual extension of its competences and continuous consultation with industry, enabled the Commission to capitalise on the inability of national governmnents to come up with new solutions to the old problem of European competitiveness. By acting as 'innovator of selective incentives' (Olson, 1971), the Commission has been able to encourage the participation of a variety of powerful industrial actors in an EU context. While, this has often been achieved with the keen cooperation of the industries involved, as in the case of ESPRIT and the mobilisation of user groups, on occasion this has been achieved with only the reluctant involvement of major actors (for example RACE). Indications are that industry, left to its own devices, would have followed a rather different path, more global and oriented towards competitive research. Thus while the Commission may not be able simply to impose its own priorities on industry, it can certainly help to influence the direction which cooperation takes. Participation in EU R&D programmes, for example, has had a significant impact upon the R&D environment in the EU. With firms increasingly participating in intra-EU cooperation, R&D staff in the various companies have come to know one another and are increasingly aware of each other's activities. To some extent the mind-set of those involved in ICT R&D can be said to have been altered, and the EU has indeed become a focus for cooperative activity; the CEU has, moreover, capitalised upon the prevailing trend towards liberalisation and deregulation in the ICT sector.[4]

The Commission has both responded adeptly to and helped to create an environment in which national governments are no longer able to protect national champion industries with the traditional instruments of public policy. In this changed environment, the Commission has successfully managed to introduce a range of standards and regulations, while attaining few significant new powers in this area. This has been as a result, not only of the Commission's ability to respond to the changing climate in the ICT sector, but also of its ability to encourage policy adaptation at the national level and to make strategic choices in the selection of policy types and policy instruments.

5   EU SOCIAL POLICY: UNDERMINING THE OPPOSITION

Unlike the relatively new DGXIII, DGV is one of the original Directorates of the Commission, it enjoys no symbiotic relationship with European industry, and has rarely enjoyed the high profile given to EU ICT initiatives. While DGXIII was able to capitalise on the strategic importance of ICT for European industry, DGV has yet to discover such a potent justification for action in the social field.[5] While the agenda changes little, officials in DGV are constantly trying to find new means of justifying old initiatives. Perhaps the most surprising feature of EU social policy is that it should have developed to the extent that it has. Yet, a number of important developments have taken place in the social policy field. This section examines the difficult relationship between DGV and the various important sectoral actors. It also highlights some of the ways in which the scope of EU competence has been increased in the area of EU social policy despite the lack of support for these developments, and the potentially important role which EU social policy plays in the integration process.

5.1 EU social policy: where are the champions?

There has been consistent opposition by employers and industry to any extension of EU competence in the area of social policy. However, more recently multinational companies have come to perceive the potential benefits of supranational legislation in avoiding the upward spiralling of consistently higher national standards (Majone, 1989a). The overt opposition of industry, combined with the almost inevitable veto by the UK government of the vast majority of social policy proposals, has left DGV with only limited room for manoeuvre in recent years.

This has proved to be extremely difficult despite the variety of attempts to extend the institutional framework for the development of social policy beyond the various directorates of DGV. In particular, attempts to involve the two sides of industry (the 'social partners') in the elaboration of EU social policy has been inherently problematic, not least because of the rather ambivalent attitudes which the various national members of these organisations have had towards the development of European social policy (Lange, 1992). Until recently, the formal involvement of the social partners in the work of DGV was fairly limited. In part at least, this was because the two frequently contradicted each other and hence prevented any progress from being made. Although the two sides of industry have been given a strengthened role in the Maastricht Treaty it is not yet clear that they will be able to overcome their internal problems sufficiently to take effective advantage of their new powers.[6] Unable to take on influential industrial actors and national governments, and without a powerful champion of the social policy cause, much of the work of DGV has thus been aimed at mobilising a constituency of support, establishing precedents for future action and the careful strategic selection of policy instruments.

5.2 A human face for Europe? Mobilising EU support

Many of the EU programmes in the social field are targeted at vulnerable groups in society, perhaps already disaffected from their national governments and perceiving the EU as an alternative arena of power. Drawing these groups into the EU policy process, providing funding for the establishment of research and information networks, and for participation in EU committees is an important way of mobilising citizen support for the Union while requiring minimal expenditure. This has, for example, been suggested as an explanation of the continued Commission interest in the poverty programme despite the fact that evaluations of its effectiveness in combating poverty have, at best, been inconclusive:

> The European authorities have jumped on this wagon in order to play a leading role in Europe in at least one aspect of social policy, which would appeal strongly to public opinion.
>
> (Langendonck, 1990: 22)

The public relations potential of the social dimension has clearly not been overlooked, as its inclusion under the headings of a 'People's Europe', a 'Citizen's Europe' and a 'Human Face' for Europe make clear. Programmes focused upon young people or students may also perform an important mobilising function for the Union. Promoting notions of a common European heritage and introducing a European dimension to the educational environment may have a significant influence upon those participating in these programmes. The Commission has noted its significant contribution 'to the construction of Europe and the European educational community' (*Social Europe*, 1989: iii) through the European Union Action Scheme for the Mobility of University Students (ERASMUS). While examining the future prospects for a 'People's Europe', it has been observed that 'a people's Europe will spring up once we are all fully aware of the roots, values and options for the future which we have in common. Culture and education now need to be tackled' (Fontaine, 1990: 33). Looked at from this perspective, EU social policy may have a wider role to play in increasing popular support for the further development of the EU and hence for the extension of the Commission's powers.

6   THE COMMISSION AS A 'MULTI-ORGANISATION'

It has become clear that, while the Commission as a whole has an important role to play in the EU policy process, it can in no way be characterised as a monolithic unit. Both of the Directorates-General observed have, however, developed certain key skills.

First, the ability to package issues in the form likely to engender least opposition in the Council of Ministers and to maximise the scope of CEU competence or indeed to bypass the Council of Ministers altogether. The need to gain member state approval and to minimise financial costs at the EU level, in part, explains the trend towards the use of regulatory policy in the social field (Cram, 1993; Majone, 1993).[7] Meanwhile, DGV has learned how to make use of soft law and small-scale direct expenditure programmes to create precedent for action and to establish its competence in a wide range of policy areas which would not have gained member states' approval for more substantial policy initiatives. For example, in areas in which it proves impossible to get a policy accepted, the Commission may propose a programme. Or, where the use of a Directive or Regulation would prove unacceptable to the member states, DGV might propose a recommendation or an opinion (as has been the case, for example, in the area of social protection).

Meanwhile, as the CEU has achieved increased credibility and legitimacy as an actor in the ICT field, it has learned to capitalise on the diverse institutional roots of EU ICT policy and to make use of the powerful competition instruments at its disposal. Thus, the CEU is able to to produce Directives and Decisions in the ICT field for which it does not require the support of the member states. The links rather than the conflict between DGXIII, DGIV and DGIII have increasingly come to the fore. Together these form a formidable alliance in the ICT field. Likewise, the Commission has managed to develop a central role for itself in a complex standard-setting process. This serves the dual purposes of not requiring national government approval (as voluntary standards are set by industry) and of allowing the Commission some input into a process from which it would otherwise be almost entirely excluded.

Of course, to maximise the likelihood of the success of any of its proposals, the CEU must await the emergence of a suitable opportunity to which it may respond *purposively*. A new Treaty provision, the Conclusions of a European Council meeting, or a high-level commitment such as that promoting the development of the information society, may provide just such an opportunity.

The second key skill is preparing the ground for future action. By establishing research projects, and relatively small-scale EU programmes, issuing communications and drawing a range of actors into the EU policy process (whether formally or informally), the Commission attempts to soften up the policy area, paving the way for the Commission's preferred course of action should a policy window open up. Similarly, the Commission carries out extensive analysis and comprehensive evaluations, both of its own actions and programmes, and, perhaps more importantly, of the policies of the member states at the national level. In this context, the persuasive role of policy analysis is worth recalling. For some, 'policy analysis is no longer an alternative to a play of power; it becomes largely an instrument of influence or power.... Policy is analysed not in an unrealistic attempt to reach conclusive determinations of correct policy, but simply to persuade' (Lindblom, 1968: 117). Part of the softening-up process is the preparation of data which requires action and, moreover, which demonstrates that the most suitable action will be that which favours the interests of the CEU, that is, action which expands the competence of the CEU. Majone's (1989b: 117) observation, that 'demonstrating that there is a problem which can be attacked by one's favourite instrument is a very real preoccupation of participants in the policy process', is nowhere more true than when applied to the activities of the European Commission.

The third key skill is facilitating the emergence of a policy window. The Commission does not simply wait passively for an opportunity to take action but is actively engaged in encouraging the emergence of policy windows through which it may push its preferred proposals. This dual role is not uncommon for institutional actors. Indeed, 'the same people pursue their goals within the given institutional framework and attempt to modify that framework in their favour' (Majone, 1989b: 96). The Commission has played an important role in providing the catalyst for collective action in both the ICT and the social field. A range of powerful selective incentives (Olson, 1971) have been offered by the EU institutions, and by the CEU in particular, to encourage the participation of Euro-interests at the EU level and the development of trans-national cooperation in the social field.

Advisory committees, networks, observatories and EU R&D programmes all faciltate the participation of traditionally domestic interests at the European level. The involvement of Euro-interests in the EU policy process, meanwhile, has a two-fold impact on the opportunities for CEU action. First, as Euro-groups push for new issues to be addressed at the EU level, officials in the CEU are often more than happy to take these issues on board. This is especially the case in areas, such as social policy, where the CEU has only limited legal competence and when the organisations can claim wider support from other Euro-interests hence providing a broader legitimation, or a constituency of support, for EU action in the policy area (Mazey and Richardson, 1994b: 178). Second, participation in EU level activities may also affect the pressures brought to bear on national governments by domestic interests at the national level.[8]

However, while overarching similiarities exist, the ways in which the two Directorates observed have operated have been quite different. In ICT, DGXIII has, to a large extent, simply attempted to hop onto the cooperative bandwagon of globalisation in the ICT industry, while creating some kind of role for itself or massaging the direction of cooperation within industry, which, although ongoing, might otherwise have taken on a more global, rather than European, character. Thus,

> the Commission's major levers are located in existing trends in the international and regional economy. However, in addition, a community-wide movement toward liberalization undermines member-government regulation and enhances the power of the Commission.
>
> (Hills, 1991: 125)

In social policy, meanwhile, faced with the opposition of powerful industrial actors and national governments, DGV has, from the outset, had to actively seek out and encourage new sources of support for EU action. Much of the work of DGV has been aimed at undermining the opposition of powerful governments and industries, by creating a constituency of support for Union action, and enticing groups to cooperate, where there is little evidence that cooperation would have emerged of its own volition. Appealing to organisations and groups, often with a high level of moral credibility (if not political power), the activities of DGV have made the issue of EU social policy difficult for national governments to ignore. The steps might seem small, and EU participation may be dismissed as ineffectual and purely symbolic. However, the importance of symbolism and rhetoric in the policy process have long been acknowledged (Edelman, 1971; Majone, 1989b).

The activities of the two Directorates have been characterised above all by very different relationships with important sectoral actors and by the different characteristics of the policy sectors themselves. Thus, in ICT, there are strong technological and market forces at work which are forcing powerful actors to collaborate and the job of DGXIII has been to capitalise on this momentum. In social policy, meanwhile, these trends have not become evident until very recently (although multinational companies have latterly come to recognise the benefits of and to push for EU standards in the social field). DGV is, therefore, constantly seeking new justifications for action and has been actively promoting the involvement of citizen groups in the social policy process. While much of the activity in DGV is focused precisely on generating a sense of European solidarity and social cohesion, activities in DGXIII are carried out with almost no citizen involvement (even conscious efforts to involve consumer interests have met only marginal success).

More recently, however, the promotion of the information society has proved to be a powerful legitimising concept not only for officials in DGXIII but also for those in DGV. Thus the underlying political strategy pursued by the Commission may have paid off:

> liberalising telecommunications risks creating new problems that will require new Community-led solutions. 'Social Europe' is precisely designed to respond to the problems that the Internal Market is almost being willed to create. The gamble is that by the 1990s the current trend towards de-regulation will have generated support for re-regulation and enhanced social policy, which would both have to be on a EC-wide basis so as not to distort the internal market.
>
> (Holmes, 1990: 28)

On 13 July 1995, for example, the Commission established an Information Society Forum. Comprising 124 members, drawn from academia, trade unions, family organisations, industry, users, public sector and consumers' groups, the forum has the task of promoting 'debate and reflection upon the social, societal, cultural and linguistic aspects of the information society' (IP/95/729). Meanwhile, following the recommendations in the Commission's action plan, *Europe's Way to the Information Society* (COM (94) 347 Final) and in the Commission's report to the Essen Council (SEC (95) 278/7), the Commission agreed, on 22 February 1995, that DGV should establish a 'High Level Group of Experts on the Social and Societal Aspects of the Information Society'. The first reflections of the High Level Group were presented to the Commission in January 1996 with a final report expected in May 1996. The Commission would, meanwhile, stated that it will be preparing a Green Paper on 'Social Policy for the Information Society' to be launched at the Information Society colloquium in Dublin in September 1996. The Commission expects to follow this up with concrete action by early 1997 (ISPO Web, 3.96).

7   CONCLUSION

The underlying theme of this book has been that the policy-making process, and the policies which emerge from this process, have in themselves a fundamental impact on the direction of European integration. The policies which ultimately emerge from the complex policy-making process in the EU, in turn, determine the environment in which future policies are promulgated.

One result of the neglect by integration theorists, of the importance of the policy-making process for future integration, has been a lack of detailed research into the internal functioning of individual EU institutions, and of their influence on the process of European integration.

National governments retain the upper-hand in EU decision-making.[9] However, as has emerged in this book, the role of the EU institutions is a crucial element in explaining the way in which policy agendas are set, the shape in which proposals are presented for approval by national governments, the means by which policy intervention is justified, the types of policy instruments which are selected for policy implementation and the way in which support is mobilised for EU action. Each time the Commission presents a new policy proposal, suggests the use of a particular policy instrument, or introduces a new justification for EU intervention, it both affects the environment in which future decisions are taken, and ensures its own place at the negotiating table in future debates in that policy area.

The aim in this chapter has been to highlight just some of the differences in the way that two of the Directorates within the European Commission operate, differences which might be overlooked if the Commission is treated as a monolithic unit. Concentrating on the role of the Commission as a monolithic unit, or solely on the activities of any of its constituent parts, might lead to very different views of the Commission's role in the integration process. Even within one institution, the policy process and the actors involved can be very different. Yet it is clear that any useful theory of European integration ignores the impact of the policy process and the role of the EU institutions at its peril. Thus, recognition of the crucial interrelationship between the internal dynamics of the EU policy process and the process of European integration is important for the development of a more rounded understanding of the integration process.

Conclusion: institutions, purposeful opportunism and the integration process

1 INTRODUCTION

Central to the argument developed in this book is the contention that an understanding of developments within the policy process may help to explain how and why the dominant actors assumed particular negotiating positions on major 'history-making' decisions.[1] Hence, that events in the 'normal' or 'day-to-day' politics of the EU may help to explain the process through which major institutional change takes place in the EU. Decisions concerning major institutional change in the European Union are taken unanimously by governments of its member states. Ultimately, the choices made by national governments, and the outcome of the bargaining between national governments, determine the direction of the integration process. It is thus crucial to understand how member state governments choose between the alternatives available to them.

In the preceding chapters the sharp distinction between 'everyday' politics and 'constitutional' decisions was questioned. By distinguishing between 'day-to-day' politics and 'constitutional' politics, it has been argued, that while semi-autonomous supranational institutions do have an important (if tightly constrained) role to play at the 'day-to-day' level, they do not have a significant impact on major 'constitutional' developments in the integration process (Moravcsik 1993: 508–514).[2] This level of decision-making is, it is said, dominated by governments which are 'assumed to act purposively in the international arena, but on the basis of goals which are defined domestically' (Moravcsik, 1993: 481). However, the relationship between interest groups, both domestic and transnational, national governments and the EU institutions is much more complex than this analysis implies.

The insights gained from the study of the EU policy process have played an invaluable role in furthering our understanding of the 'nature of the fundamental social actors, their preferences, and the constraints they face' (Moravcsik, 1993: 477). The policies which emerge from the policy-making process, and the impact on the various actors of their participation in this process, have been critical factors in determining the role which national governments play and the positions which they adopt in negotiations on the future of the EU.

By altering the environment in which the dominant actors (member states) take critical 'history-making' decisions, the activities of the institutions and other interests have also had a major impact upon the integration process. Not least, the Commission has played a key role in catalysing the process of collective action at the EU level.[3] In this context, it must be asked to what extent the process of national preference formation can be considered to be entirely exogenous, or whether this should be recognised as an endogenous process (hence influenced at least in part by the participation of key actors in the existing EU policy process (see Sandholtz, 1993: 3)). Likewise, activities and events in the 'day-to-day' EU policy process act as constraints or opportunities which impact upon the choices made by national governments when negotiating 'history-making' decisions. In understanding the outcome of negotiations at the 'constitutional' level of EU decision-making it is, therefore, vital to take into account the learning and adaptation processes which iterated contact between the various actors in the policy-making process has made possible.

2 INTEGRATION THEORY AND THE INSIGHTS OF THE POLICY PROCESS

The increased understanding of the intricacies of the policy process which has been generated by recent studies of the EU as a system of governance has been important in at least two major respects. First, new questions to be addressed by integration theorists have been highlighted and the shortcomings of existing explanatory approaches have been exposed. Second, some of the commonly acknowledged explanatory failings of existing theories of integration have been addressed. Critically, evidence derived from the study of the policy process has helped analysts to address the recognised shortcomings in existing macro-theories of integration. For example, by justifying the various analysts' focus on particular actors, explaining the process of preference formation through empirical observation, examining the nature of the actors involved (to what extent they may be characterised as rational actors, for example), and by identifying the relationship between the policy environment and the taking of major constitutional decisions.

Traditional theories of regional integration have, quite appropriately, been extensively criticised: sometimes they failed by their own standards (probably no school of integration scholars has, for example, been more self-critical than the neo-functionalists); sometimes they have been criticised for their choice of key actors or analytical focus; and sometimes, perhaps most importantly, they have been criticised for their failure to specify or justify the underlying assumptions on which their conceptualisations are based.[4] Clearly, the analytical focus adopted by the neo-functionalist and the communications schools, for example, overestimated the importance of day-to-day political processes and underestimated the persistent central role which national governments have played in the decision-making process. Evidence from both the EU policy process and from major treaty negotiations has consistently reinforced the evidence of the critical role which national governments play in the integration process. In this context, the insights offered by theories of international relations, and developed and refined by Moravcsik (1991, 1993) in his theory of liberal intergovernmentalism, that national governments are the dominant actors in the integration process and that bargaining between these relatively more or less powerful actors determines the final outcome of most decisions in the EU policy-making and integration processes, have been invaluable in developing our understanding of European integration. However, while the criticism of the early approaches is valid and appropriate, it is important to ensure that, in contemporary analyses of the integration process, the proverbial 'baby' is not thrown out with the 'bath water'.

3   INSTITUTIONS, AGENCY SLACK AND PURPOSEFUL OPPORTUNISM

Clearly, 'institutions matter' in the EU context. As a growing body of literature emerges on this issue, this has become less and less of a startling statement. A range of studies, which recognise the role of EU institutions in the integration process, has begun to emerge, both from authors favouring an intergovernmentalist perspective and from those who emphasise the central role of semi-autonomous supranational institutions. Institutions have been characterised in a number of ways: as passive structures; as actively shaping expectations and norms; and as purposive actors seeking to influence the development of the EU. Traditionally, analyses which focus on the role of supranational institutions have been characterised as existing in direct conflict with analyses which adopt an intergovernmental focus. However, as current scholarship on the role of institutions becomes more sophisticated this can no longer be said to be the case (see for example Moravcsik, 1993: 507).

The notion of institutions recognised as passive structures, that is as providing the norms, values and procedures, alterable only with unanimous consent, within which the day-to-day policy choices and major 'constitutional' decisions are taken, is quite consistent with the intergovernmentalist perspective which focuses predominantly on the structural leadership exerted by national governments in international negotiations (see for example, Moravcsik, 1993: 509). Following international regime theory, the critical role played by EU institutions in providing a passive structure which enhances the efficiency of intergovernmental decision-making is recognised. EU institutions provide a framework within which to negotiate major 'history-making' decisions by ensuring a shared negotiating forum, joint decision-procedures, a set of shared legal and political norms, institutions to monitor cooperation and defection and, not least, by disseminating ideas and information (Moravcsik, 1993: 508).

However, it is increasingly recognised that EU institutions also play an active role in the EU policy process. Thus, while emphasising the crucial role which national governments play in selecting between available alternatives when taking decisions in the EU, Garrett and Weingast (1993) have argued that EU institutions also play an important role in coordinating expectations and in shaping a 'shared belief system'. Analysing the role of institutions and ideas in EU policy-making, they have argued that 'by embodying, selecting and publicising particular paths on which all actors are able to co-ordinate, institutions may provide a *constructed focal point*'. In this way, 'institutions not only provide individuals with critical information about defection but also help to construct a shared belief system that defines for the community what actions constitute co-operation and defection' (Garrett and Weingast, 1993: 176).

Garrett and Weingast's (1993) emphasis on the development of a shared belief system is consistent with recent studies in which, drawing on new institutionalist perspectives, of both its rational choice and its historical institutionalist variants (Hall, 1989; March and Olsen, 1989; Shepsle, 1989; Thelen and Steinmo, 1992), present institutions as more than simply 'arenas within which political action is played out' (Bulmer, 1994a: 357) but as playing a role in shaping norms, values and conventions. Analysts applying the tools of historical institutionalism in the EU context have, moreover, gone further by stressing the dual role played by institutions (Bulmer, 1994a). Thus, not only the 'strategies' pursued by actors in the EU context but also the very 'goals' which they pursue are seen to be shaped by the institutional context (cf. Thelen and Steinmo, 1992: 8). Perhaps most importantly, the question of preference formation has been problematised by analysts and EU institutions are increasingly viewed as being able to 'generate endogenous institutional impetuses for policy change that go beyond the usual representation of institutional mediation' (Bulmer, 1994a: 372). It is with this historical institutionalist analytical perspective that the evidence developed in this book lies most comfortably.

Institutions are also increasingly recognised as playing an independent role as actors in the policy process, able to 'develop their own agendas and act autonomously of allied interest groups' (Peterson, 1995: 81). Thus, the agency of the EU institutions is increasingly recognised and studies reveal how EU institutions have influenced the agenda-setting, policy formulation and implementation processes.[5] There is considerable evidence that institutions, as purposive actors, have an important role to play. Approaches which emphasise the purposive role of EU institutions are usually, however, portrayed as representing a direct contrast to intergovernmentalist approaches, as a result of their focus on the agency of semi-autonomous institutions. Indeed, this view is traditionally presented as being most consistent with the neo-functionalist emphasis on the role of the EU institutions. However, even within the liberal intergovernmentalist framework it is explicitly recognised that within the 'everyday' process of legislation, administration and enforcement, the semi-autonomous EU institutions, to whom national governments have chosen to delegate certain powers, have a role to play (Moravcsik, 1993: 508). This role is said to be strictly circumscribed by the national governments and 'is acceptable to member governments only insofar as it strengthens, rather than weakens, their control over domestic affairs, permitting them to attain goals otherwise unachievable' (Moravcsik, 1993: 507). Institutional autonomy, following this argument, is permitted only to the extent that the advantages to national governments outweigh the political risk. Thus to emphasise the role which EU institutions play, for example, in the agenda-setting process is, from the liberal intergovernmentalist perspective, simply to emphasise a role which governments, operating as self-interested, rational, actors, have delegated to these institutions as a means of increasing the efficiency of collective decision-making and which may be curtailed if the political risk becomes too great.

The most interesting debate on the significance of EU institutions is not then whether or not they have a role to play. Rather, the interesting question is whether the role played by EU institutions is simply that ascribed to them by the national governments of the EU member states, and strictly limited by these member states, or whether the EU institutions have developed a role for themselves which extends beyond that delegated to them by the member states. Even within the liberal intergovernmentalist approach, the decisions of one supranational institution, the European Court of Justice, are acknowledged to have had a greater impact than many national governments either anticipated or desired (Moravcsik, 1993: 513). Importantly, the Court is not alone in enjoying some limited room for manoeuvre within the constraints placed upon it by the dominant role of national governments. Indeed, it is possible to develop a conceptualisation of the behaviour of the Commission as a purposeful opportunist which is largely compatible with the line of reasoning developed in the liberal intergovernmentalist approach to explain the relationship between national governments and the domestic interests which are said to shape the preferences of those governments and from which national governments consistently seek to loosen their ties.

Within the framework of liberal intergovernmentalism, Moravcsik (1993: 484 and 488) allows for a degree of what he terms 'agency slack'. Thus, within the principal–agent relationship, in which societal principals delegate power to governmental agents, there is on occasion some limited discretion allowed to those agents. Where the interests of societal groups are ambiguous or divided, the constraints upon government are loosened, allowing politicians 'a wider range of *de facto* choice in negotiating strategies and positions'. Yet, just as national governments enjoy, under certain circumstances, some limited autonomy from domestic interests, so too the Commission and its Directorates-General have been able to pursue a wider set of interests than those delegated to them by the member states. In Table 3, the parallels between the behaviour of the Commission *vis-à-vis* the member states, which ultimately constrain its actions, and the behaviour of national governments *vis-à-vis* the domestic societal interests, which Moravcsik argues determine the actions of these governmental agents, are illustrated.

Building upon the work of Majone (1992a, 1993), which has emphasised the European Commission's ultimate goal of extending the scope of its competence, the argument developed in this book is that the European Commission, acting within the tight constraints placed upon it by national governments, has consistently enjoyed

Table 3   The principal–agent relationship

	Domestic interest–national governments	*National governments– Commission*
Relationship	Societal principals delegate power to governmental agents (Moravcsik, 1993: 483)	Governments delegate power to international institutions (Moravcsik, 1993: 481)
Preferences/role of agent	Determined by domestic societal pressures (Moravcsik, 1993: 483)	Determined by member states (Moravcsik, 1993: 513)
Primary goal of agent	To remain in power (Moravcsik, 1993: 483)	Not to have its powers curtailed (Cram, 1993: 141)
Secondary goal of agent	To maximise autonomy from domestic interests (Moravcsik, 1993: 515)	To maximise the scope of its competences (Majone, 1992b: 138)
Constraints	Where domestic societal interests are clear and powerful views are expressed; actions of governmental agents tightly constrained (Moravcsik, 1993: 483)	Where national governments have clear and strongly expressed stances on an issue the actions of the CEU are tightly constrained (Moravcsik, 1993: 513)
Opportunities	Where domestic societal interests are ambiguous, where a range of potentially acceptable solutions exist: some 'agency slack' and greater discretion for governmental agent (may pursue strategies to promote re-election) (Moravcsik, 1993: 491)	Where national governments' opinion is ambiguous, where a range of potentially acceptable solutions exist: greater discretion for CEU, may pursue strategies to increase the scope of its competences (Cram, 1994a: 199)
Choice of bargaining strategy	Governmental agents respond to strategic opportunities according to the particular constraints and opportunities prevailing	CEU responds to strategic opportunities according to the particular constraints and opportunities prevailing

some limited autonomy from these governments (see also Cram, 1993, 1994a; Peters, 1992; Pollack, 1995). Importantly, this approach does not ignore the central role played by national governments although it emphasises the crucial role which supranational institutions play. The question remains, of course, whether the impact of the supranational institutions is restricted to influencing events in the 'day-to-day' policy process or to those events which do not significantly impact upon the broader process of European integration. The weight of evidence would suggest that the impact of the European Commission is not so easily constrained.

First, continuing to follow the line of reasoning developed by Moravcsik (1993), national governments have not simply passively enjoyed the benefits of the occasional discretion allowed to them by divided or unclear domestic pressures, but have actively sought to maximise their room for manoeuvre. Thus, Moravcsik (1993) has argued that national governments have used EU institutions as part of a two-level game (cf. Putnam, 1988) to increase the policy autonomy of national governments in relation to domestic interests: 'particularly where domestic interests are weak or divided, EC institutions have been deliberately designed to assist national governments in overcoming domestic opposition' (Moravcsik, 1993: 515). As Wincott (1995b) has pointed out this raises an important question: namely, in the absence of clearly defined domestic 'demand' how are national government preferences formed?

A crucial aspect of the preference formation of national governments has resulted from their participation along with other transnational interest groups and domestic interests in the EU policy process. Importantly, the EU institutions, for example, the European Court (Alter and Meunier-Aitsahalia, 1994) and also the Commission have played a crucial role in drawing a range of interests into the policy process. In this way they have influenced the constitution of policy networks and epistemic communities (Haas, 1992) in the EU policy process which may ultimately influence the 'socialisation' of transnational and domestic interests (Sandholtz, 1993; Sbragia, 1994). EU institutions, including the European Commission, have, therefore, enjoyed a degree of active input into the preference formation of national governments (both directly and through the socialisation of domestic interests) and thus a degree of influence over not only the 'strategies' chosen but also the 'goals' (Thelen and Steinmo, 1992: 8) pursued by national governments in intergovernmental negotiations over 'history-making' decisions.

Second, just as the liberal intergovernmentalist approach (Moravcsik, 1993) allows for the potential of governments to maximise the extent of their autonomy from domestic interests, by promoting ambiguity and the diffusion of entrenched domestic opposition, EU institutions have also sought to maximise their autonomy from the constraints placed upon them by the member states. Thus by promoting particular types of policies, the Commission and its Directorates-General have sought to minimise the likelihood of member states adopting entrenched positions in opposition to particular issues.[6] National governments do not always possess full or adequate information with which to accurately predict the impact of their actions.

The Commission has often capitalised upon this fact by packaging particular issues in such a way as to maximise the likelihood of their acceptance by national governments at the history-making level, while enhancing the degree of room for manoeuvre enjoyed by the CEU at the level of the day-to-day policy process.

In particular, it emerged in Chapter 4 that by promoting the use of regulatory policy it has been possible for the Commission to disguise the 'winners and losers' in particular policy debates or to pursue a 'hands-off' approach in sensitive policy areas. In this way significant increases CEU competence have been achieved in policy areas in which national governments and industry remain divided over the development of an increased EU presence. While the intention of national governments may have been to restrict the role of the EU institutions to activities in the day-to-day politics of the policy process, the implications of EU activities at this level have, in fact, had far-reaching implications for the choices made by national governments at the 'constitutional' level.

4   CONCLUSION

Clearly national governments play the dominant role in negotiating the future of the integration process. However, events in the day-to-day policy process have also had a crucial impact on the direction of the integration process. By altering the environment in which the dominant actors (member states) take critical history-making decisions, the activities of the institutions and other interests at the day-to-day level have also had a major impact upon the integration process.

National governments simply do not always possess full or adequate information with which to accurately predict the impact of their actions. The EU institutions, however, also operate under similar constraints. In this context, it has been argued that the impact of past policy participation and the processes of learning and adaptation within the policy process are crucial weapons in the various actors' battle to minimise surprises. Thus, an understanding of the importance of policy learning and adaptation, in informing the actions of both the EU institutions and those of the member states, is crucial for any rounded explanation of the manner in which European integration has proceeded.

NOTES

INTRODUCTION

1 Since the Maastricht Treaty, the terminology which applies to the European Union/European Community has become increasingly complicated. Throughout this text I refer to the European Union except when I am specifically referring to events which occurred prior to the ratification of the Treaty on European Union (TEU/Maastricht Treaty) in 1993. To avoid confusion I have included a list of abbreviations (see p. xiii–xvi).

2 I refer to the Commission throughout this book as either the Commission or the CEU. These terms are used interchangeably.

3 The Commission is divided into an Executive Commmission and an Administrative Commission. The Administrative Commission is further subdivided into twenty-four Directorates-General, each with responsibilities for particular policy areas.

4 I have tried throughout this book to refer to 'the Commission' only when I am in fact referring to the generalisable characteristics of this body. However, the Commission is not a monolithic unit (see Chapter 6). Only in the case studies, when it is clear that I am talking about different policy sectors, have I used the terms Commission and the relevant DG interchangeably.

5 See Chapter 1.

6 See Chapters 2 and 3.

7 See Chapter 4.

8 Sixty elite interviews were carried out for this book: see list of interviews.

9 See Chapter 4.

10 See Chapter 5.

11 See Chapter 6.

12 See Conclusion.

13 For an excellent overview and application of the principal–agent literature to the member state–Commission relationship see Pollack (1995b).

1 INTEGRATION THEORY AND THE STUDY OF THE EUROPEAN POLICY PROCESS

1 see Section 2.4.

2 In his advocacy of functionally organised international organisations Mitrany referred, for example, to the organisation of the International Labour Organisation (1966: 83–85).

3 Schuman Declaration, 9 May 1990, reproduced in part in Weigall and Stirk (1992: 59).

4 Thanks to James Mitchell for this characterisation.

5 See Groom (1978) on this point and also below.

6 For example, in a footnote to his 1965 article in the *Journal of Common Market Studies*, Mitrany notes one misplaced critique of 'functionalism': 'the experience of the European communities shows the unreality of the "functionalist" thesis that starting from small, autonomous specialized authorities one could build a complete state!' (M.J. Petot cited in Mitrany 1966: 198). Yet, as Mitrany (ibid.) reminds us: 'A complete state and its introverted nature happens to be the very idea which functionalism seeks to overcome internationally'. The critique, in fact, relates more closely to Monnet and Schuman's deracinated version of functionalism rather than to Mitrany's functionalist thesis.

7 Haas (1958: 4) notes in particular: the Organisation for European Economic Cooperation; the Council of Europe; the Western European Union; and the European Coal and Steel Community.

8 See Section 2.5 for a summary of the key aspects of the realist approach to international relations.

9 Later this was to result in the criticism that neo-functionalism, which based its analysis on results from the study of only one example of the integration process, did not travel well. Thus, that its strengths as a generalisable theory of integration were diminished (see Caporaso and Keeler, 1995 on this point).

10 Although both of these were recognised as crucial aspects of European integration.

11 Although Haas specifically points out that the central institutions need not be federal but could equally be unitary state structures (Haas, 1958: 8).

12 Although, they may equally become opposed to the integration process as they recognise its costs (Haas, 1958: 287–288).

13 Interestingly, Haas had found the ECSC legislature rather wanting in this respect – it had clearly not lived up to the expectations Monnet had of a federal executive – Haas felt, however, that the Assembly might prove to be a more 'faithful prototype' of a federal parliament (Haas, 1958: 311).

14 Applications for membership came from Denmark, Ireland and the UK in 1961 and from Norway in 1962.

15 Recall Haas's (1958: 29) emphasis on the important role of institutions as 'agents of integration'.

2 THE DEVELOPMENT OF EU SOCIAL POLICY

1   DETERMINED to establish the foundations of an ever closer union among the European peoples,
    DECIDED to ensure the economic and social progress of their countries by common action in eliminating the barriers which divide Europe,
    DIRECTING their efforts to the essential purpose of constantly

improving the living and working conditions of their peoples,
ANXIOUS to strengthen the unity of their economies and to ensure
their harmonious development by reducing the differences existing
between the various regions and by mitigating the backwardness of the
less favoured,
INTENDING to confirm the solidarity which binds Europe and over-
seas countries, and desiring, to ensure the development of their prosper-
ity, in accordance with the principles of the Charter of the United
Nations.

(Preamble, Treaty of Rome, 1957)

2 Articles 117 and 118 of the Rome Treaty rather neatly exemplify the
tension between the identification of broad social ends envisioned by the
Treaty (Art 117) alongside the provision of only limited means for their
realisation (Art 118):

Member states agree upon the need to promote improved working
conditions and an improved standard of living for workers, so as to
make possible their harmonisation while the improvement is being
maintained.
   They believe that such a development will ensue not only from the
functioning of the common market which will favour the harmonisation
of social systems, but also from the procedures provided for in this
Treaty and from the approximation of provisions laid down by law,
regulation or administrative action.

(Article 117, Treaty of Rome, 1957)

Without prejudice to the other provisions of this Treaty and in confor-
mity with its general objectives, the Commission shall have the task of
promoting close cooperation between member states in the social field,
particularly in matters relating to:

– employment
– labour law and working conditions
– basic and advanced vocational training
– social security
– prevention of occupational accidents and diseases
– occupational hygiene
– the right of association, and collective
  bargaining between employers and workers

To this end, the Commission shall act in close contact with Member
States by making studies, delivering opinions and arranging consulta-
tions both on problems arising at national level and on those of concern
to international organisations.
   Before delivering the opinions provided for in this Article, the Commission shall consult the Economic and Social Committee.

(Article 118, Treaty of Rome, 1957)

3 DETERMINED to work together to promote democracy on the basis
of the fundamental rights recognised in the constitutions and laws of the
Member States, in the Convention for the Protection of Human Rights

and Fundamental Freedoms and the European Social Charter, notably freedom, equality and social justice,

DETERMINED to improve the economic and social situation by extending common policies and pursuing new objectives, and to ensure a smoother functioning of the Communities by enabling the Institutions to exercise their powers under conditions most in keeping with Community interest.

(Preamble, Single European Act, 1987)

4 See Section 2.5 of this chapter.

5 See Agence Europe no. 2583, 17 December 1966 for a summary of the Veldkamp Memorandum and the EC Bulletin no. 2, 1967: 33 for the conclusions of the meeting of the Ministers of Social Affairs.

6 This was the first action programme to be submitted after the Veldkamp agreement. The earlier memorandum, 'Guidelines for the EEC Commission's work in the social sector', was submitted to the Council on 22 December 1966 and thus does not indicate the impact that the agreement was to have upon the CEU's activities.

7 See Introduction, Section 4.

8 The Council of Ministers, of course, is not a homogeneous unit but reflects a variety of national positions. The minutes of Council meetings often reflect the level of diversity of opinion in the Council. See Nicoll (1993).

9 See Introduction, Section 3 for an outline of the principal–agent relationship and see Chapter 1, Section 4 for the use of this approach in Moravcsik's (1993) 'liberal intergovernmentalism'.

10 See Introduction, Section 1.

11 See Sections 2.4 to 2.7 of this chapter.

12 See Introduction to this chapter.

13 *Community Charter of Fundamental Social Rights For Workers*: a Solemn Declaration signed by eleven member states of the European Community on 8/9 December 1989.

14 See Introduction to this chapter.

15 Except, of course, 'administrative costs entailed for the institutions' (TEU: Protocol 14).

16 Table 1 is taken from COM (93) 600 Final, 14 December 1993. I have, however, updated it slightly to incorporate the changed number of votes required since the accession of Sweden, Finland and Austria in 1994.

17 Case 242/87, *Commission* v *Council*, para. 11, at 1453 cited in Lenaerts (1995: 19).

18 See the annual report *Review of the Council's Work (The Secretary-General's Report)*.

19 See Chapter 4 for a further elaboration of this argument.

20 See Section 2.4 in this chapter.

21 See Section 2.7 for the Commission's ambivalent attitude towards the use of the Protocol procedure.

22 The Council to act by QMV except where Article 2(3) issues are to be dealt with.

23 Unless this is agreed to by both the social partners and the Commission.

24 Martin Rhodes (1995: 88n) describes these organisations: 'UNICE was formed in 1958; its membership comprises thirty-two national employer

and industrial federations from twenty-two countries. ETUC was established in 1972 and has forty affiliated confederations from twenty-one countries, including all of the most important EU national union confederations, apart from the Communist French CGT and the Portuguese CGTP-IN. The third important interest organization, CEEP (European Centre of Public Enterprises), was formed in 1965; it represents 260 of the European Union's public enterprises (from all states except Britain and Denmark) and provides them with information and research on EU activities.'

25 See Section 2.6 in this chapter.

26 See Section 2.5 in this chapter.

27 It should not be taken from this that the other fourteen national governments have suddenly become ardent supporters of EU social policy. On the contrary, member states continue to press largely for only those policies which fit in with their national priorities. Meanwhile, there have been some notable shifts in the positions of those member states which have signed up to the social protocol: most notably perhaps the blocking by Germany of four social action programmes currently before the Council. It could be argued that the position traditionally adopted by the UK is coming to be adopted by other member states forced to come out from behind the UK's coat-tails.

28 See Section 2.7 in this chapter.

29 Hence the importance attached to the establishment of the European Centre for Industrial Relations in Florence.

30 See, for example, Whiteford (1993) on the *acquis communitaire*.

31 The current Conservative government in the UK has made its position on EU social policy very clear in its submission to the 1996 Intergovernmental Conference: 'Within the Social Chapter the UK would risk being outvoted on a wide range of possible Directives on work conditions. The potential costs, in money and in jobs, are enormous. The UK will not give up its opt-out and cannot be forced to do so' (*A Partnership of Nations* (March 1996: 25) London: HMSO). However, the Commission must also consider the possibility of a change in the current UK government at the general election (to be held before July 1997).

32 Portugal abstained in the final vote (Agence Europe, 12.10.94, 1902).

33 The Commission has calculated these to be 20 Deutschmarks per person in a company (Agence Europe, 22.9.94, 6321: 6).

34 The introduction, with the SEA, of qualified majority voting in the area of health and safety for workers does appear to have had a significant effect on the pattern of EC social policy development since 1986 (see Chapter 4, Figure 5). The impact of the Social Protocol agreed upon at Maastricht by all member states, with the exception of the UK, has yet, of course, to become clear.

35 See Chapter 4 for an elaboration of this argument.

36 Although see Pollack (1995a) for a more general attempt to examine the policy types emerging in the EU policy process.

3   THE DEVELOPMENT OF EU ICT POLICY

1 Although the Telecommunications and the Information Technology sectors have, in practice, been very different, the two have traditionally been

closely integrated for the purposes of EU activities. Initially, the CEU 'managed to treat telecommunications as a sub-field of IT policy' (Fuchs, 1994: 181). However, more recently, with the increasing convergence of high technologies and the development of the information society, support for IT policy has come to be heavily dependent on advances in telecommunications. DGXIII, the focus of this chapter, deals with 'Telecommunications, Information Industry and Innovation'. Thus, the focus on ICT policy seems appropriate. Moreover, as the development of the EU policy sector has closely intertwined the two sectors, these links are explored in this chapter.

2 See also Chapter 4 for an elaboration of this point.

3 For example, in Council discussions on the liberalisation of telecommunications infrastructures, the Council was rather predictably divided into three camps: the ardent liberalisers (Germany, United Kingdom and the Netherlands), the ambivalent liberalisers (particularly France) and those nervous of liberalisation altogether (Spain, Greece, Portugal, Denmark and Belgium). (Agence Europe, 29.9.94, 6325: 7).

4 For example, Jacques Stern, former Chairman of France's Groupe Bull, has argued that to return the European ICT industry to health will require 'a strong lead from Brussels with the full support of the national governments of the community' (*Financial Times* (FT) 17.3.94). Meanwhile, Mr Vitorio Cassoni, Olivetti's managing director, referring to Europe's weakness in computer technology, has said that the Commission should not spend money trying to catch trains that Europe has already missed' (FT 17.3.92: ii).

5 For example, the Memorandum from British Telecommunications Plc on the 1996 Intergovernmental Conference recommends: 'the single market in telecommunication should be regulated – or deregulated – far more at the EU level than the case is today... there is logic in the establishment of a Single EU Communications regulatory body'. Meanwhile, the Bangemann Report on the Information Society (1994: 13) recommends: 'the establishment at the European level of an authority whose terms of reference will require prompt attention'.

6 In the UK, in particular, R&D was heavily integrated with broader national policies and goals (Nau, 1975: 630).

7 See Section 5 in this chapter.

8 Indeed in the mid-1980s the strictly intergovernmental EUREKA programme enjoyed 'high profile encouragement from some national governments anxious to play down Commission initiatives' (Sharp, 1990: 103) and was 'an attempt to get away from what some saw as the too bureaucratic and excessively research-oriented EEC programmes' (Williams, 1989: 167). EUREKA was established in Paris on 17 July 1985. For a detailed study of the EUREKA project see Peterson (1993).

9 See Section 3 in this chapter for more details on this programme.

10 For example, International Organization for Standardization (ISO), International Electrotechnical Commission (IEC), International Telecommunications Union (ITU) and European Conference of Postal and Telecommunications Administrations (CEPT).

11 The European Standards Boards are the European Committee for Standardisation (CEN), European Committee for Electrotechnical Standardisa-

tion (CENELEC) and European Telecommunications Standards Institute (ETSI).

12 See Section 4 of this chapter.
13 Title VI, Articles 130f–q of the SEA reinforced the competence of the EU in the ICT field (see also Section 6.1 of this chapter).
14 France – interventionist, Germany – committed to free market and the UK – ambivalent (Sharp and Shearman, 1989: 39), Italy and Benelux – keen to extend centralised, integrated programmes (Nau, 1975: 636).
15 Much of the impetus behind the establishment of this body came from France and its desire to create a European 'protectionist' policy (Nau, 1975: 632).
16 Council Resolutions of 28 May 1969, OJ C 076 17.06.69: 1 and 7.
17 COST is above all a framework for cooperation – allowing either the coordination of national research or the participation of non-member countries in EU programmes – which generally take the form of precompetitive or basic research or activities of public utility.
18 For a list of the extra-EU countries see Section 2.2 in this chapter.
19 'Memorandum from the Commission on the Technological and Industrial Policy Programme' Bull. EC, Supplement 7/73.
20 See Section 6.3 in this chapter and Chapter 4.
21 See Chapter 6 for some of the problems inherent in treating the European Commission as a monolithic unit.
22 See EC Yearbook (1983) 4th edn Brussels: Delta
23 See Chapter 4.
24 ICL, GEC and Plessey of the UK; Thomson, Bull and CGE from France; AEG, Nixdorf and Siemens from Germany: Olivetti and STET from Italy; and Philips from the Netherlands.
25 Indeed, by 1983, Mitterrand, for example, had already launched a campaign for increased European cooperation in technology and himself became a vigorous supporter of the ESPRIT initiative (Sandholtz, 1992 c: 11).
26 EC R&D spending, for example, accounted for 2% of total R&D spending in the EC in 1980 and 4.3% in 1991 (*The Economist*, 9.1.93).
27 See Chapter 4.
28 In particular through the use of Directive 90/531/EEC.
29 See Chapter 4.
30 See Chapter 4.
31 These guidelines are to be adopted on the basis of the co-decision procedure (TEU: Title XII, Article 129d).
32 The members of this high level group included, for example, Pehr Gyllenhammar (Volvo), Carlo de Benedetti (Olivetti), Etienne Davignon (Ex-Commissioner for Industry), Gaston Thorn (ex-President of the European Commission), Peter Bonfield (ICL).
33 'Europe and the Global Information Society' 26 May 1994.
34 Teleworking, distance learning, university and research networks, telematic services for SMEs, road traffic management, air traffic control, health care networks, electronic tendering, trans-European public administration network, city information highways (Bangemann Report, 1994: 34).
35 See Chapter 5 for the range of ways in which the ICT industry seeks to influence EU ICT policy.
36 For example, prior to the main thrust of EC policy, a number of firms had begun to collaborate of their own volition in the area of R&D, but

cooperation with extra-EC firms was far more common than intra-EC collaboration (Mytelka and Delapierre, 1987: 241).

4 POLICY TYPES AND POLICY INSTRUMENTS IN THE EU POLICY PROCESS

1 See Chapter 5.
2 Importantly, even in the area of social policy there are no redistributive policies at the EU level. Distribution takes place through competition for funds from the various social action programmes and, in practice, the principle of *juste retour* has come to dominate distribution in the EU.
3 This category includes, for example, EU Recommendations, Opinions and Declarations. For an elaboration of the concept of soft law in the context of the European Union see Wellens and Borchardt (1989). See also Introduction of this volume.
4 Although see Introduction to Chapter 2 for the extent of soft law provisions in these areas.
5 This section does not, for example, include all policies in the area of vocational training although this is one of the specific areas of competence of DGV (Directorate-General for Social Affairs). These policies are also included in the Directory under the heading 'Education, Training and Cultural Questions'.
6 Figures 2 to 9 indicate the number of pieces of EU legislation occurring in each of the categories employed.
7 It is important not to confuse EU Regulations, which are a legal instrument for the enactment of EU policies, with regulatory policy which is examined in this chapter. EU Regulations are the strongest legal instruments available to the Community institutions and are directly applicable. For a definition of regulatory policy see Introduction, Section 4.
8 See Chapter 2, Section 2.7.
9 In this case the willingness of multinationals to implement EWCs throughout Europe may, of course, be explained by the relatively cheap nature of this innovation (see Chapter 2).
10 Article 118 specifies the following areas:
   • employment
   • labour law and working conditions
   • basic and advanced vocational training
   • social security
   • prevention of occupational accidents and diseases
   • occupational hygiene
   • the right of association, and collective bargaining between employers and workers.
11 See Chapter 2, Section 2.4.
12 But see Chapter 2, Section 3 for the Commission's response.
13 See Chapter 3.
14 CEN had produced in total 2,403 standards by 4.1.96 and CENELEC 1,874 standards by 13.3.96 (information from CEN and CENELEC).
15 Italy v Commission (Case 41/83).
16 Full liberalisation was to be achieved by 1 January 1998.

17 French Republic, supported by Italy, Belgium, Germany and Greece v Commission of the European Communities.
18 See next section.
19 This characterisation is an inversion of Falcone and Van Loon's (1983) title: 'Public Attitudes and Intergovernmental Shifts in Responsibility for Health Programmes: Paying the Piper without Calling the Tune?' The authors investigate the relationship between system support and responsibility for the provision of health services in the Canadian federal system. They conclude that while the Canadian federal government provides a large proportion of funding for provincial public health programmes, the provincial governments receive the credit for providing these much valued public goods. The federal government, on the other hand, tends to be associated with the unenviable task of collecting taxes to pay for them. The federal government thus finds itself in the undesirable position of 'paying the piper without calling the tune'.
20 See, however, Chapter 5 for the spill-over effects of this participation.

5 COLLECTIVE ACTION AT THE EU LEVEL

1 By Euro-interests I mean those non-governmental actors that are *involved* in the EU policy process. These may be individual organisations or groups of organisations. McLaughlin *et al.* (1993: 193) have used the term 'policy participant' when referring to organisations 'attempting to influence policy outcomes on their own account'. I have not adopted this term because part of my argument is that organisations involved in EU policy-making are not always actively seeking to *influence* that process. I use the term Euro-group only to refer to those organisations in which national organisations or groups of organisations have joined together in a collective European forum.
2 While most Euro-organisations will attempt to influence policy, there are also a wide range of less formal organisations which are largely concerned with soliciting funds or gaining information from the European institutions.
3 Binding EU regulations in the area of EU social policy are restricted to the areas of Health and Safety, Equal Treatment of Men and Women, Protection of Workers and Social Security for Migrant Workers (see Chapter 4).
4 See list of organisations and EU programmes on pp. xiii–xvi for details of organisations and programmes cited.
5 TACIS is the EU Initiative in the Area of Telematics. FORCE is the EU Initiative on Continuing Vocational Training.
6 Although it should be noted that many of COFACE's members were already represented in national consumer bodies.
7 HORIZON is the EU Initiative Concerning Handicapped Persons and Certain Other Disadvantaged Groups. EUROFORM is the EU Initiative Concerning New Qualifications, New Skills and New Employment Opportunities. NOW is the EU Initiative for the Promotion of Equal Opportunities for Women in the Field of Employment and Vocational Training.
8 As the ICT sector is dominated by a number of important multinational companies I have concentrated on the strategic alliances forged between these firms throughout this chapter. While there have been a number of European Commission and national government incentives employed to

increase the role of small and medium size enterprises in the ICT sector, major multinational industries continue to dominate industrial representation in the policy process.

9 This, of course, is not unique to the ICT sector – various Directorates-General have developed close relationships with their client industries, for example, DGVI and the agriculture industry.

10 Information presented in this section was derived from interviews with senior industrialists in the ICT sector.

11 For details on the organisation of the telecommunications sector in Europe see Schneider (1992) and Dang-Nguyen *et al.* (1993).

12 For details on the organisation of the consumer electronics sector see Cawson (1992, 1995).

13 As one industrial representative pointed out – this is not always how those paying for such organisations would characterise them. Indeed there is enormous variation in the levels of resources allocated to sectoral organisations as well as in the levels of staffing. However, it is often the case that a relatively small number of staff are expected to cover a very wide range of issues.

14 As McLaughlin (1994) shows, this phenomenon is not restricted only to the ICT industry.

15 ICL, GEC and Plessey of the UK; Thomson, Bull and CGE from France; AEG, Nixdorf and Siemens from Germany; Olivetti and STET from Italy; and Philips from the Netherlands.

16 See Chapter 3, Section 5.

17 For an overview of the extent of technological concentration in the ICT sector in the late 1980s see Sharp (1993: 217–218).

18 EWOS (European Workshop for Open Systems) was created by the following:

- COSINE – Cooperation for Open Systems Interconnection Networking in Europe
- ECMA – European Computer Manufacturers' Association
- EMUG – European MAP Users' Group
- OSITOP – Open Systems Interconnection Technical and Office Protocols
- RARE – Reseaux Associés pour la Recherche Européene
- SPAG – Standards Promotion and Application Group

19 See Chapter 3.

20 see Sharp and Pavitt (1993) for a list of the major EU programmes for promoting new technologies.

21 The approach of Japanese ICT firms to the policy process in the EU has been rather different from that pursued by the US and European firms and deserves more research. For some insight into the Japanese approach to lobbying in the EU, see McLaughlin (1994).

6 THE INSTITUTIONAL DIMENSION OF EU POLICY-MAKING

1 The organisational strategy of 'purposeful opportunism' used is drawn from that elaborated by Klein and O'Higgins (1985). 'Purposeful oppor-

tunism' refers to the activities of an organisation which has a notion of its overall objectives and aims but is quite flexible as to the means of achieving them.

2 These discussions are most notably held at the level of the Commissioners' cabinets, and at the meetings of the Chefs de Cabinet, where any difficulties are ironed out before proposals reach the executive Commission.

3 For an excellent insight into precisely this type of in-fighting in the area of industrial policy see Ross (1993).

4 See Chapter 3.

5 Although see below for the emerging focus on the social dimension of the information society.

6 See Chapter 2.

7 See Chapter 4.

8 See Chapter 5.

9 However, this observation should not distract commentators from analysing the political process through which national governments formulate their positions on important issues. As Allison (1971) noted, 'treating national governments as if they were centrally coordinated, purposive individuals provides a useful shorthand for understanding problems of policy. But this simplification – like all simplifications – obscures as well as reveals. In particular, it obscures the persistently neglected fact of bureaucracy: the "maker" of government policy is not one calculating decisionmaker but is rather a conglomerate of large organisations and political actors' (Allison, 1971: 3). National governments are subject to a whole variety of pressures from various interests at the national level and increasingly (i) these interests are able to pursue alternative routes of influencing policy via the European Union and (ii) national decisions are taken in a context defined or at least influenced by the influence of the European Union.

CONCLUSION

1 See Moravcsik 1993 and Peterson 1995 on the distinction between 'history-making' and 'day-to-day' politics in the EU context. See also Chapter 1, Section 5 on the dangers of overstating the distinction between the two.

2 See Wincott (1995b) on this point.

3 See Chapter 5.

4 See Chapter 1.

5 See Chapter 1 for details of these studies.

6 See Chapter 4.

Bibliography

Adler, E. and Haas, P. (1992) 'Conclusion: Epistemic Communities, World Order, and the Creation of a Reflective Research Programme' *International Organization* 46, 367–390.

Alber, S. (1986) *Speech Made on Occasion of the Signing of the Single European Act on 17 February 1986* Council of the European Communities, Luxembourg.

Allison, G. (1971) *Essence of Decision: Explaining the Cuban Missile Crisis* Boston, MA: Little, Brown.

Altenstetter, C. (1994) 'European Responses to AIDS/HIV and Policy Networks in the Pre-Maastricht Era' *Journal of European Public Policy* 1: 3, 413–440.

Alter, K. and Meunier-Aitsahalia, S. (1994) 'Judicial Politics in the European Union: European Integration and the Pathbreaking Cassis de Dijon Decision' *Comparative Political Studies* 26: 4, 536–561.

Andriessen, F. (1986) *Speech Made on the Occasion of the Signing of the Single European Act on 17 February 1986* Council of the European Communities, Luxembourg.

Armstrong, K. and Bulmer, S. (1997) *The Governance of the Single European Market* Manchester: Manchester University Press.

Bangemann Report (1994) *Europe and the Global Information Society: Recommendations to the European Council* Report of the High Level Group on the Information Society, Brussels, 26 May.

Barry, A. (1990) 'Technical Harmonisation as a Political Project' in Locksley, G. (ed.) *The Single European Market and the Information and Communication Technologies* London: Belhaven Press.

Bercusson, B. (1990) 'The European Community's Charter of Fundamental Social Rights for Workers' *The Modern Law Review* 53: 5, 624–642.

Besen, S. (1990) 'The European Telecommunications Standards Institute' *Telecommunications Policy* 14: 6, 521–530.

Bomberg, E. (1994) 'Policy Networks on the Periphery: EU Environmental Policy and Scotland' *Regional Politics and Policy* 4, 45–61.

Bonfield, P. (1988) 'UK, Europe or the World? What Should the Perspective Be?' *Information Technology and Public Policy* 7: 1, ii–iii.

Brewster, C. and Teague, P. (1989) *European Community Social Policy: Its Impact on the UK* London: Institute of Personnel Management.

Bulmer, S. (1983) 'Domestic Politics and EC Policy-Making' *Journal of Common Market Studies* 21: 4, 349–363.

Bulmer, S. (1994a) 'The Governance of the European Union: A New Institutionalist Approach' *Journal of Public Policy* 13: 4, 351–380.

Bulmer, S. (1994b) 'Institutions and Policy Change in the European Communities: The Case of Merger Control' *Public Administration* 72, 423–444.

Burley, A. and Mattli, W. (1993) 'Europe Before the Court: A Political Theory of Legal Integration' *International Organization* 47, 41–76.

Caporaso, J. and Keeler, J. (1995) 'The European Union and Regional Integration Theory' in Mazey, S. and Rhodes, C. (eds) *The State of the European Union* vol. 3 Boulder, CO: Lynne Rienner/Longman.

Cawson, A. (1992) 'Interests, Groups and Public Policy-Making: the Case of the Consumer Electronics Industry' in Greenwood, J., Grote, J. and Ronit, K. (eds) *Organised Interests and the European Community* London: Sage.

Cawson, A. (1995) 'Public Policies and Private Interests: the Role of Business Interests in Determining Europe's Future' in Greenwood, J. (ed.) *European Casebook on Business Alliances* London: Prentice Hall.

Cawson, A., Holmes, P., Webber, D., Morgan, K. and Stevens, A. (1990) *Hostile Brothers* Oxford: Clarendon Press.

CEN (1993) *Standards for Access to the European Market* Brussels: CEN.

CENELEC (1993) *Electrotechnical Standards Europe* no. 1 Brussels: CENELEC.

CEU (1989) *Guide to the Programmes of the European Community in the Areas of Education, Training and Youth* Luxembourg: CEU.

CEU (1994) *Europe's Way to the Information Society: An Action Plan* 29 July 1994 (IP/94/683).

Cobb, R., Ross, J. and Ross, M. (1976) 'Agenda Building as a Comparative Political Process' *American Political Science Review* LXX, 126–138.

COFACE (1994) *COFACE Contacts* January/February, Brussels: COFACE.

Cohen, M.D., March, J.G. and Olsen, J.P. (1972) 'A Garbage Can Model of Organizational Choice' *Administrative Science Quarterly* 17: 1, 1–25.

Collie, L. (1993) 'Business Lobbying in the European Community: the Union of Industrial and Employers' Confederations of Europe' in Mazey, S. and Richardson, J. (eds) *Lobbying in the European Community* Oxford: Oxford University Press.

Collins, D. (1975) *The European Communities: The Social Policy of the First Phase* London: Martin Robertson.

COM (80) 421 Final. *Proposal for a Council Regulation (EEC) Concerning Community Actions in the Field of Microelectronic Technology* Brussels, 1 September 1980.

COM (80) 422 Final. *Recommendations on Telecommunications* Brussels, 1 September 1980.

COM (85) 350 Final. *Towards a European Technology Community* Brussels, 25 June 1985.

COM (87) 290. *Towards a Dynamic European Economy: On the Development of the Common Market for Telecommunications Services and Equipment* Green Paper, Brussels, 30 June 1987.

COM (89) 568 Final. *Communication from the Commission Concerning its Action Programme Relating to the Implementation of the Community Charter of Basic Social Rights for Workers* Brussels, 29 November 1989.

COM (90) 80 Final. *Proposal for a Council Decision on Community Actions for the Elderly* Brussels, 24 April 1990.

COM (91) 161 Final. *Recommendation on Common Criteria Concerning Sufficient Resources and Social Assistance in the Social Protection Systems* Brussels, 13 May 1991.

COM (91) 228 Final. *Proposal for a Council Recommendation on the Convergence of Social Protection Objectives and Policies* Brussels, 27 June 1991.

COM (91) 511 Final. *First Report on the Application of the Union Charter of the Fundamental Social Rights of Workers* Brussels, 27 June 1991.

COM (93) 457. *European Dimension of Education* Green Paper, Brussels, 24 September 1993.

COM (93) 551. *European Social Policy: Options for the Union* Green Paper, Brussels, 17 November 1993.

COM (93) 600 Final. *Communication Concerning the Application of the Agreement on Social Policy* Brussels, 14 December 1993.

COM (93) 700 Final. *Growth, Competitiveness, Employment: The Challenges and Ways Forward into the 21st Century* White Paper, Brussels, 5 December 1993.

COM (94) 333 Final. *European Social Policy: A Way Forward for the Union* White Paper, Brussels, 27 July 1994.

COM (94) 347 Final. *Europe's Way to the Information Society: An Action Plan* Brussels, 19 July 1994.

COM (94) 440 Final. *Liberalisation of Telecommunications Infrastructure and Cable Television Networks* Green Paper, Brussels, 25 October 1994.

COM (94) 682 Final. *Liberalisation of Telecommunications Infrastructure and Cable Television Networks Part II A Common Approach to the Provision of Infrastructure for Telecommunications in the European Union* Green Paper, Brussels, 25 January 1995.

COM (95) 134 Final. *Medium-Term Action Programme 1995–1997* Brussels, 12 April 1995.

Community Charter of Fundamental Social Rights for Workers (1990) Luxembourg: Commission of the European Communities.

Coombes, D. (1970) *Politics and Bureaucracy in the European Community* London: Allen and Unwin.

Coudenhove-Kalergi, R.N. (1923) *Paneuropa* Vienna–Leipzig, trans (1926) *Pan-Europe* New York: A.A. Knopf.

Coudenhove-Kalergi, R.N. (1934) *Europa erwacht! (Europe Awake)*. Zurich–Vienna–Leipzig.

Coudenhove-Kalergi, R.N. (1938) *Europe Must Unite* Glarus, Switzerland: Editions Ltd.

Cowles, M. Green (1995) 'Setting the Agenda for a New Europe: The ERT and EC 1992' *Journal of Common Market Studies* 33: 4, 501–506.

Cram, L. (1993) 'Calling the Tune Without Paying the Piper? Social Policy Regulation: the Role of the Commission in European Union Social Policy' *Policy and Politics* 21: 135–146.

Cram, L. (1994a) 'The European Commission as a Multi-Organization: Social Policy and IT Policy in the EU' *Journal of European Public Policy* 1: 2, 195–217.

Cram, L. (1994b) 'Rationalising EU Intervention: Rhetoric and Soft Law in European Union Policy-Making' Paper presented to the Conference of Europeanists, Chicago, 31 March–2 April.

Cram, L. (1994c) 'Providing the Catalyst for Collective Action: The EU Institutions and Euro-Interests in EU Social Policy' Paper presented to the panel on 'The Logic of Group Membership in the New Europe' ECPR, Madrid, 17–22 April.

Cram, L. (1995) 'Rhetoric and Soft Law as Resources in the EU Policy Process: Has the Commission Become a Victim of its Own Success?' Paper presented to the American Political Science Association Annual Conference, Chicago, September.

CREW Reports (1994) vol. 13, no. 12/14 - no. 1 CREW: Brussels.

Dahl, R.A. and Lindblom, C.E. (1976) *Politics, Economics and Welfare* (2nd edn) London: University of Chicago Press.

Dahlberg, J. (1968) 'The EEC Commission and the Politics of the Free Movement of Labour' *Journal of Common Market Studies* 6, 310–333.

Dang-Nguyen, G., Schneider, V. and Werle, R. (1993) 'Networks in Europen Policy-Making: Europeification of Telecommunications Policy' in Andersen, S.S. and Eliassen, K.A. (eds) *Making Policy in Europe: The Europeification of National Policy-Making* London: Sage.

Darnton, J.E. and Wuersch, D.A. (1992) 'The European Commission's Progress Toward a New Approach for Competition in Telecommunications' *The International Lawyer* 26, 111–124.

Dehousse, R. (1993) 'Integration v Regulation: On the Dynamics of Regulation in the European Community' *Journal of Common Market Studies* 330: 4, 383–402.

Deutsch, K. (1954) *Political Community at the International Level: Problems of Definition and Management* Garden City, NY: Doubleday.

Deutsch, K. (1964) 'Communication Theory and Political Integration' in Jacob, P. and Toscano, J. (eds) *The Integration of Political Communities* Philadelphia, PA: J.B. Lippincott.

Deutsch, K. with others (1957) *Political Community and the North Atlantic Area: International Organization in the Light of Historical Experience* Princeton, NJ: Princeton University Press.

Deutsch, K. (1966) *Nationalism and Social Communication: An Inquiry into the Foundations of Nationality* 2nd edn Cambridge, MA: MIT Press.

Deutsch, K. (1967) *Arms Control and the Atlantic Alliance* Chichester: Wiley.

Deutsch, K. (1968) *The Analysis of International Relations* London: Prentice Hall.

Donnelly, M. (1993) 'The Structure of the European Commission and the Policy Formation Process' in Mazey, S. and Richardson, J.J. (eds) *Lobbying in the European Union* Oxford: Oxford University Press.

Downs, A. (1967) *Inside Bureaucracy* Boston, MA: Little, Brown.

Drake, H. (1995) 'Political Leadership and European Integration: The Case of Jacques Delors' *West European Politics* 18: 1, 140–160.

Edelman, M. (1971) *Politics as Symbolic Action: Mass Arousal and Quiescence* Chicago: Markham.

Edelman, M. (1985 [1967]) *The Symbolic Uses of Politics* 2nd edn, Urbana: University of Illinois Press.

Eichenberg, R. and Dalton, R. (1993) 'Europeans and the European Community: the Dynamics of Public Support for European Integration' *International Organization* 47: 4, 507–534.

Euro-Citizen (1990) Newspaper of the European Citizen Action Service no. 1, May/June.

Eurolink Age (1993) *Ageing Well* Brussels, March.

European Women's Lobby (EWL) (1993–4) *Report of Activities* Brussels: EWL.

European Women's Lobby (1994a) *Work Programme* Brussels: EWL.

European Women's Lobby (1994b) *European Women's Lobby Election Newsletter* special issue no. 1, Brussels: EWL.

European Workshop for Open Systems (EWOS) (1993) *General Information on EWOS* 21 June 1993, Brussels: EWOS.

Falcone, D. and Van Loon, R.J. (1983) 'Public Attitudes and Intergovernmental Shifts in Responsibility for Health Programmes: Paying the Piper Without Calling the Tune?' in Kornberg, A. and Clarke, H. (eds) *Political Support in Canada* Durham, NC: Duke University Press.

FEANTSA (1993) *Annual Report: Homeless in the Single Market* Brussels: FEANTSA.

Findlay, G. (1991) 'International Collaboration' in Nicholson, R., Cunningham, C. and Gummett, P. (eds) *Science and Technology in the United Kingdom* London: Longman.

Fontaine, P. (1990) *Europe, a Fresh Start: the Schumann Declaration 1950–90* Periodical 3/1990, Brussels: Commission of the EU.

Frohlich, N., Oppenheimer, J.A. and Young, O.R. (1971) *Political Leadership and Collective Goods* Princeton, NJ: Princeton University Press.

Froman, L.A. Jr (1968) 'The Categorization of Policy Contents' in Ranney, A. (ed) *Political Science and Public Policy* Chicago: Markham.

Fuchs, G. (1994) 'Policy-Making in a System of Multi-Level Governance: the Commission of the European Community and the Restructuring of the Telecommunications Sector' *Journal of European Public Policy* 1: 2, 178–194.

Galtung, J. (1973) *The European Community: A Super Power in the Making* London: Allen and Unwin.

Garrett, G. (1992) 'International Cooperation and Institutional Choice: the European Community's Internal Market' *International Organization* 46: 2, 533–560.

Garrett, G. and Weingast, B. (1993) 'Ideas, Interests and Institutions: Constructing the European Community's Internal Market' in Goldstein, J. and Keohane, R. (eds) *Ideas and Foreign Policy: Beliefs, Institutions and Political Change* London: Cornell University Press.

Goldenstein, J. (1991) 'Participating in European Cooperative R&D Programmes' *Journal of European Business* 3: 1, 51–53.

Grant, W. (1995) *Pressure Groups, Politics and Democracy in Britain* 2nd edn, London: Harvester Wheatsheaf.

Green, M. (1993) 'The Politics of Big Business in the Single Market Program' Paper presented to the 1993 Biennial International Conference of the European Community Studies Association.

Greenwood, J. and Ronit, K. (1992) 'Established and Emergent Sectors: Organised Interests at the European Level in the Pharmaceutical Industry and the New Biotechnologies' in Greenwood, J., Grote, J. and Ronit, K. (eds) *Organised Interests and the European Community* London: Sage.

Greenwood, J., Grote, J. and Ronit, K. (eds) (1992) *Organised Interests and the European Community* London: Sage.

Groom, A.J.R. (1978) 'Neofunctionalism: A Case of Mistaken Identity' *Political Science* 30: 1, 15–28.

Haas, E. (1958) *The Uniting of Europe: Political, Social and Economic Forces, 1950–1957* Stanford, CA: Stanford University Press.

Haas, E. (1960) 'International Integration: The European and the Universal Process' *International Organization* XV, 366–392.

Haas, E. (1964) *Beyond the Nation-State: Functionalism and International Organization* Stanford, CA: Stanford University Press.

Haas, E. (1970) 'The Study of Regional Integration: Reflections on the Joys and Anguish of Pre-theorizing' *International Organization* 4, 607–646.

Haas, E. (1975) *The Obsolescence of Regional Integration Theory* Berkeley, CA: Institute of International Studies.

Haas, P. (1992) 'Epistemic Communities and International Policy Coordination' *International Organization* 46, 1–35.

Hall, P.A. (1989) *The Political Power of Economic Ideas* Princeton, NJ: Princeton University Press.

Harvey, B. (1992) *Networking in Europe* London: National Council for Voluntary Organizations and Community Development Foundation.

Hayes, M.T. (1978) 'The Semi-Sovereign Pressure Groups: a Critique of Current Theory and an Alternative Typology' *Journal of Politics* 40, 134–161.

Heclo, H. (1972) 'Review Article: Policy Analysis' *British Journal of Political Science* 2, 83–108.

Heclo, H. (1978) 'Issue Networks and the Executive Establishment', in King, A. (ed.) *The New American Political System*, Washington DC: American Enterprise Institute for Public Policy Research.

Heclo, H. and Wildavsky, A. (1974) *The Private Government of Public Money* London: Macmillan.

HELIOS II (1993) *GENERAL RULES concerning the co-financing of activities organised by Non Governmental Organisations in the framework of Helios II* Doc 31 CC-F/93 Brussels: CEC.

Hepple, B. (1990) 'The Implementation of the Community Charter of Fundamental Social Rights' *The Modern Law Review* 53: 5, 643–654.

Hills, J. with Papathanassopoulos, S. (1991) *The Democracy Gap: The Politics of Information and Communications Technologies in the United States and Europe* London: Greenwood Press.

Hix, S. (1994) 'The Study of the European Community: The Challenge to Comparative Politics' *West European Politics* 17: 1, 1–30.

Hodges, M. (ed.) (1972) 'Introduction' in *European Integration* Harmondsworth: Penguin.

Hoffmann, S. (1966) 'Obstinate or Obsolete? The Fate of the Nation State and the Case of Western Europe' *Daedalus* 95: 892–908.

Hogwood, B.W. and Gunn, L.A. (1984) *Policy Analysis for the Real World* Oxford: Oxford University Press.

Hogwood, B.W. and Peters, B.G. (1983) *Policy Dynamics* Brighton: Wheatsheaf.

Holloway, J. (1981) *Social Policy Harmonisation in the European Community* Farnborough: Gower.

Holmes, P. (1990) 'Telecommunications in the Great Game of Integration' in Locksley, G. (ed.) *The Single European Market and the Information and Communication Technologies* London: Belhaven Press.

Hood, C.C. (1983) *The Tools of Government* London: Macmillan.

Hood, C. and Dunsire, A. (1981) *Bureaumetrics* Farnborough: Gower.

Hood, C. and Jackson, M. (1991) *Administrative Argument* Aldershot: Dartmouth.

Inglehart, R. (1967) 'An End to European Integration' *American Political Science Review* 61, 91–105.

International Labour Organization (1975) *The European Community and Social Policy* Geneva: ILO.

IRIS (1990) *An Evaluation of the IRIS Network by its Members* Network Dossier, Brussels: CREW.

IRIS (1992) *Building Bridges* Annual Report, Brussels: CREW.

Jordan, A.G. and Richardson, J.J. (1987) *British Politics and the Policy Process* London: Allen and Unwin.

Judge, D., Earnshaw, D. and Cowan, N. (1994) 'Ripples or Waves: the European Parliament in the European Community Policy Process' *Journal of European Public Policy* 1: 1, 27–52.

Kay, N. (1990) 'The Single European Market: Industrial Collaboration and the Single European Market' in Locksley, G. (ed.) *The Single European Market and the Information and Communication Technologies* London: Belhaven Press.

Keohane, R. and Hoffmann, S. (1991) 'Institutional Change in Europe in the 1980s' in Keohane, R. and Hoffmann, S. (eds) *The New European Community: Decision-Making and Institutional Change* Boulder, CO: Westview.

Keohane, R. and Nye, J. (1974) 'Transgovernmental Relations and the International Organisations' *World Politics* 26: 1, 39–62.

Keohane, R. and Nye, J. (1977) *Power and Interdependence: World Politics in Transition* Boston, MA: Little, Brown.

Kingdon, J.W. (1984) *Agendas, Alternatives and Public Policies* New York: HarperCollins.

Kirschen, E.S. (1964) *Economic Policy in our Time* Amsterdam: North Holland.

Klabbers, J. (1994) 'Informal Instruments Before the European Court of Justice' *Common Market Law Review* 31: 997–1023.

Klein, R. and O'Higgins, M. (1985) 'Social Policy after Incrementalism' in Klein, R. and O'Higgins, M. (eds) *The Future of Welfare* Oxford: Basil Blackwell.

Knieps, G. (1990) 'Deregulation in Europe: Telecommunications and Transportation' in Majone, G. (ed.) *Deregulation or Reregulation? Regulatory Reform in Europe and the United States* London: Pinter.

Koebel, P. (1990) 'Deregulation of the Telecommunications Sector: a Movement in Line with recent Technological Advances' in Majone, G. (ed.) *Deregulation or Reregulation? Regulatory Reform in Europe and the United States* London: Pinter.

Lange, P. (1992) 'The Politics of the Social Dimension' in Sbragia, A. (ed.) *Euro-Politics: Institutions and Policy-Making in the 'New' European Community* Washington, DC: Brookings Institution.

Lange, P. (1993) 'Maastricht and the Social Protocol: Why Did They Do It?' *Politics and Society* 21: 1, 5–36.

Langendonck, G. (1990) *The Role of the Social Security Systems in the Completion of the Internal Market* Leuven: European Institute of Social Security.

Layton, C. (1967) *European Advanced Technology: A Programme for Integration* London: Allen and Unwin.

Lenaerts, C. (1994) 'Education in European Community Law after "Maastricht"' *Common Market Law Review* 31, 7–41.

Lindberg, L. (1963) *The Political Dynamics of European Economic Integration* Stanford, CA: Stanford University Press.

Lindberg, L. and Scheingold, S. (1970) *Europe's Would-Be Polity: Patterns of Change in the European Community* Englewood Cliffs, NJ: Prentice Hall.

Lindblom, C.E. (1959) 'The Science of "Muddling Through"' *Public Administration Review* 19, 79–88.

Lindblom, C.E. (1965) *The Intelligence of Democracy: Decision Making through Mutual Adjustment* New York: Free Press.

Lindblom, C.E. (1968) *The Policy-Making Process* Englewood Cliffs, NJ: Prentice Hall.

Lindblom, C.E. (1990) *Inquiry and Change: The Troubled Attempt to Understand and Shape Society* New Haven, CT: Yale University Press.

Locksley, G. (ed.) (1990) *The Single European Market and the Information and Communication Technologies* London: Belhaven Press.

Lowi, T. (1964) 'American Business, Public Policy, Case Studies and Political Theory' *World Politics* 16: 4: 677–715.

McLaughlin, A. (1994) 'Outsiders Inside? Japanese Lobbying in the European Union' Paper presented to the Conference of Europeanists, Chicago, 31 March –2 April.

McLaughlin, A. and Jordan, G. (1993) 'The Rationality of Lobbying in Europe: Why are Euro-Groups so Numerous and So Weak? Some Evidence from the Car Industry' in Mazey, S. and Richardson, J. (eds) *Lobbying in the European Community* Oxford: Oxford University Press.

McLaughlin, A., Jordan, G. and Maloney, W. (1993) 'Corporate Lobbying in the EC' *Journal of Common Market Studies* 31: 2, 191–212.

McNeil, G. (1991) 'IT in Europe: The future' *Information Technology and Public Policy* 10: 1, 11–18.

Maes, M. (1990) *Building a People's Europe: 1992 and the Social Dimension* London: Whurr.

Majone, G. (1989a) 'Regulating Europe: Problems and Prospects' *Jarbuch zur Staats- und Verwaltungswissenschaft* Baden-Baden: Nomos Verlagsgesellschaft.

Majone, G. (1989b) *Evidence, Argument and Persuasion in the Policy Process* New Haven, CT: Yale University Press.

Majone, G. (ed.) (1990) *Deregulation or Reregulation? Regulatory Reform in Europe and the United States* London: Pinter.

Majone, G. (1991a) 'Cross-National Sources of Regulatory Policymaking in Europe and the United States' *Journal of Public Policy* 11: 1, 79–106.

Majone, G. (1991b) 'Regulatory Federalism in the European Community', Paper presented to the Annual Meeting of the American Political Science Association, Washington, DC, August–September.

Majone, G. (1991c) 'Market Integration and Regulation: Europe after 1992' *European University Institute Working Paper* 91/10, Florence.

Majone, G. (1992a) 'Regulatory Federalism in the European Union' *Government and Policy* 10, 299–316.

Majone, G. (1992b) 'Market Integration and Regulation: Europe after 1992' *Metroeconomica* 43, 131–156.

Majone, G. (1992c) 'Ideas, Interests and Policy Change' *European University Institute Working Paper* 92/21, Florence.

Majone, G. (1993) 'The European Community: Between Social Policy and Social Regulation' *Journal of Common Market Studies* 31: 2, 153–169.

Majone, G. (1994) 'Ideas, Interests and Institutions: Explaining the Revival of Policy Analysis in the 1980s' Paper presented to XVIth World Congress of the International Political Science Association, Berlin, 21–25 August.

March, J. and Olsen, J. (1989) *Rediscovering Institutions: The Organizational Basis of Politics* New York: Free Press.

Marks, G. (1992) 'Structural Policy in the European Community' in Sbragia, A. (ed.) *Euro-Politics: Institutions and Policy-Making in the 'New' European Community* Washington, DC: Brookings Institution.

Marsh, D. and Rhodes, R. (eds) *Policy Networks in British Government* Oxford: Oxford University Press.

Mazey, S. and Richardson, J. (eds) (1993a) *Lobbying in the European Community* Oxford: Oxford University Press.

Mazey, S. and Richardson, J. (1993b) 'Introduction: Transference of Power, Decision Rules and Rules of the Game' in Mazey, S. and Richardson, J. (eds) *Lobbying in the European Community* Oxford: Oxford University Press.

Mazey, S. and Richardson, J. (1993c) *Policy Coordination in Brussels: Environmental and Regional Policy* EPPI Occasional Papers 93/5, Warwick.

Mazey, S. and Richardson, J. (1994a) *EC Policy-Making: An Emerging European Policy Style*? EPPI Occasional Papers 94/2, Warwick.

Mazey, S. and Richardson, J. (1994b) 'The Commission and the Lobby' in Edwards, G. and Spence, D. (eds) *The European Commission* London: Longman.

Meehan, E. (1993) *Citizenship and the European Community* London: Sage.

Mitnick, B.M. (1980) *The Political Economy of Regulation: Creating, Designing, and Removing Regulatory Forms* New York: Columbia University Press.

Mitrany, D. (1966a [1943]) *A Working Peace System* Chicago: Quadrangle.

Mitrany, D. (1966b [1965]) 'The Prospect of European Integration: Federal or Functional' *Journal of Common Market Studies* reprinted in *A Working Peace System* Chicago: Quadrangle.

Moravcsik, A. (1991) 'Negotiating the Single European Act: National Interests and Conventional Statecraft in the European Community' *International Organization* 45, 19–56.

Moravcsik, A. (1993) 'Preferences and Power in the European Community: A Liberal Intergovernmentalist Approach' *Journal of Common Market Studies* 31: 4, 473–524.

Moravcsik, A. (1994) 'Why the European Community Strengthens the State: Domestic Politics and International Cooperation' Paper presented to the Conference of Europeanists, Chicago, 31 March–2 April.

Morgenthau, H. (1967 [1948]) *Politics Among Nations: The Struggle for Power and Peace* 4th edn, New York: Knopf.

Mosely, H. (1990) 'The Social Dimension of European Integration' *International Labour Review* 129: 2, 147–164.

Mytelka, L. and Delapierre, M. (1987) 'The Alliance Strategies of European Firms in the Information Technology Industry and the Role of ESPRIT' *Journal of Common Market Studies* 26: 2, 231–253.

Nau, H.R. (1975) 'Collective Responses to RandD Problems in Western Europe 1955–1958 and 1965–1968' *International Organization* 29: 2, 617–653.

Nicoll, W. (1993) 'Note the Hour – and File the Minute' *Journal of Common Market Studies* 31: 4, 559–566.

Nielsen, R. and Szyszczak, E. (1993) *The Social Dimension of the European Community* 2nd edn, Denmark: Handelschjskolens Forlag.

Niskanen, W. A. (1971) *Bureaucracy and Representative Government* Chicago: Aldine-Atherton.

Nye, J. (ed.) (1968) *International Regionalism* Boston, MA: Little, Brown.

Olson, M. (1971 [1965]) *The Logic of Collective Action* Cambridge, MA: Harvard University Press.

Peters, B.G. (1992) 'Bureaucratic Politics and the Institutions of the European Union' in Sbragia, A. (ed.) *Euro-Politics: Institutions and Policy-Making in the 'New' European Community* Washington, DC: Brookings Institution.

Peters, B.G. (1994) 'Agenda-Setting in the European Community' *Journal of European Public Policy* 1: 1, 9–26.

Peterson, J. (1991) 'Technology Policy in Europe: Explaining the Framework Programme and Eureka in Theory and Practice' *Journal of Common Market Studies* 29, 269–290.

Peterson, J. (1992) 'The European Technology Community: Policy Networks in a Supranational Setting' in Marsh, D. and Rhodes, R. (eds) *Policy Networks in British Government* Oxford: Oxford University Press.

Peterson, J. (1993) *High Technology and the Competition State* London: Routledge.

Peterson, J. (1995) 'Decision-Making in the European Union: Towards a Framework for Analysis' *Journal of European Public Policy* 2: 1, 69–93.

Pierson, P. (1993) 'When Effect Becomes Cause: Policy Feedback and Political Change' *World Politics* 45: 4, 595–628.

Pollack, M. (1995a) 'Creeping Competence: The Expanding Agenda of the European Community' *Journal of Public Policy* 14, 97–143.

Pollack, M. (1995b) 'Obedient Servant or Runaway Eurocracy? Delegation, Agency and Agenda Setting in the European Community' Paper presented to the Annual Meeting of the American Political Science Association, Chicago, 31 August–4 September.

Pressman, G.L. and Wildavsky, A. (1973) *Implementation* Berkeley, CA: University of California Press.

Puchala, D. (1970) 'International Transactions and Regional Integration' *International Organization* 24: 732–763.

Puchala, D. (1975) 'Domestic Politics and Regional Harmonization in the EC' *World Politics* 27: 4, 496–520.

Puchala, D. (1983) 'Worm Cans and Worth Taxes: Fiscal Harmonisation and the European Policy Process' in Wallace, H., Wallace, W. and Webb, C. (eds) *Policy Making in the European Community* 2nd edn, Chichester: Wiley.

Putnam, R.D. (1988) 'Diplomacy and Domestic Politics' *International Organization* 42, 427–461.

Quintin, O. (1990) 'EEC Social Policy' Paper presented at University of Bath, 12 July.

Rhodes, M. (1991) 'The Social Dimension of the Single European Market: National Versus Transnational Regulation', *European Journal of Political Research* 17, 245–280.

Rhodes, M. (1995) 'A Regulatory Conundrum: Industrial Relations and the Social Dimension' in Leibfried, S. and Pierson, P. (eds) *European Social Policy* Washington, DC: Brookings Institution.

Richardson, J. (1982) *Policy Styles in Western Europe* London: Allen and Unwin.

Rifflet, R. (1985) 'Evaluation of the Community Policy (1952–1982)' in Vandamme, J. (ed.) *New Dimensions in European Social Policy*. Beckenham: Croom Helm.

Ripley, R.A. and Franklin, G.A. (1986) *Policy Implementation and Bureaucracy* 2nd edn, Chicago: Dorsey Press.

Robbins, D. (1991) 'Voluntary Organisations and the Social State in the European Community' *Voluntas* 1: 2, 98–128.

Room, G. (ed.) (1991) *Towards a European Welfare State?*, Bristol, School of Advanced Urban Studies.

Ross, G. (1993) 'Sidling into Industrial Policy: Inside the European Commission' *French Politics and Society* 11: 1, 20–43.

Ross, G. (1995) 'The Delors Era and Social Policy' in Leibfried, S. and Pierson, P. (eds) *European Social Policy* Washington, DC: Brookings Institution.

Sandholtz, W. (1992a) *High-Tech Europe: The Politics of International Cooperation* Berkeley, CA: University of California Press.

Sandholtz, W. (1992b) 'Institutions and Collective Action: The New Telecommunications in Western Europe' *World Politics* 45: 2, 242–270.

Sandholtz, W. (1992c) 'ESPRIT and the Politics of International Collective Action' *Journal of Common Market Studies* 30: 1, 1–21.

Sandholtz, W. (1993) 'Choosing Union: Monetary Politics and Maastricht' *International Organization* 47: 1, 1–39.

Sandholtz, W. and Zysman, J. (1989) '1992: Recasting the European Bargain' *World Politics* 42: 1, 95–128.

Sbragia, A. (1992) 'Introduction' in Sbragia, A. (ed.) *Euro-Politics: Institutions and Policy-Making in the 'New' European Community* Washington, DC: Brookings Institution.

Sbragia, A. (1994) 'From 'Nation-State' to 'Member-State': the Evolution of the European Community' in Lutzeler, P.M. (ed.) *Europe After Maastricht* Oxford: Berghahn.

Schmitter, P. (1970) 'A Revised Theory of Regional Integration' *International Organization* 24, 836–868.

Schneider, V. (1992) 'Organized Interests in the Telecommunications Sector' in Greenwood, J., Grote, J. and Ronit, K. (eds) *Organised Interests and the European Community* London: Sage.

Servan-Schreiber, J.J. (1968) *Le Defi Americain*, trans. Steel, R. (as *The American Challenge*) London: Hamilton.

Shanks, M. (1977) *European Social Policy Today and Tomorrow* Oxford: Pergamon Press.

Shapiro, M. (1992) 'The European Court of Justice' in Sbragia, A. (ed.) *Euro-Politics: Institutions and Policy-Making in the 'New' European Community* Washington, DC: Brookings Institution.

Sharp, M. (1990) 'The Single Market and Policies for Advanced Technologies' in Crouch, C. and Marquand, D. (eds) *The Politics of 1992* Oxford: Basil Blackwell.

Sharp, M. (1993) 'The Community and New Technologies' in Lodge, J. (ed.) *The European Community and the Challenge of the Future* 2nd edn, London: Pinter.

Sharp, M. and Pavitt, K. (1993) 'Technology Policy in the 1990s: Old Trends and New Realties' *Journal of Common Market Studies* 31: 2, 129–151.

Sharp, M. and Shearman, C. (1989) *European Technological Collaboration* London: Routledge and Kegan Paul.

Shepsle, K. 'Studying Institutions: Some Lessons from the Rational Choice Approach' *Journal of Theoretical Political* 1: 2, 131–147.

Simon, H. A. (1976) *Administrative Behavior* 3rd edn New York: Free Press.

Snyder, F. (1993a) 'The Effectiveness of European Community Law: Institutions, Processes, Tools and Techniques' *Modern Law Review* 56, 19–54.

Snyder, F. (1993b) 'Soft Law and Institutional Practice in the European Community' *European University Institution Working Paper LAW* 93/5 Brussels.

Spicer, M. (1992) *A Treaty Too Far?* London: Fourth Estate.

Spicker, P. (1991) 'The Principle of Subsidiarity and the Social Policy of the European Community' *Journal of European Social Policy* 1: 1, 3–14.

Spinelli, A. (1966) *The Eurocrats: Conflict and Crisis in the European Community* Baltimore, MD: Johns Hopkins University Press.

Stein, E. (1981) 'Lawyers, Judges and the Making of Transnational Constitutions' *American Journal of International Law* 70, 1–27.

Taylor, P. (1983) *The Limits of European Integration* Beckenham: Croom Helm.

Teague, P. (1989) *The European Community: The Social Dimension* London: Cranfield School of Management and Kogan Page.

Thatcher, M. (1993) *The Downing Street Years* London: HarperCollins.

Thatcher, M. (1994) 'Regulatory Reform in Britain and France: Organizational Structure and the Extension of Competition' *Journal of European Public Policy* 1: 3, 441–464.

The Report of the Information and Communications Technologies Review Board, June 1992, Brussels.

Thelen, K. and Steinmo, S. (1992) 'Historical Institutionalism in Comparative Politics' in Thelen, K., Steinmo, S. and Longstreth, F. (eds) *Structuring Politics: Historical Institutionalism in Comparative Analysis* Cambridge: Cambridge University Press.

Tranholm-Mikkelsen, J. (1991) 'Neo-functionalism: Obstinate or Obsolete? A. Reappraisal in the Light of the New Dynamism of the European Community' *Millennium* 20, 1–22.

Tsebelis, G. (1994) 'The Power of the European Parliament as a Conditional Agenda-Setter' *American Political Science Review* 88: 1, 128–142.

Tsoukalis, L. (1993) *The New European Economy* 2nd edn, Oxford: Oxford University Press.

Tyszkiewicz, Z. (1989) 'Employers' View of the Community Charter of Basic Social Rights for Workers' *Social Europe* 1: 90, 22–24.

Ungerer, H. (1990) 'Comments on Telecommunications Regulatory Reform in the European Community' in Majone, G. (ed.) *Deregulation or Reregulation? Regulatory Reform in Europe and the United States* London: Pinter.

Usher, J. (1994) 'The Commission and the Law' in Edwards, G. and Spence, D. (eds) *The European Commission* London: Longman.

Van den Broek, H. (1986) *Speech made on the Occasion of the Signing of the Single European Act in Luxembourg on 17 February 1986* Luxembourg: Council of the EC.

Van Schendelen, M. (ed.) (1993) *National Public and Private EC Lobbying*, Aldershot: Dartmouth.

Venturini, P. (1989) *1992: The European Social Dimension* Brussels: Commission of the EC.

Vickers, G. (1965) *The Art of Judgement* London: Chapman and Hall.

Wallace, H. Wallace, W. and Webb, C. (eds) (1977, 1983) *Policy-Making in the European Community* Chichester: Wiley.

Watson, P. (1993) 'Social Policy After Maastricht' *Common Market Law Review* 30, 481–513.

Weigall, D. and Stirk, P. (eds) (1992) *The Origins and Development of the European Community* Leicester: Leicester University Press.

Weiler, J. (1982) 'Community, Member States and European Integration: Is the Law Relevant?' *Journal of Common Market Studies* 20: 1/2, 39–56.

Weiler, J. (1991) 'The Transformation of Europe' *Yale Law Journal* 100, 2403–2483.

Weiss, M. (1992) 'The Significance of Maastricht for European Community Social Policy' *International Journal of Comparative Labour Law and Industrial Relations* 8, 3–14.

Wellens, K.C. and Borchardt, G.M. (1989) 'Soft Law in European Community Law' *European Law Review* 14: 267–321.

Whiteford, E. (1993) 'Social Policy After Maastricht' *European Law Review* 18: 3, 202–222.

Williams, R. (1989) 'The EC's Technology Policy as an Engine for Integration' *Government and Opposition* 24: 2, 158–176.

Wincott, D. (1995a) 'The Maastricht Treaty: An Adequate "Constitution" for the European Union?' *Public Administration* 72: 4, 573–590.

Wincott, D. (1995b) 'Institutional Interaction and European Integration: Towards an Everyday Critique of Liberal Intergovernmentalism' *Journal of Common Market Studies* 33: 4, 597–609.

Wincott, D. (1996) 'The Court of Justice and the European Policy Process' in Richardson, J. (ed.) *Policy-making in the European Union* London: Routledge.

Wyatt-Walker, A. (1995) 'Globalisation, Corporate Identity and European Technology Policy' *Journal of European Public Policy* 2: 3, 427–446.

Young, O. (1991) 'Political Leadership and Regime Formation: On the Developments of Institutions in International Society' *International Organization* 45: 3, 281–308.

Index

Action Committee for a United
States of Europe 69
Action Programme for Employment
Growth (1986) 41
Adler, E. 133
Advisory Committee on the Joint
Data Projects 74
AEG 183 n24
agency slack 24, 170–176
Alber, S. 50
Alcatel 85, 145
Allison, G. (1971) 2, 26, 36, 187 n9
Altenstetter, C. 46, 132
Alter, K. 26, 175
Andriessen, F. (Vice President of
CEU) 40
Armstrong, K. 108
authority-legitmacy transfers 14–16
Article 2, part one, Title II, Treaty of
European Union 30, 47
Article 51, Treaty of European
Union 103
Article 100a, Single European Act
30, 41
Article 57, Treaty of European
Union 44, 45
Article 85, Treaty of Rome 90, 91
Article 86 Treaty of Rome 90, 91,
115
Article 90, Treaty of Rome 91, 115,
116
Article 117, Treaty of Rome 29, 179
n2, 31, 32
Article 118, Treaty of Rome 29, 31,
32, 33, 103, 179 n2,

Article 118a, Single European Act
30, 42, 43, 103, 105
Article 118b, Single European Act
49, 103
Article 119, Treaty of Rome 105
Article 125, Treaty of European
Union 43
Article 126, Treaty of European
Union 44–45
Article 127, Treaty of European
Union 43
Article 128, Treaty of Rome 43, 45
Article 129, Title X, Treaty of
European Union 46
Article 129, Title XII, Treaty of
European Union 93
Article 235, Treaty of Rome 70, 109
atypical work 52
Austria 67

Bangemann, M. 94, 117
Bangemann Report 94, 121, 147,
182 n5, 183 n33
Barry, A. 70
Belgium 130, 182 n3
Benedetti, C. 183 n32
BENELUX 183 n14
Besen, S. 92, 118, 145
BEUC 129
Blüm, Norbert 51
Bomberg, E. 2, 132
Bonfield, P. 81, 183 n32
Borchardt, G.M. 4, 29, 71, 107, 111,
184 n3
Bosch 140

Brewster, C. 39, 40, 41
BRITE 87
British Telecommunications 115, 116, 121, 182 n5
BSI 146
Bull 81, 143, 145, 148, 182 n4, 183 n24
Bulmer, S. 2, 21, 25, 26, 98, 108, 120, 152, 171–172
burden of proof directive 51–52
bureaucratic politics 26, 30, 104, 107, 155, 157
Burley, A. 26
business elites *see* multi-national companies, ICT industry or specific firms

Canada 95
Caparaso, J. 20, 22, 25, 26, 178 n9
Carpentier, M. 77
Cassoni, V. 182 n4
Cawson, A. 66, 146, 186 n12
CBEMA 151
CBI 51, 55
CEEP 49, 56
CEN 99, 113, 118, 145–146, 182 n11, 184 n14
CENELEC 99, 113, 118–119, 143–146, 182 n11, 184 n14
Centre for Research into European Women (CREW) 130
CEPT 92, 182 n10
CERD 74
CGE 183 n24
cheap talk 59, 60, 109, 110
Citizen's Europe 162
Coats Viyella 54
collective action 4, 62, 123–153, 164
Collie, L. 141
Collins, D. 29, 32, 33, 43, 60, 108
COMETT 43
Commission: adaptability 57; as agenda setter 26, 37, 58, 79–85, 120, 125–132, 152, 164, 169; attitude to UK opt-out from social agreement 42, 54; and dynamic treaty interpretation 29, 31, 33, 36, 41, 42, 70, 90; and 'gate-keeper' role 49–50; as a maturing bureaucracy 69, 76, 77–79; and member states 32–33, 37; as a 'missionary bureaucracy' 31; as a 'multi-organisation' 4, 26, 154–167, 183 n21; as a policy entrepreneur 23, 155–157; as a 'purposeful opportunist' 6, 34, 107–108, 114–120, 152, 154–167; as a regulator 63, 88–90, 103–107, 114–122; as a victim of its own success 109–110; catalytic role of 37, 58, 79–85, 125–132, 152, 164, 169; creating a constituency of support 137–139, 161–162, 165; organisation 75, 76, 155–156, 180 n3; preparing the ground for future action 107–111, 121, 161, 163–164; problems with coordination 77–78, 158; relationship with Council of Ministers 31, 33, 36, 37, 53, 57, 75–76, 91, 107–108, 114, 115, 162; *see also* Directorates-General
Common Agricultural Policy 18
communications school 8, 20, 170; *see also* transactionalism
Community Charter of Fundamental Social Rights for Workers 5, 41, 43, 59, 109, 180 n13
competition policy 76, 81, 83, 88, 89, 90, 91, 96, 114, 115–118, 163
conceptual lenses 2, 26, 34, 36, 52, 63
Confederation of Family Organisations in the EU 126, 129, 130, 131, 133–134, 135, 137
Confederation of Independent Trade Unions 56
constitutional decisions 2, 25, 26–27, 168, 171, 175, 176
consultation (by CEU) 57, 58, 92, 99, 140
Consumer Consultative Committee 133
Coombes, D. 76
Coppe, Albert 34
COREPER 75
corporatism 53
COSINE 186 n18
COST 67, 71, 183 n17
Coudenhove-Kalergi, R. 8
Council of Europe 178 n7

Council of Ministers 31–32, 54, 56, 57, 58, 59, 60, 63, 70, 72, 80, 83, 91, 106, 107, 109, 110, 111, 113, 114, 115, 129, 130, 162
Council of Science Ministers 70, 71
Cowles, M. Green 23, 140
CREST 72
Cram, Laura 2, 6, 25, 26, 157, 162, 174

Dahl, Robert 98
Dahrendorf, Ralf 72
Daimler-Benz 140
Dang-Nguyen 186 n11
Darnton, J. 63, 115, 116
data processing 74
Davignon, E. 76, 79–80, 144, 183 n32
day-to-day policy process 2, 6, 26–27, 168, 171, 174, 176
Decker, W. 140
Dehousse, R. 26
Delapierre, M. 67, 183–184 n97
Delors, Jacques 39, 41, 109
Defrenne cases 110
Denmark 126, 127, 182 n3
De Gaulle, Charles 18
deregulation/reregulation 88–90, 93, 118, 122, 160
Deutsch, K. 8, 152,
Digital 151
DIN 146
Directorate-General III 71, 73, 77, 78, 93, 163
Directorate-General IV 76, 89, 93, 96, 117, 163
Directorate-General V 3, 28–60, 138, 154, 160–162, 165
Directorate-General VI 140
Directorate-General X 138
Directorate-General XI 138
Directorate-General XII 76, 78
Directorate-General XIII 3, 45, 76, 77–79, 78, 80, 83, 88, 89, 96, 97, 139, 154, 158–160, 163, 165
Directorate-General XXII 45
Directory of Community Legislation in Force and Other Acts of the Community Institutions 4, 28, 100
domestic politics approaches 21, 23–24

Donnelly, M. 158
Dooge Committee 5
Downs, A. 30
Drake, H. 109

EACEM 143
ECAS 127–128, 134
ECMA 186 n18
economic and monetary union 34, 37
economic and social cohesion 40, 47
Economic and Social Committee 129
ECTEL 142, 143
Edelman, M. 5, 33, 165
education 44–45, 106
EECA 143
EFTA 17, 18, 68
employers' organisations 32, 39, 41
EMUG 186 n18
epistemic communities 132, 175
equal treatment of men and women 28, 38, 44, 101–103 (Figs 3–5), 105–106, 107, 108, 185 n3
ERASMUS 45, 162
ERDA 74
L'Espace Sociale 39
ESPRIT 65, 77, 79–85, 139, 144, 152, 159
ETSI 92, 99, 113 (Table 2), 118, 145, 151, 182 n11, 184 n14
ETUC 49, 55, 56
EUCREA 128, 132
Euratom 17, 70, 76
EUREKA 82, 182 n8
EUROBIT 142, 143–44, 150, 151
Eurocommerce 57
EUROFORM 134
Eurolink Age 129, 131, 134, 135, 136
Europe's Way to the Information Society: An Action Plan 95, 147, 166
European Anti-Poverty Network 126, 127, 128, 131, 132, 135
European Centre for Industrial Relations 50
European Coal and Steel Community 7, 11, 17, 108, 178 n7, 178 n13
European Conference on Social Security 32
European Council 4, 104

European Court of Justice 26, 45, 91, 110–111, 115–116, 158, 159, 173, 175; and interaction with CEU 2, 26; role in the integration process 22; and UK opt-out 56

European Executive Confederation (CEC) 56

European Forum for Disabled People 126, 134

European Foundation for the Improvement of Living and Working Conditions 28, 38

European IT Round Table 79, 83, 144–145, 150

European Monetary System 25

European Network of Women 130

European Parliament 26, 33, 51, 56, 129, 130, 135, 138

European Public Health Alliance 129, 134

European Round Table of Industrialists 140, 150

European Social Fund 28, 43, 99, 130

European Union: as a polity/system of governance 21, 25–27, 170–176; as strengthening the nation state 24–25, 170–176

European Union Technology Community 62, 66, 79–85, 152

European Women's Lobby 129, 130, 131, 135, 138, 139

European Works Councils 51–52, 54–57, 105, 121

EWOS 118, 146

Falcone, D. 185 n19

FAST 75

FEANTSA 129

federalism 7–8; 'the perplexities of', Mitrany, D. 9

Fiat 140

Findlay, G. 82

Finland 67

Flynn, Padraig 46, 51, 52, 54

Fontainebleau European Council 39

Fontaine, P. 162

FORCE 130

Framework Programmes: (1984–87) 82; (1987–91) 82; (1990–94) 82; (1994–98) 82; (1987–91) 87

France 95, 127, 135, 137, 182 n3, 183 n14, 183 n15

Franklin, G.A. 98

freedom of establishment 29, 44

freedom of movement for workers 29, 36, 44

Froman, L. A. Jnr 98

Fuchs, G. 69, 78, 182 n1

Fujitsu 144

functionalism 9–11; deracination of 11, 12, 178 n6; impact of 11; limits of functionalist method 19

G7 95; Ministerial Conference on the Information Society 95

Galtung, J. 153

Garret, G. 26, 171

GEC 183 n24

Germany 95, 109, 130, 131, 135, 137, 143, 146, 182 n3, 183 n14

global competition/globalisation 63, 64, 66, 67–68, 85, 96

Global System for Mobile Telecommunications 85

Goldenstein, J. 68

Grant, W. 140, 143, 144

Greece 127, 136, 192 n3

Green Papers: Education 138; European Social Policy: Options for the Union 58, 131; Liberalisation of Telecommunications Infrastructure and Cable Television Networks: Parts I & II 93, 116; Towards a Dynamic European Economy: On the Development of the Common Market for Telecommunications Services and Equipment 86, 90, 91, 92, 93, 116

Green, Maria *see* Cowles, Maria Green

Greenwood, J. 2, 26, 123, 141, 144

Groom, A. J. R. 12, 13, 178 n5

Grote, J. 2, 26, 123, 141, 144

Gunn, L. 98

Gyllenhammar, P. 140, 183 n32

Haas, Ernst 8, 11–18, 19, 20, 25, 123, 153, 178 n15

Haas, Peter 132, 133, 175

habits of cooperation/integration: in
Deutsch, K. 8; in Haas, E. 14; in
Mitrany, D. 10–11
Hague Summit 37, 72, 85
Hall, P. 137, 171
Hallstein, W. 8, 18
Harvey, B. 125, 129
Hayes, M.T. 98
HDTV 112–114
health and safety 28, 40, 43, 44,
101–102 (Figs 3–5), 105, 107, 108,
110, 185 n3; action programme
for 37
Helios programme 29, 126, 129, 131,
132, 134, 135, 136, 138
High Level Group of Experts on the
Social and Societal Aspects of the
Information Society 166
High Level Group of Industrialists
121, 147
high politics 20
Hills, J. 69, 76, 83, 84, 90, 165
historical institutionalism 171–172;
see also institutionalist
approaches
history-making decisions *see*
constitutional decisions
Hix, S. 27
Hodges, M. 8
Hoffmann, S. 19–20
Hogwood, B. 98
Holloway, J. 29, 32, 33, 34, 36
Holmes, P. 86, 90, 91, 115, 117, 166
Hood, C. 98
HORIZON 134, 137

IBM 143, 151
ICL 81, 144, 151, 183 n24
ICT policy 3–4; and collective action
134–152; development of 61–97;
legislative pattern 111–120; and
regulatory policy 120–122; and the
role of the CEU 158–160
ICT industry: and collective action
124, 134–152; loss of autonomy 89;
participation in standards process
145–147; role in ICT policy 79–81,
82, 86, 87, 97, 117, 158–160; *see
also* specific firms
ICT industry associations 140–145

ICT Standards Board 95
IEC 182 n10
implementation 84, 87
incentives for collective action 80–81,
83, 86, 124–132, 159
industrial policy 61, 65, 66, 70, 73,
78, 86, 111, 117, 159, 187 n3
information and communication
technology policy *see* ICT policy
information and consultation of
workers 44, 52, 54, 56
information society 78, 93–95, 97,
117, 121, 147, 165–166, 187 n5
Information Society Forum 166
Information Society Project Office 95
Inglehart, R. 8
institutions: as 'agents of
integration' 13, 18, 178 n15; and
the EU policy process 27; as
'honest broker' 13; and the
integration process 170–176; in
neo-functionalist theory 13–14; as
passive structures 171; as
purposive actors 172; as shaping a
'shared belief system' 171–172; *see
also* specific institutions
institutionalisation 45, 48, 50, 63, 69,
86–88, 94, 95
institutionalist approaches 2, 36, 53,
68–69, 171–172
Integrated Broadband
Communications 83–84
integration theory: development of
7–27; and the EU policy process
168–176; synthetic approach
to 21
interdependence/regime theory
21–22, 24
interest groups 2, 14–16, 26, 62,
123–153, 168
Intergovernmental Conference 1996/
7 (IGC) 42, 54, 56
intergovernmentalism 19–20, 23, 26,
53, 59, 60, 123, 169–176
internal market 30, 39, 40, 41, 44, 58,
69, 81, 85, 86, 88, 104, 106, 111,
166
international context 19, 23
International Labour Organisation
106, 178 n2

international relations approaches 2, 3, 62, 157
Ireland 41, 126
ISDN 84
IRIS 127, 129, 1130, 132, 134, 135, 137
ISO 182 n10
Italy 41, 95, 126, 127, 137, 183 n14
ITU 182 n10
IUFO 130

Japan 61, 64, 67, 68, 70, 95, 96, 142, 143, 144, 149, 151, 186 n21
Joint Research Centre 72
Jordan, G. 2, 84, 123, 125, 141, 144, 146, 149
Judge, D. 26

Kay, N. 68, 81
Keohane, R. 18, 21
Kingdon, J.W. 38
Kirschen, E.S. 98
Klabbers, J. 111
Klein, R. 5, 186–187 n1
Koebel, P. 66

Lamborghini, B. 143
Lange, P. 59, 60, 109, 161
Langendonck, G. 162
Language of justification 3, 34–35; see also rationalisations for action
Layton, C. 71, 73, 74, 76
law and integration 22; see also European Court of Justice and specific Treaty Articles
League of Nations 10
learning process 37, 104–105, 121, 158, 168; through collective action 133, 152; in Deutsch/communications school 8; in Haas/neofunctionalism 14–16; in ICT policy 87; importance for integration 176; in Mitrany/functionalism 10–11; in social policy 57; and UK opt-out 109
legal basis for action 3, 28–30, 43–51, 44 (Table 1), 49, 58, 70, 75, 81, 93–94, 109, 111
Lenaerts, C. 44, 45, 180 n 17

Levi-Sandri, Vice President of the CEU 33
Liberal intergovernmentalism 23–25, 170–176
liberalisation 65, 74, 76, 84, 85, 88, 90, 91, 92, 93, 95, 118, 160; of telecommunications infrastructure 182 n3
Lindberg, L. 15, 17, 20
Lindblom, C.E. 36, 38, 98, 164
LINGUA 45
Lobbying 2
Locksley, G. 89
low politics 20
lowest common denominator bargaining 23
Lowi, T. 98, 99

McLaughlin, A. 2, 123, 125, 141, 144, 146, 148, 149, 185 n1, 186 n21
McNeill, G. 81
Maastricht Treaty see Treaty on European Union
Majone, G. 25, 26, 28, 38, 60, 63, 88, 89, 90, 98, 104, 105, 107, 120, 156, 157, 162, 164, 165, 174
March, J. 171
Marks, G. 25
Mattli, W. 26
Mazey, S. 2, 25, 26, 123, 124, 138, 141, 153, 164
Medium Term Social Action Programme (1984) 39
Medium Term Social Action Programme (1995) 51, 57–58, 109
Meehan, E. 130
member states: autonomy of 24; and ICT policy 64–66, 72, 74, 78, 85, 86, 91, 96, 119–120; impact of collective action on 123, 126, 149; and the integration process 168–176; as key decision-makers 30, 62, 167; preference formation of 6, 24–25, 168–176; in realist/intergovernmentalist theories 18–21; and social policy 58–59, 104–110; and the social protocol/agreement 52–53
Memorandum from the Commission on the Technological and

Industrial Policy Programme 73, 183 n 19
Meunier-Aitsahalia, S. 26, 175
Migrant's Forum 129
Milan Council (1985) 85
Mitnick, B. 5
Mitrany, D. 8, 9–11, 13, 16, 17
Mitterrand, F. 183 n25
Monnet, J. 8, 10, 12, 199, 69, 178 n6, 178 n13
Moravcsik, A. 23, 152, 168–176, 187 n1
Morgenthau, H. 18
Mosely, H. 31
Motorola 151
multi-national companies 21, 55, 62, 99, 105, 120, 121, 139, 141, 142, 146, 150, 161, 165, 185–186 n8
mutual recognition 71, 90
Mytelka, L. 67, 183–184 n97

national champion strategy 61, 64–66, 139
national governments *see* member states
Nau, H.R. 62, 71, 72, 73, 74, 75, 182 n6, 183 n14, 183 n15
neo-functionalism 8, 11–20, 26, 123, 170; contrast with functionalism 13; intellectual parentage of 12; intergovernmentalist critique of 19–20; revitalisation of 23; role of supranational institutions in 13–14
The Netherlands 126, 127, 135, 137, 182 n3
Nicoll, T. 180 n8
Nielsen, R. 5
Nixdorf 183 n24
non-governmental organisations 126, 127, 130, 134, 138
Norway 67
NOW 134
Nye, J. 18, 20, 21

O'Higgins, M. 5, 186–187 n1
OEEC 178 n7
Olivetti 140, 143, 145, 148, 182 n4, 183 n24, 183 n32
Olson, J. 171

Olson, M. 61, 80, 96, 124, 125, 140, 149, 159, 164
opt-out from social agreement 30, 42, 51, 53–54, 55, 58, 109–110
ORGALIME 142, 143
organised interests *see* interest groups
OSITOP 186

Papandreaou, V. 42
parental leave 51–52, 56–57
Paris Summit (1972) 37, 72, 73, 85
Pavitt, K. 139, 186 n20
People's Europe 162
Peters, B.G. 2, 25, 26, 104, 157, 174
Peterson, J. 2, 25, 26, 75, 107, 132, 139, 172, 182 n8, 187 n1
Philips 140, 143, 145, 146, 149
Pierson, P. 124
Plessey 183 n24
policy instruments 4, 29, 43, 44–45, 62, 66, 70, 96, 98–122, 156, 160, 161, 167
policy networks 2, 132, 175
policy types 4, 60, 98–122, 160, 175
Pollack, M. 26, 98, 157, 174, 177 n13, 181 n36
Portugal 84, 137, 182 n3
Poverty Programme 37, 108–109, 129, 162
preference formation: in Deutsch 8; as endogenous process 25, 169, 172; in Haas/neo-functionalist theory 14–15, 25; impact of collective action on 152–153; in interdependence/regime theory 22; of member states 6, 24–25, 168–176; in Moravcsik/liberal intergovernmnentalism 24, 160–176; in Sandholtz 25, 169, 172
Preliminary Guidelines for a Community Social Policy (1971) 57
Pressman, G. 84, 157
PREST 71, 75
principal–agent relationship 5–6, 24, 35, 36, 173–176
protection of workers 28, 44, 101–102 (Figures 3–5), 105, 107, 185n3

PTTs 61, 63, 65, 76, 77, 83–84, 89, 91, 92, 93
public health 46
public procurement 62, 71, 73, 76, 86, 89, 91, 92
Puchala, D. 8, 21
Putnam, D. 24
purposeful opportunism 5, 27, 34, 170–176, 186–187 n1

qualified majority voting *see* voting procedures

R&D 62, 64, 70, 74, 75, 76, 78, 79, 81, 82, 84, 86, 89, 94, 97, 113, 139, 155, 160
RACE 65, 83–85, 139, 159
Radley, P. 85
rationalisations for action 3, 35, 39, 66, 67, 90, 106, 107, 158, 160, 165, 167; *see also* language of justification
RARE 186 n18
realist school 12, 18–20, 21, 23–24, 178 n8
Reflection Group 54
regime school *see* interdependence/ regime theory
regulation 5, 40, 60, 62, 66, 69, 70, 78, 88, 98–122, 125, 160, 176, 184 n7
regulatory policy *see* regulation
rhetoric 4, 29, 37, 59–60, 67, 107–111
Rhodes, M. 30, 42, 50, 110, 181–182 n24
Rifflet, R. 59
Richardson, J. 2, 25, 26, 123, 124, 138, 141, 153, 159, 164
Ripley, R.A. 98
Robbins, D. 126
Ronit, K. 2, 26, 123, 141, 144
Ross, G. 39, 187 n3

Sandholtz, W. 23, 25, 27, 63, 65, 66, 69, 77, 79, 80, 83, 84, 88, 91, 140, 169, 175
satellite 114
Sbragia, A. 25, 175
Schmitter, P. 20
Schneider, V. 143, 186 n11

Schuman Declaration 11, 12, 177 n3
Schuman, R. 11, 178 n6
Scheingold, S. 15, 20
Scientific and Technology Policy Programme 76
Senior Official's Group for Telecommunications 91
sense of community 8, 124, 137–139, 152–153
Servan-Schreiber, J. 64
Shanks, M. 31, 37
Shapiro, M. 26
Sharp, M. 61, 62, 69, 70, 71, 75, 76, 80, 81, 86, 87, 139, 140, 144, 152, 182 n8, 183 n14, 186 n17, 186 n20
Shearman, C. 61, 62, 69, 71, 75, 76, 140, 144, 183 n14
Shepsle, K. 171
Siemens 140, 145, 148
de Silguy, Y.T. 46
Simon, H. 149
Single European Act 2, 22, 23, 30, 39, 40, 50, 58, 62, 70, 86, 87, 90, 103, 105, 109, 110, 179 n2, 181 n34
single market *see* internal market
small and medium size enterprises 82
SNI 145
Snyder, F. 4
social action programme (1974) 37, 107, 108; (1989) 42–43, 57, 109–110
social agreement (TEU) 30, 42, 43–58
social dialogue 41, 47, 49, 56–57; *see also* social partners and Val Duchesse
social partners 39, 47, 48 (figure 1), 49, 52, 53, 94, 134, 161, 180 n23
social policy 3–4; and the CEU 160–162; and collective action 125–139; development of 28–60; as human face of the EU 161–162; legislative pattern 100–111; and regulatory policy 120–122
social protection 108–109
social protocol (TEU) 43–58, 109–110, 80 n15
social security 108–109
social security for migrant workers 28, 44, 101–102 (figures 3–5), 105, 185 n3

socialisation 175
SOCRATES 138
soft law 4, 29, 60, 71, 99, 101 (figure
  2), 103, 107–111, 111–113, 112
  (figure 6), 162
softening-up process 38, 39, 53, 55,
  69, 75, 86, 94, 99, 159, 163–164
SPAG 186 n18
Spain 127, 182 n3
Spicer, M. 156
Spicer, P. 35
spill-over: from collective action 4,
  87; functional/sectoral spill-over
  16, 18; geographical spill-over 17,
  18; political spill-over 16, 18; spill
  back/spill round 20; and Treaty of
  Rome 18
Spinelli, A. 8, 73
standards/standardisation 62, 66, 67,
  69, 77, 81, 84, 87, 88, 89, 94, 95, 97,
  99, 100, 113 (Table 2), 114,
  118–120, 121–122, 139, 145–147,
  151–152, 159–160, 163; *see also*
  CEN/CENELEC/ETSI/EWOS/
  ISO/IEC/ITU/CEPT
Standing Committee on Employment
  38, 49
state-centred approaches 3, 22, 60,
  64, 120, 153, 155; *see also*
  realist/intergovernmentalist
  approaches
Stein, E. 22
Steinmo, S. 171–172, 175
Sterne, J. 182 n4
STET 183 n 24
Sweden 67
Switzerland 67
symbolic politics 5, 29, 30, 34–36,
  59–60, 67, 86, 90, 96, 107–111,
  138–139, 165
Szyszczak, E. 5

TACIS 130
Task Force on 'Education, Training
  and Youth' 45
Task Force for Information and
  Communication Technologies 77,
  80
Taylor, P. 31, 59
Teague, P. 39, 40, 41

technical self-determination, 10–11,
  16
technological convergence 78
technological imperative 66–68, 85
technology gap 64, 65
telecommunications policy 83–85,
  90–93, 112–114, 115–118
temporal dimension 28–30, 34, 48, 69
TEMPUS 45
Thatcher, Margaret 5, 40
Thatcher, Mark 62, 88
Thelen, K. 171–172
Thomson 146, 183 n24
Thorn, G. 183 n32
trade unions 32, 39; *see also* ETUC
  and TUC
transactionalism 8; *see also*
  communications school
Trans-European Networks (TENS)
  93
transfer of undertakings 56
Treaty of Paris 70
Treaty of Rome 29, 58, 70, 105, 115,
  178–179 n1
Treaty on European Union 2, 22,
  30, 39, 42, 43–57, 58, 59, 62,
  93–95, 109–110, 161, 180 n15,
  181 n34
Tsoukalis, L. 29
Turkey 67
TUC 55
two-level game 24
Tyszkiewicz, Z. 42

unanticipated consequences 5–6, 40,
  124
Ungerer, H. 79, 116
UNICE 49, 53, 54, 56, 141
United Biscuits 54
United Kingdom 40–41, 43, 51,
  53–54, 55–56, 59, 91, 95, 109–110,
  126, 127, 129, 135, 146, 161, 182
  n3, 182 n6, 183 n14
United States 61, 64, 67, 68, 70, 95,
  96, 142, 143, 144, 151
Usher, J. 30

Val Duchesse dialogue 39, 49
Van Loon, R. 185 n19
Van Miert, K. 88, 116

Van Schendelen, M. 123
VDMA 143
Veldkamp Memorandum 33, 34, 57, 180 n5&6
Venturini, P. 29, 41
Vickers, G. 152, 153, 154
VLSI 79
vocational training 43, 44, 106, 184 n5
Volvo 140, 183 n32
voting procedure 30, 40, 42, 43, 46, 47, 51, 59, 60, 70, 103, 110, 168, 180 n22, 18 n34, 183 n31
Vredling Directive *see* information and consultation of workers

Wallace, H. 21
Wallace, W. 21
Watson, P. 50
Webb, C. 21
Weiler, J. 22, 26
Weingast, B. 26, 171
Weiss, M. 50

Wellens, K.C. 4, 29, 71, 107, 111, 184 n3
West European Union 178 n7
White Paper on Growth, Competitiveness and Employment 94
White Paper on the Internal Market 86
White Paper on Social Policy 51
Whiteford, E. 46, 50
Wildavsky, A. 84, 157
Williams, R. 182 n8
Wincott, D. 2, 22, 26, 110, 175
windows of opportunity 38, 40, 162–167
working conditions 44
Working Peace System 9
Wuersch, D. 63, 115, 116
Wyatt-Walker, A. 67, 68

Youth for Europe 45
Yugoslavia 67

Zysman, J. 23, 140